KOMMANDO

German Special Forces
of World War Two

KOMMANDO

German Special Forces of World War Two

James Lucas

ARMS AND ARMOUR PRESS

Published in 1985
by Arms and Armour Press
2-6 Hampstead High Street, London NW3 1QQ.

British Library Cataloguing in Publication Data
Lucas, James, *1923*–
Kommando: German Special Forces of World War Two
1. Germany. *Heer* – Commando troops
2. World War, 1939–1945 – Commando troops
3. World War, 1939–1945 – Campaigns – Germany
I. Title 940.54'87'43 D757
ISBN 0-85368-707-2

1 2 3 4 5 6 7 8 9 0

Designed by David Gibbons; edited by Michael Boxall;
diagrams by Anthony A. Evans. Typeset by Typesetters
(Birmingham) Limited. Printed and bound in Great
Britain by R. J. Acford, Chichester.

The Publishers wish to
acknowledge the kind assistance of
Brian L. Davis and K. Green with
the cover illustration. Photograph
by Michael Dyer Associates,
Endell Street, London.

CONTENTS

LIST OF DIAGRAMS

PREFACE

The conflict between Germany and Poland which began on 1 September 1939, spread to involve so many nations that it became, eventually, a world-wide war. This book is concerned with the Armed Services of just one European nation – Germany – and specifically with the special forces, military, naval and aerial, which she raised and employed during the five years of that war.

At this juncture I must define what to me constitutes a special force. This will be a formation fulfilling one of three criteria. First, units from a conventional Arm of Service which have been grouped to form a unique fighting detachment. The pilots who formed the Luftwaffe's ramming squadron come into this category. Secondly, those who conduct operations using tactics or weapons of an original nature. The glider-borne troops who attacked the fortress of Eben Emael with hollow-charge grenades fulfil that criterion. Thirdly, units which are raised to conduct a specific type of military operation, such as the German guerrilla movement, Werewolf.

It must be emphasised here that the special forces of Germany are not to be confused with Battle Groups (Kampfgruppen), which were men or units brought together to carry out a single, specific military operation. The basic difference between special forces and battle groups is that the former have a permanence which the latter were not intended to have.

ACKNOWLEDGMENTS

It is with a deep sense of gratitude that I acknowledge the assistance and collaboration of a great many people and institutions in the production of this book.

Chief among the latter are the Departments of Documents, of Photographs and of Printed Books at the Imperial War Museum; the various Historical Branches of the Ministry of Defence; and the Public Record Office. I am also grateful to foreign museums and archives, particularly those in the United States of America, Germany and Austria.

Among the ex-Service organisations upon whose help I depended were those of my own regiment, the Parachute Regiment, the Bund deutscher Fallschirmjäger, the Traditionsverband Panzerkorps 'Grossdeutschland' and the HIAG. The number of those individual people whose help was invaluable, is too many for me to acknowledge by name, but Matthew Cooper, Terry Charman, George Clout and John Harding in Britain, Oberst Erich Busch, Oberst Rudolf Witzig, Karl Heinz Bruch, Rudi Hambuch, Franz Josef Kugel and Paul Beck in Germany were particularly helpful.

Nothing could have been achieved without the support and encouragement of my dear wife, Edeltraude, or of our daughter, Barbara Shaw, who typed the manuscript. Finally, my very special thanks to my publisher, Lionel Leventhal, whose staff turned the manuscript into this book, particularly David, Beryl, Tessa and Lynda of the production side of Arms and Armour Press.

As I sit here, now that the book is completed and with only this thank-you page to complete, I see in my mind's eye those contributors whose letters, anecdotes and visits form the fabric of this book. It is hard to connect the gentle, elderly gentlemen I met and with whom I corresponded, with the daring men who carried out the exploits recorded here. Of all those who served in the special forces, one name stands out – that of Leutnant Grabert, one of the original Brandenburgers, who fell for his country on the Eastern Front. To his memory and as the representative of all the men of the German special forces, this book is respectfully dedicated.

James S. Lucas, London.

INTRODUCTION

Today an aura of glamour surrounds the special forces of the world's armies. It is produced in part, perhaps, by their élitist nature and by the secrecy in which they operate. Little official information is released on the missions they undertake and, lacking such authoritative, precise information, the public has to use imagination to reconstruct the deeds of daring, and speculation to picture the special weapons, the arduous training and the brilliantly executed plans.

Special forces are unquestionably an élite. They carry the nimbus of success. They recruit discreetly and accept only those few who attain the unusual standards that are set. Theirs is a reputation for iron-hard toughness. They have the appeal of unknown but undisputed potency, attributes which operate the military 'seduction principle', but which are more effective recruiting agents than the handsome, coloured uniforms of former days. Today's special units wear no bright and distinctive clothing to identify themselves, but dress in dull camouflage or even plain clothes, for much clandestine work is conducted in mufti. The aim of special forces these days is to be unobtrusive, to be undistinguished and, thereby, to avoid being identified as soldiers on active service. The allure of becoming one of a group of anonymous, drably-dressed men, undertaking secret operations, is a contemporary phenomenon and inseparable from the attitudes and mores of the middle decades of the twentieth century.

Considering the aura which today surrounds the camouflaged men of the special forces it is surprising to recall that the employment of such troops, the use of disguise and the tactics of guerrilla warfare which they operate are aspects of warfare that were repugnant to the orthodox military mind as recently as the first decades of this century. The conduct of today's special forces would have been incomprehensible to the conventional soldiers of former days.

In earlier and more colourful days soldiers of élite units had gloried in the panoply of power and had been proud of those distinctions which marked them out as the chosen men of immediately identifiable regiments. Within the regiment one was part of a special and select body. Outside it one was one of the mob. Arrogant in this association with proud regiments, orthodox soldiers considered partisans and guerrillas to be nothing but bandits; as *francs tireurs* who should be given no quarter, for the danger of those criminals was that they wore civilian clothes and could not, therefore, be identified as being part of an armed enemy force. Then, too, partisans often used underhand tricks to attain their goals; disguising themselves in the uniform of the occupying Power, carrying out sabotage and using unconventional means to win victories, but never staying to fight a proper battle. Rather did they vanish into darkness or submerge themselves among the local population. Such tactics were considered to be unfair.

The attitude of the German professional soldier to special forces was one of total abhorrence. In Germany the status of a soldier, and especially an officer, was a high one. He was a dedicated man. A weapon-bearer whose duty it was to defend his Fatherland and whose pride it was to wear his country's uniform. There existed in the German Army, as indeed in most other European military forces of former days, a mystical bond between the warrior and his Sovereign or his country; the strongest strand of which was that of honour. The honour of his Nation and his honour as a soldier. Both had to be kept unblemished and it was considered that the use of civilian clothes to avoid being identified as a soldier, or the wearing of an enemy uniform to gain a tactical advantage were deeds which would tarnish a soldier's honour and, therefore, that of his country. Indeed, such deceptions were considered almost as reprehensible as spying. They were underhand, deceitful and ungentlemanly.

Shortly before the outbreak of the Second World War, the idea was mooted among the senior commanders of the German Army that the Service should raise special forces which would use partisan tactics or conduct guerrilla warfare, possibly using disguise. Those traditionally-minded men, with their almost mystic regard for the uniform they wore, rejected as perfidious the use of disguise to deceive and were of the opinion that men serving in partisan-type units were either misfits within the military system or were spies and agénts. Despite this rejection by senior officers, the German counter-Intelligence Section, die Abwehr, formed small commandos, later to be known as 'Brandenburg' units, which were to be employed in penetration and on anti-sabotage operations. During the war it was demonstrated to the senior officers of the Army that the use of 'Brandenburg'-type troops or undercover tactics produced good results for minimum casualties. Nevertheless, many commanders maintained this opposition to special units throughout much of the war.

But if the conservative-minded commanders of the Army saw in the employment of unconventional units a slur upon their own concept of honour, there were officers in other German organisations who did not. The men who accepted with enthusiasm new ideas and methods of warfare were the leaders of the SS. The commanders of this Force were not hidebound by military dogma, but were sufficiently flexible to see that there were practical advantages to be gained through the use of irregular forces fighting along unorthodox lines. Many of the SS officers were veterans of the street battles fought in the Party's early days of struggle and were, thus, personally familiar with the potential of small units aggressively handled. Before the outbreak of the Second World War the Security Service of the SS (the Sicherheitsdienst or SD) had employed some of its men in Bohemia as *agents provocateurs* to foment political crises, the outcome of which was the invasion of Czechoslovakia. When war did come such men were prepared to use any means to disconcert the enemy and to give their own men every possible advantage; for the SS was less concerned with ethics than with victory.

The SS commanders and their colleagues in the SD were ambitious men. In view of the Army's rejection of irregular units, contrasted with the pragmatic approach of the SS to those forces, it is understandable that when the time came for unconventional forces to be raised it was the SS which could offer the best chance of success for they knew the potential offered and the rewards which could be gained by the employment of small detachments of well-armed and determined men.

The greatest number of Germany's special forces were created out of a struggle between an Admiral and an SS General for control of the Intelligence agencies of the Third Reich. The Admiral, Wilhelm Canaris, moulded the German High Command's espionage and counter-espionage departments, die Abwehr, into a powerful weapon. His opponent was SS General Reinhard Heydrich, sometime Head of the SS Security Services. These are the principal characters. Other men played important parts. There were commanders of special units who showed ingenuity, courage and flair in leading their determined men on land, on the sea or in the air. But every one of these units and the weapons which they used, were the product, however indirectly, of the efforts made, the directions given or the orders initiated, by one of the principals of this story.

PART ONE

GROUND FORCES

THE ABWEHR AND SPECIAL UNIT BRANDENBURG

In the beginning there was only the Abwehr, the Counter-Intelligence agency of the Armed Forces High Command, which can be said to have been formed on 21 January 1921. Two and a quarter years had elapsed since the armistice of November 1918 brought an end to the Great War, and the bankrupt Germany of those immediate, post-war years had little money to spare on its armed forces. Not that the defeated Germany was to be allowed large military contingents. The victorious Allies had directed that the Army was to number no more than one hundred thousand men and that it was forbidden to have heavy artillery or armour. The Navy could have neither heavy units nor submarines and the Air Force existed only in name. The small budget for the armed forces did not allow the setting up of a large Intelligence system and the modest sums which were allocated for that purpose were sufficient to form only two Sections: an Eastern and a Western. Officers were seconded from these Sections to carry out Intelligence duties at one of the seven military Commands into which Germany was divided. The task of the Abwehr officers was to obtain detailed information about the armies and military intentions of Germany's neighbours.

The Abwehr's first commander, a naval officer, Kapitän zur See Patzig, appreciated that, in her weakened state, Germany's greatest danger was from the East. The vigorous, new republic of Poland had already made several attempts to invade and occupy part of the German provinces of Silesia, Prussia and Saxony. Each invasion had been flung back by militias of ex-servicemen hastily raised and grouped into units described as Freikorps, but the danger might perhaps come again.

It did not, and the dangerous political tension in the East eventually eased. But the financial crises of the late 1920s and early 1930s continued to prevent the Abwehr from increasing its staff or expanding its operations. Forced by circumstances to work within the tightest limits, the frugal officers of the German Intelligence organisation became adept in making do with very little, but they did produce plans for expansion which were to be implemented when Germany's fortunes improved. This came about in 1935, in the first years of the Nazi government, a government formed from a Party dedicated to the task of raising Germany to pre-eminence among the nations of Europe.

The revolutionary National Socialist German Workers' Party – the Nazi Party – believed, as have fanatical creeds in all centuries, that the end justifies the means. Political terror, racial intolerance and religious persecution were the means whereby opposition to the policies of Hitler's government would be crushed. Inevitably those officers, those politicians, those elements in German social, political, religious and cultural life, who believed in liberalism and tolerance were removed from office, were forced to emigrate or were placed in the camps which had been built to hold the dissidents and enemies of the new Faith.

Kapitän zur See Patzig of the Abwehr was a man who made no secret of his hatred of National Socialist ideals, nor did he hide his contempt for those German officers who subscribed to them. His bluntness offended many leading soldiers, not least the Minister for War, Feldmarschall von Blomberg. This officer's relationship with Hitler was so close that the Führer had attended von Blomberg's wedding. Von Blomberg, with two senior SS officers, Himmler and Heydrich, prevailed upon Admiral Raeder, Commander-in-Chief of the Navy, to retire Patzig prematurely. Raeder, another senior officer sympathetic to Nazi policies, acted swiftly and with Patzig gone cast about for a replacement. He found him in the person of Wilhelm Canaris.

On 1 January 1935, Kapitän zur See Canaris, a man of only forty-seven, took up his appointment as Chief of Counter-Intelligence in the High Command. During the years of his incumbency the Abwehr became a large and formidable Intelligence apparatus and from it evolved Germany's first special force – the Brandenburg detachments.

The qualifications which Canaris brought to his new post had been acquired during the First World War when, after sea service and an escape from internment, he had gone on to become an assistant to the German Naval Attaché in Madrid. There he had set up a network of agents who reported the movements of Allied ships. Seconded from his Intelligence duties to serve again at sea, he had joined the U-boats and operated in the Mediterranean until the Armistice. He was kept on in the small, post-war Navy of the Republic and began secretly to rebuild U-Boat Command. At first Canaris believed that Hitler and the Nazi Party were the strongest opponents of the Communist revolution which had destroyed the Imperial Navy, and he supported the new ideas. They seemed to work and certainly the Führer was intent upon supporting the armed forces.

Within two years of his accession to power Hitler had expanded the German Armed Forces. Money, formerly lacking, was now available and among those agencies which benefitted from the increase in allowances was the Abwehr. Freed from the repressions of years of famine its officers could now finance the plans which, in leaner days, had had to remain vague hopes. Under the skilful control of the Admiral and his subordinates, the counter-Intelligence organisation grew until it had absorbed not only the entire Intelligence agency but also, in 1938, the Foreign Section which had as its function the relations with other Powers. Eventually, the Abwehr became so important that it was granted ministerial status. Its expansion, which had begun in 1936, was completed in 1938 and in its final form consisted of three Sections: Abwehr I, II and III, directly subordinated to the Supreme High Command (OKW). Abwehr Section I was concerned with active espionage and the collection of Intelligence information. Section II controlled special units and sabotage. It was Hauptmann Hippel of Section II, who organised the Brandenburg special troops. Abwehr Section III dealt with counter-espionage activities.

Each of the three principal Sections had an Army, a Navy and an Air Force Sub-Section from which Abwehr officers received and passed Intelligence of interest. In addition to the three Armed Services sub-Sections into which Abwehr I and II were sub-divided, Section III was also responsible for counter-Intelligence operations in industry, trade and the civil service. It was also the task of III to plant false information, to penetrate foreign Intelligence agencies and to investigate acts of sabotage. Shortly after the outbreak of war, Abwehr Section III was also made responsible for counter-espionage work in military and civil communications and among enemy prisoners of war.

Officers from Abwehr headquarters carried out liaison duties with active service units from the level of High Command down to that of Division or its equivalent in the Air Force or the Navy. In time the entire German armed forces were covered by a network of Abwehr-trained officers: those in Section I obtaining and disseminating Intelligence information; those in Section II organising clandestine operations and those in Section III frustrating the attempts by Germany's enemies to gain her military secrets or disrupt her military plans.

A network of Abwehr agents was also set up in foreign countries, building on the foundations and using the techniques initiated by Patzig against Poland in the 1920s. Strangely, Hitler ordered that no Intelligence operations of any nature be directed against Great Britain, a ban which was lifted partially in 1936 and totally in 1937. A similar total ban made in respect of the United States was not lifted until war broke out between America and Germany. Under this proscription, the establishing of an Abwehr network in the Anglo-Saxon countries was seriously inhibited and it says much for the ability of Canaris that, so far as the United Kingdom is concerned, he was able to infiltrate agents very quickly and to obtain from them, well before the outbreak of war in 1939, a dossier which included much classified information on both the Royal Air Force and the Royal Navy. For the Abwehr the situation in America remained a total ban and there were no agents to undertake

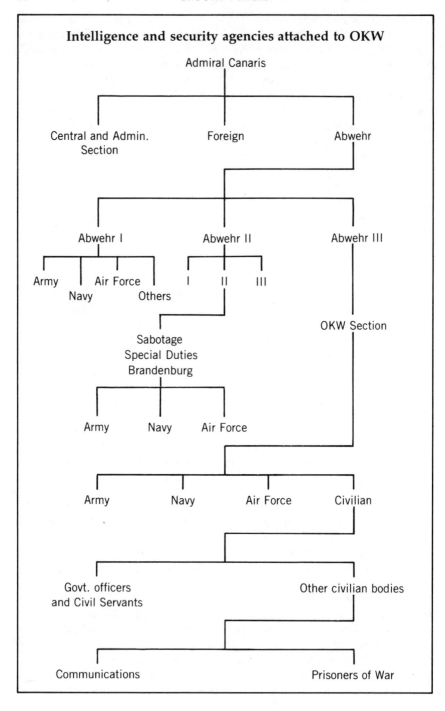

Intelligence and security agencies attached to OKW

Admiral Canaris

Central and Admin. Section — Foreign — Abwehr

Abwehr I — Abwehr II — Abwehr III

Abwehr I: Army, Navy, Air Force, Others

Abwehr II: I, II, III

Sabotage Special Duties Brandenburg: Army, Navy, Air Force

Abwehr III: OKW Section

Army, Navy, Air Force, Civilian

Govt. officers and Civil Servants — Other civilian bodies

Communications — Prisoners of War

spying or to conduct sabotage operations until the outbreak of war in 1941.

Well before the war, Canaris had established the most friendly relations with certain countries bordering Germany, particularly with Italy and Hungary. Old friendships played a great part in the establishing of cordial relations. Horthy, the Regent of Hungary, had been an Admiral in the Navy of the former Austro-Hungarian Empire and, therefore, Canaris's comrade in arms during the Great War. During the late 1930s German influence spread throughout Europe, much of it due to the subtle, charming, gentlemanly approach of Canaris and his subordinates. This smooth penetration of foreign countries was soon threatened by the abrasive attitudes and tactics of the SS Intelligence group led by the skilful, ambitious and ruthless, Reinhard Heydrich.

Before the sinister Gruppenführer Heydrich enters the story, let us examine the reasons why this SS officer came to have the power to disrupt the Abwehr's plans; why, indeed, it was necessary for the SS to be involved in the Intelligence activities of the Reich. Quite simply, the Abwehr was an agency whose terms of reference restricted it solely to the collection and dissemination of information on Intelligence matters outside the Reich's frontiers. This information was passed without analysis or comment to the appropriate branch of the armed services. The Abwehr had no power to act upon the information it received, it possessed no executive power at all and no authority to do more than transmit Intelligence. When positive action had to take place: surveillance undertaken or raids carried out and arrests made, the Abwehr was dependent upon the help of the police force which, by 1936, had been brought under SS control *de jure*, but which was, *de facto*, within the competence of Reinhard Heydrich, Commander of the Security Service (the SD) and the man responsible for the internal security of the Third Reich.

Even in Imperial days the police force had not had a centralised authority; each force had worked for its own state, its own province. Under the Nazi idea of central control, moves were begun, as early as March 1933, that is two months after the Party came to power, to amalgamate the separate states' forces into one comprehensive body. The moves began in Bavaria where Himmler was appointed Chief of the Political Police. Next the forces of the other states were absorbed one by one and without any opposition until it came to Prussia, whose police were under the control of Hitler's closest Party comrade, Hermann Goering. He refused to relinquish his authority and Himmler had to content himself as Goering's deputy. As Chief of the Prussian police, Goering had had original ideas. In order to combat the Berlin Communists, whose control of the streets through a system of sentries had enabled wanted men to escape from a police raid, Goering formed a detachment of parachutists who dropped from the air on to suspected

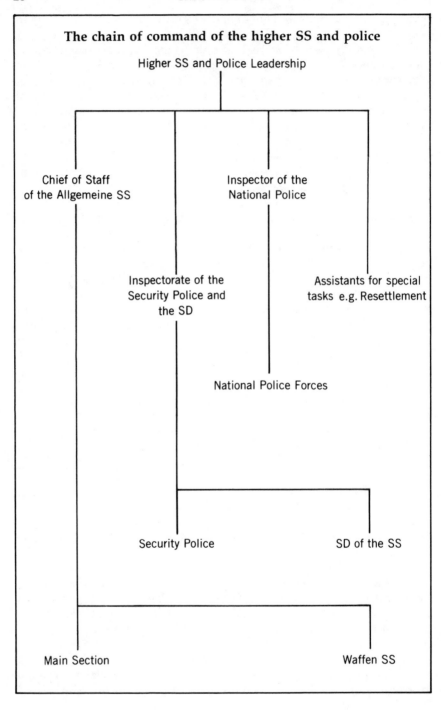

The chain of command of the higher SS and police

Higher SS and Police Leadership

Chief of Staff
of the Allgemeine SS

Inspector of the
National Police

Inspectorate of the
Security Police and
the SD

Assistants for special
tasks e.g. Resettlement

National Police Forces

Security Police

SD of the SS

Main Section

Waffen SS

buildings. Out of that small 'Hermann Goering Para Detachment', grew the paratroop formations, of the Third Reich, some of whose exploits are recorded in this book. He had also formed a Secret State Police, the Gestapo, which was a kind of Intelligence unit with executive functions and designed to fight political enemies as distinct from the Kripo which dealt with ordinary crime. Secret Police detachments (Gestapo) formed along the lines of the Prussian force, then became standard in all parts of Germany.

Himmler, the Gestapo chief for the whole of the Reich, first merged the Criminal Police and the Gestapo into one body, and then linked this with the Nazi Party's police and security organisations so that the entire German police organisation dedicated to the internal security of the Reich, reposed in the hands of his protégé, Reinhard Heydrich.

Feeling even this great power to be insufficient, Heydrich next looked at the authority of the Abwehr to deal with Germany's external enemies, and determined to incorporate as soon as he could, that element within the SD, upon whose political loyalty he could depend. He set to work and soon achieved success. As part of the order directing the amalgamation of the German police forces under one authority, Hitler had decreed that the SD alone was to be the political information-gathering service of the Nazi Party. It became, thereby, the single Intelligence organisation for the Party's internal administration, and as the Party encroached more and more into every sphere of German life, so did the influence and power of the SD grow. By clever manipulation and by creating diversions, Heydrich was able to avoid precise delineation of the areas of his influence. There were 'grey' areas and it was in Intelligence matters concerning these ill-defined sectors that the first conflicts arose between Heydrich and Canaris. These first clashes were conducted upon very friendly and informal levels, as between shipmates, for Canaris and Heydrich had served together as naval officers in the cruiser *Berlin* until a matter of honour concerning a lady had forced the handsome and virile young Heydrich to leave the Service. He found acceptance in the Nazi Party and, specifically, in its élite, paramilitary arm, the SS. It was within the party police of that dread organisation that he had found his true role and in which he rose quickly under the aegis of Himmler.

Heydrich was a contradiction, a paradox. He was a sensitive musician, a violinist of such accomplishment that he might have achieved world fame – yet he operated extermination squads. As an athlete he had, in the pre-war years, represented Germany in foils. He was an excellent oarsman and an even better horseman. During the first years of the war his skill as a fighter pilot brought him a number of confirmed victories. Yet he was a man with a fanatical devotion to the darker and more sinister principles of National Socialism, who was driven, because of overweening ambition, to authorise the commitment of appalling atrocities, if thereby he could extend the influence of the organisations which he led and the political faith in which he believed. He was a romantic. Not a romantic of hearts and flowers, although he could be sentimental enough, but a romantic believer in the world of espionage and Intelligence as portrayed in works of fiction. He admired, almost to adoration, the British Secret Service and aware, through the novels which he read, that its Head was identified by a single initial, adopted that idea and insisted upon being addressed – when wearing his spy hat – as 'C'. References to 'C' can be found in many letters dealing with Heydrich. But for all his vanity he saw what Canaris had perhaps not seen, that the lack of a centrally-organised, single Intelligence and counter-Intelligence service led to overlapping and wasted efforts which in turn produced gaps in the collecting of information and enabled enemy agents to slip through the net. The German Intelligence organis-ations were still very new. The Germany of the nineteenth century had been a collection of independent kingdoms, principalities, duchies and states, lacking a common policy until 1866. Heydrich envied the cen-turies of experience which the British had gained and the mastery which the various British secret services showed in the planning and execution of their tasks and he was determined to make the German agencies as powerful. The single and basic difference was that his organisation would serve the interests of the Nazi Party and only the Party.

Since the Abwehr was concerned with external enemies and the SD was responsible for internal security, the two should have been the halves of a perfect whole. Instead they were deadly rivals. Heydrich was tirelessly ambitious, a persuasive speaker and a very imposing figure; a man who had presence. And he was able to influence Hitler on the matter of Intelligence in a way that the short, grey-haired, unmilitary Canaris could not. Soon Hitler had ordered that the Abwehr files on the Party's senior members were to be handed over to the SD. At the same time the Abwehr was forbidden to collect details of political or economic Intelligence for this task now came within the competence of Heydrich's organisation. Nor could the Abwehr involve itself with enemy agents who were caught in Germany. The authority to round-up and interrogate foreign agents now lay with the Gestapo, which was part of the Reich Security (RSHA) complex. Information obtained from overseas organisations of the Nazi Party went directly to Heydrich, never to the Admiral. There were thus two Intelligence organisations both working overseas and each acting independently of the other, a situation which led to confusion in the reports which they produced; to the obstruction of each other's plans and, sometimes, to the danger of the agents in the field.

The lunacy of having two agencies competing with each other pro-duced difficulties enough, but this ridiculous situation was com-pounded by the pragmatic manner in which Hitler conducted his government. His method of ensuring that there was no rival to his authority was to divide his Party comrades and thus rule them. Each of those comrades, as a defensive measure to his own position, sought to produce Intelligence information about his cabinet colleagues. To reduce SD interference in their own ministries as well as to gain power over their rivals, each minister then set up his own information-gathering agency. The Intelligence scene degenerated from the ridiculous to the farcical. The Minister for Propaganda and Enlighten-ment, Josef Goebbels, needed to know the reactions of the foreign Press to Nazi speeches and policies. His research department supplied these, but the knowledge gained was hoarded, not used and its value was lost. The foreign office network released no details or information to anyone but von Ribbentrop, the Foreign Minister, who often drew from them the wrong conclusions. Himmler had his own contacts and his own organisations; Goering had his Forschungsamt from which he obtained various types of information as well as receiving Intelligence from the Abwehr in his role as Head of the German Air Force. But Goering, too, hoarded these nuggets of information so as to drop them as *bons mots* among his dinner guests and thereby increase his reputa-tion of being close to the centre of power.

German political life was riven with gangs of agents each seeking to supply their own particular master with secret information. And Hitler encouraged this. A demonic character, who lived for the tingling excite-ment of politics, he demanded instant answers, immediate victories and sensational coups. The Abwehr could not supply such things. Canaris had frequently reminded the Führer that Intelligence work was a slow growth, not concerned with the immediate and the now, but with results which would only show after years or even decades. The Führer decided to replace Canaris and his negative attitude with the new and dynamic Heydrich. Heydrich, for his part, continued his work to isolate the Abwehr and to prove that the SD could be just as influen-tial and successful outside Germany's borders as it was within them. In 1936, for example, Heydrich's organisation demanded from the Abwehr specimen signatures of leading Red Army commanders. The SD is thought to have leaked to Stalin incriminating but false letters above the forged signatures of those commanders. If there is any truth in this suspicion, the Soviet purges of 1937 and 1938 may well have been the outcome of the plan produced by Heydrich and his sinister associates.

Early in 1938, *agents provocateurs*, SD men disguised as Czech patriots, instigated anti-German riots which led eventually to a political crisis and paved the way for the occupation of the Sudetenland. In the summer of the following year, the Abwehr received a requisition for the supply of a number of Polish uniforms. Research traced the origin of that peculiar demand back to Heydrich's office. The use to which the SD put those uniforms is recorded in this book.

While Heydrich was organising undercover activities and employing his bands of agents, Canaris and the Abwehr had completed the raising of a Company, out of which there was to grow, in time, a great number of special units, known collectively as 'Brandenburg'.

During the years following the Great War, officers of several commissions set up by the German Army sought to establish why Germany had not won the war for which she had prepared for so many years. Among the men who considered the reasons was Hauptmann von Hippel. His war had been fought in the former German African colonies. Because of his experience in a non-standard type of military operation, he was assigned to study the Allied use of irregular forces.

Von Hippel examined the role of Colonel T. E. Lawrence, Lawrence of Arabia, and his contribution to the Allied victory. The German officer was fascinated by the exploitation of Arab nationalist feelings and the potential which guerrilla warfare offered; that an elusive band of saboteurs could create chaos in the enemy's rear; could bring confusion to his military plans and win for themselves victories out of all proportion to their numbers, even though they lacked heavy weapons, firm bases or proper supply routes. The successes enjoyed by Lawrence, the ease with which he penetrated the Turkish lines in disguise, coupled with his ability to keep large numbers of enemy soldiers tied down in searching for him and his Arab bands, dominated von Hippel's thoughts. The belief that such a guerrilla unit might aid Germany in any future war was one which he imparted to his friend and confidant, Admiral Canaris, Head of the German Intelligence and counter-Intelligence organisation, the Abwehr. The Admiral, too, saw how a military David could destroy a Goliath.

Drawing upon his own experiences in German East Africa, von Hippel explained how a small German Colonial Force, commanded by von Lettow-Vorbeck, had conducted military operations against the Allies. Although, admittedly, these were of a minor nature, the *threat* they posed had tied down large numbers of British and Imperial troops who might otherwise have been released to fight in Flanders. Strong British forces had had to be kept in Africa throughout the whole of the First World War in pursuit of the small groups of Germans under von Lettow. Von Hippel then considered the prospect of a new European war, whose outbreak he saw as being only a matter of time. He saw that Germany would need such guerrilla units: élite formations, highly skilled, highly trained and with specialist abilities. Such groups could spearhead the new campaigns. They could infiltrate the enemy's lines before war had been declared, or before an offensive was launched and be in a position to seize vital targets or tactical areas as soon as operations began. The men of such units would not have their abilities wasted in conventional infantry battles. They would be held in readiness to attack by land, sea or air and would be withdrawn once they had gained their objectives; possibly even before the enemy had become aware of their presence. He appreciated that the existence of the new units could not be kept forever secret, but once knowledge of them had become public, fear of their skills and the awareness that they were in action would force an enemy to flood his sensitive areas with troops to combat them; men who would otherwise be used in the front line. The need for conventional units would, of course, remain. But what if in a new war the advance of those conventional units and formations could be aided by raids? What if raiders could attack and destroy enemy headquarters? Then, blows would have been struck at the foe which might paralyse him completely or at least slow the speed of his counter-actions and thereby reduce the effectiveness of his defence.

How much, if at all, von Hippel was influenced by German military thought on the use of armoured blitzkreig warfare is not known, but the two concepts were in parallel: a strike at the nerve-centre of the enemy by small units whose mobility would counter enemy superiority in mass.

The concepts of guerrilla warfare were accepted by Canaris, whose officers then made approaches to, and interviewed, the type of men whom they intended to recruit for the new units. These would be men who had lived abroad and who had been engaged in open-air toil. In short, independently-minded, tough and resilient men, inured to hardship and with knowledge of foreign languages, customs and cultures. And such men were available in large numbers. In the years after 1918 many Germans had emigrated to South America and to Africa, hoping to find there the employment that was unavailable in the Fatherland. In the late 1930s these men were encouraged to return to the new Germany which Hitler had created and they came home in thousands to offer their skills and abilities to the Third Reich.

All those who served in von Hippel's detachments were volunteers and this was a cardinal rule maintained throughout most of the Second World War. Indeed, it has been claimed that there were always more men coming forward than could be accepted; volunteers willing and eager to serve in unusual and secret units. They found, upon being accepted, that they belonged to an Abwehr formation which was, as has already been stated, an Intelligence/counter-Intelligence organisation. It must be emphasised here, that these new men were not, nor would be, spies or agents, but were soldiers with specialist aptitudes who had been grouped together to carry out, under the aegis of the Abwehr, the type of military operation for which conventional military units would have been unsuited. They belonged, in those first years, less to the Army than to Admiral Canaris, and the power of the Abwehr was sufficient to deflect those military commanders who asked too many awkward questions about these uniformed men who did not appear on anybody's establishment.

As early as the summer of 1939, Hippel's first groups had been formed and trained. The men of this original unit were Volksdeutsche, that is racial Germans who lived in German communities outside the Reich's borders. These first men were either Sudeten Germans or Volksdeutsche who had lived in areas along the Polish frontier or even in Poland itself. For the sake of administrative convenience and secrecy the detachments were formed into a single group and given the cover name of No. 1 Construction Training Company (German Company) for special purposes. Their first commander was Leutnant Grabert.

At this point we might consider the ease with which men having language skills could be obtained for the 'German Company'. Any nation which touches a foreign country will have along its border zone villages, sometimes even small towns, in which the use of both languages is accepted for social and commercial intercourse. There are parts of Austria, particularly those frontier regions which border Hungary, Yugoslavia and Czechoslovakia, where not one but three languages are in more or less common use.

A colleague of mine, born in Poland during the years of the Habsburg Empire, spoke Polish as his native tongue as well as German which he needed both as a student and later as a Habsburg Army officer. His family's estate bordered on Russia and he therefore knew Russian as a third language. His formal education gave him Latin, Greek and French so that by the age of twenty or so he had command of six tongues. This linguistic fluency could be matched by thousands of people who lived in pre-war Europe. It was from men with such talents that Hippel drew his volunteers.

2

PRETEXT FOR WAR

SD operations in August 1939

Among the evidence presented during the trials of the major war criminals at Nuremberg was proof positive that Adolf Hitler was obsessed with bringing about a conflict in Europe. It is, perhaps, too little understood that Hitler was not a normal politician, but a revolutionary who lived by the evil slogan that the end justifies the means. As the Führer saw it, the end, which was to make Germany supreme, justified the means, which led in time to the Second World War. During 1939 Hitler determined that he would tidy up Germany's eastern frontier, for he was offended by the Corridor, a stretch of land which gave Poland access to the sea, but which cut off East Prussia from the rest of Germany. Hitler resolved to go to war with Poland but it was not possible simply to invade his eastern neighbour state without cause. That would be open aggression. He had to act more subtly than that. War when it came must show the Poles to be the aggressors; in the eyes of the world Germany had to be seen as the victim responding to that assault. And yet it seemed to Hitler that the Poles could not or would not be forced into aggression. The government in Warsaw showed no intention of invading and, outwardly at least, gave no signs of reacting to the threats and hostile propaganda which poured from the radio-transmitters of the Reich. Inaction frustrated the Führer. Germany could not attack Poland and if that country would not invade the Reich, there was no possibility of war.

Once again the revolutionary slogan 'the end justifies the means' was to prove its perverted validity. To provoke the end Hitler intended to fake the means. A series of violent attacks against German property would be so executed as to appear to have been launched from Polish territory. With the plea that Germany had a duty to protect herself against aggression, the Third Reich would invade Poland and war would result. That it would have been provoked by lies was irrelevant, according to Hitler's revolutionary and pragmatic mind. At a meeting in Obersalzburg on 22 August 1939, the Chancellor declared to the commanders of his armed forces, 'I shall supply a propaganda justification to bring about hostilities. It is of little consequence whether the reasons are believed. No one asks the victor whether he had told the truth.' In making that declaration Hitler was not announcing a scheme which he might implement at some future date, but was proclaiming a plan which he had already discussed, which he had already approved and which had been set in motion by his creatures.

It is an unusual mind that will accept an order to fabricate a pretext to precipitate a major war. Surely, no one could be found who could accept so monstrous a commission. Hitler knew such a man. Reinhard Heydrich, Chief of the SD. Heydrich was, as we have already learned, an unusual person. A man of action and blindly obedient, but not so blind that he did not have an eye to the main chance, the extending of his organisation's influence. Hitler knew that Heydrich would accept the perverted order and mobilise his SD to carry out the grisly task.

It was the type of duty of which the Sicherheitsdienst already had some experience. In the spring of 1939, for example, there had been demonstrations in the rump of the violated State of Czechoslovakia during which German property was attacked and burned. These, and similar acts of provocation and the need to protect his fellow nationals against such oppression, were used by Hitler as the justification for the invasion of the Czech state. There were many who suspected that these convenient demonstrations were the work of sinister influences, and the suspicions were justified. The agitators who aroused the mobs were SD agents, German nationals who had lived in Czechoslovakia and who were fluent in the language.

With the Czech State gone, unrest flared next in Danzig when arms caches were discovered. To the Nazis these convenient finds were proof that the Poles had violated the neutrality of the Free City of Danzig. That the hidden supplies of weapons had been so easily found was due to the fact that they had been hidden by agents of the German Foreign Office and then 'uncovered' by the SD. The whole plot was a ruse to bring about a state of unease, not merely in Danzig, but throughout the whole of Europe. The peoples of the Continent were being conditioned to accept the certainty of a new war.

The unrest in Danzig was part of Hitler's propaganda plan, but now direct action was needed. Together with the Reichsführer SS, Heinrich Himmler, and the Chief of the SD, Reinhard Heydrich, the Führer planned the series of attacks which would be the pretext for the invasion of Poland. The scheme was simple and was known only to the three conspirators. Other men had to be brought in – officers to organise the supply of uniforms, weapons and SD personnel – which widened the circle of those involved in the operation and the increase in numbers heightened the risk of a security leak. The deterrent against such a leak was brutal. Each conspirator was warned that disclosure of any part of the plan would result not only in the execution of himself but of all his blood-relations. His entire family would be wiped out. It was a terrible threat and the fear of it kept mouths shut and security watertight. There is no record of the meetings which took place between Hitler, Himmler and Heydrich to decide the tactics of the plan

1

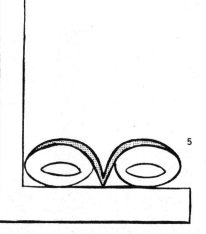

2

3

4

5

Tactical signs worn by Brandenburg units.
1 The cuff band worn by the whole Division.
2 The tactical sign of the Panzer Corps 'Gross-deutschland' was the outline of a German steel helmet; the Brandenburg eagle was worn within this shape to indicate that the unit was on the Brandenburg establishment.
3 The Brandenburg Signals Battalion.
4 The Koenen units that served in North Africa.
5 The Parachute Battalion.

Above left Admiral Canaris with some of the Officers of the Abwehr in 1940.
Above The headquarters of the Abwehr in the Bendlerstrasse in Berlin.
Left Reinhard Heydrich, here seen as a general of the Waffen SS and wearing the distinctions he had gained as a fighter pilot.

Right Volksdeutsche were Germans living outside the borders of the Third Reich. The men seen in this photograph were Polish Volksdeutsch who had been conscripted into the Polish Army, but from which they had deserted in order to enlist in the German armed forces. It was men of this type who entered Brandenburg service.
Below Men of Brandenburg detachment in training for the campaign in the west, 1940.

Above The DFS 230 assault glider, the type of machine that carried German paratroops into action at Eben Emael, the invasion of Crete and the rescue of Mussolini.
Below A training flight for the gliders of the para group that carried out the attacks in Belgium during May 1940.

Above right One of the immensely thick armoured cupolas of the Eben Emael fortress complex. Even the largest of hollow-charge grenades had little effect on them.
Below right A member of Para Assault Detachment Koch waiting for the order to move forward, May 1940.

Above German troops standing on the roof of part of the Ebe[...] Emael complex.
Left Oberleutnant Rudolf Witzig, commander of the group tha[...] captured Eben Emael on 10 May 1940.
Below Men of Witzig's 'Granite' assault detachment at Ebe[...] Emael after their relief on 11 May.

Above More of the victors of Eben Emael: part of Hauptfeldwebel Wenzel's detachment of the 'Granite' group. Wenzel, centre, wears a bandage round his head.

Below General Student, Commander-in-Chief of the German parachute arm, accompanied by Koch and Witzig, inspect and thank the men of Para Assault Detachment Koch after their return from Belgium.

Above Major Rudloff, commanding the 3rd Battalion of the Brandenburg Regiment, inspects his men before their move to France, preparatory to the planned invasion of Great Britain.
Below Leutnant Gräbert, one of the two Brandenburg men who removed the explosive charges from the Nieuport bridge in 1940.
Right Brandenburg soldiers disguised as civilian Serbs before going out on a mission at the opening of the campaign in Yugoslavia in April 1941.

to which was given the cover name 'Hindenburg'. It is not known whose idea it was to carry out the mock attacks, nor which of the conspirators decided the locations or conceived the macabre touch of using the bodies of murdered concentration-camp victims as proof of Polish attacks against German property on German territory.

Evidence from the testimony at Nuremberg indicates the probability that, to begin with, a large number of sites were chosen where simulated raids would take place, but that in time these were reduced to only three: the radio-station at Gleiwitz, a Customs post at Hochlinden and a gamekeeper's house at Pitschen. It was intended that the Gleiwitz raid should produce the best propaganda results for it would reach the widest audience. The scenario was that it would sound to listeners as if the radio-station were under attack. Live, over the air, would come the noise of shouting and of gunfire. An excited voice would proclaim in Polish that the time had come for old scores to be settled and the speaker would go on to call for the destruction of Germany. Seven men, dressed in civilian clothes, would form the attack group. The second raid would take place at Hochlinden where a very large group of men, dressed in Polish uniform, would attack and destroy the Customs post. At Pitschen, the third raid would be against an isolated house by a 'Polish' mob dressed in civilian clothes.

Having established the strategy, the chief conspirators left the tactical details to be arranged by their subordinates, but Heydrich was determined to remain in total control of the operation and chaired all the important planning meetings. The first of these was in Berlin on 8 August, when the SD Commander briefed his field commanders. One SS officer, Melhorn, raised doubts. Not as to the legality of what would be done, nor the morality of it, but as to whether the undertaking would encroach upon the Army's traditional role of carrying out operations along the German border and upon foreign territory. Heydrich's response to any doubts was to announce, 'It is the Führer's order.' To this statement there could be neither discussion nor objection. The Führer's command could not be questioned, it could only be obeyed – immediately and unconditionally.

A second conference, two days later, brought in Alfred Naujocks of the SD Foreign Intelligence Section. Detailed planning went ahead swiftly. Heydrich told the successive meetings that the Führer had decided that war should begin on 26 August – the anniversary of the military victory which von Hindenburg had gained during the First World War. It would be a good omen for Hitler's war. The first important task was to establish a communications network between the senior SD officers and the offices which they would establish in those areas where the attacks would be made. The network was kept deliberately simple, a telephone and a telex machine. The one to be used in the event of a breakdown of the other.

During the second week of August the SD Main Office sent out instructions to all its regional offices that the names of middle-aged men with military experience and a knowledge of Polish were to be forwarded. While the recruiting of the men was under way the task of obtaining uniforms and equipment was begun. The relationship between Admiral Canaris of the Abwehr and Reinhard Heydrich of the SD had never been cordial and by the autumn of 1939 they were strained almost to breaking-point. The SD leader did not wish to make a direct approach to the Admiral for the provision of the Polish uniforms. He did not want to be questioned about the operation or to have it changed in any way through the interference of the Abwehr. At a meeting with Hitler, the SD commander asked for the Führer's assistance and was given assurance that the matter would be dealt with immediately. And so it was. The order was given. Inquiries by the Abwehr were ignored and Canaris's point-blank questions to Naujocks were evaded or at best only partially answered. Interviews which the Admiral had with Hitler and then with Keitel, Head of the OKW, brought no comfort to the Head of the Abwehr. Hitler advised Canaris not to probe too deeply. The operation, claimed the Führer, was one which by its nature had to be a purely SS one in order not to involve the armed forces in actions which might be illegal. Not until the operation had been concluded did Canaris, the Head of the German counter-Intelligence organisation, learn what had lain behind the demand for Polish uniforms and weapons.

All over Germany, during that second week of August, SD men received orders from the SS or the Gestapo, to report in civilian clothes to the SS Fencing School at Bernau. The school building, empty at that time because of the political crisis, had not been designed to accommodate the hundreds of men who arrived. The conditions were spartan and the food inadequate. The SD men were ordered to surrender all personal belongings including wedding-rings, jewellery, paybooks, identity documents, photographs, letters and identity-discs. Nothing was to be retained that could identify them as being German or as belonging to the SD. They were given the same dire warning about breaches of security and were refused passes into the town. For as long as they remained at the Fencing School, they might not leave the premises and for the first few days, until fatigue uniforms were issued, they were not allowed outside the building during daylight. They were, in fact, incommunicado except that they might write and receive one letter every fourteen days. All mail would be censored.

The denim uniforms, when they arrived, were those of the Frontier Police and, dressed as recruits to that formation, the SD men were drilled and instructed in Police procedure. One of the things that each of them had in common was a knowledge of the Polish language. To improve their grasp of that tongue conversations were conducted in

Polish and community singing in the wet canteen each evening included, by order, Polish as well as German songs. Men who had served in the Polish Army gave instructions in Polish arms drill and military etiquette. Hair was close-cropped in the Slav military fashion. The uniforms arrived and the men whose role would be to form the 'Polish' attackers were changed from German SS men into infantrymen of the Polish Army. No details at all of what task it was that they were to undertake had been given to the rank and file. As a consequence rumours abounded. The emphasis on all things Polish, the uniforms and the weapons could only mean that they were to undertake some type of suicide mission inside Poland.

As already stated, the first part of the 'Hindenburg' plan called for an assault on the Customs post at Hochlinden which had been selected because of its tactically important features: it could not be seen from the nearest German or Polish villages, and on its southern side was a salient of Polish territory which jutted into Germany. Therefore, riflemen and machine-gunners standing on German soil could fire across Polish territory onto the Customs house, and the bullets would be seen as coming from Polish territory. The very isolated spot had the additional advantage that the raid could take place and the attackers could be taken away in trucks before genuine Polish personnel could move into the salient to determine the cause of the shooting.

There were certain factors to be considered. The 'Polish' group would be firing rifles and the noise might prompt the German frontier police to engage in a fire-fight with the 'attackers'. To prevent this the frontier police detachment on duty at Hochlinden was withdrawn and replaced by SD men from the Bernau school, dressed as policemen. In order to give substance to the official report of an armed assault by 'Polish' aggressors, there would have to be return fire from the German side and this would be supplied by other SD men who, disguised as German infantry, would be positioned on a hill to the north of the Customs post and who would reply to the 'Polish' fire by shooting into the air. The assault upon the gamekeeper's house would employ SD men who, dressed as Polish civilians, would act as a frenzied mob. The game-keeper and his wife would be given leave of absence before the attack began. Of all the SD groups from the Fencing School at Bernau, it was the Pitschen detachment which would need to contain the greatest number of Polish speakers. The Gleiwitz radio-station raid would need only one fluent Polish speaker to make the provocative announcements. The other members of the party would also be heard, but their contribution would be restricted to shouts and curses in Polish. A radio technician would accompany the group, to ensure that the broadcast went without a hitch.

By the end of the third week of August, everything was ready. The Naujocks group had arrived singly in Gleiwitz and had taken rooms in an hotel in the town. All had registered as businessmen and were not seen to mix socially in the hotel's public rooms. While they were waiting for D-Day, last-minute preparations were in hand to ensure that they would not be hindered during the raid. The police guard at the entrance to the radio-station was withdrawn and was replaced by SD men. It was not until 23 August that a convoy of trucks left Bernau carrying the Hochlinden and Pitschen detachments. At Oppeln the column divided and each group drove to its billeting area. On arrival the commanders reported direct to Heydrich by telephone that they were ready for action.

For the Pitschen detachment there was a period of unpleasant strain. They were billeted in a barn without any facilities and they were not allowed to go out into the farmyard to wash. Guards were posted to ensure that there was no contact between the men and the local people, and the men were forbidden to write home. Alcohol was prohibited. The Pitschen group lay for days in their barn, badly fed, lacking water, unable to wash and completely ignorant of the mission that lay before them.

Those at Hochlinden fared a little better. They were quartered in an hotel, but were confined to their rooms and forbidden to make unnecessary movement. Their presence was to be kept as quiet as possible even though they were in civilian clothes and were registered as businessmen. A reconnaissance of the Customs post area alarmed the group leader. There was a great number of Army units in this sensitive border area who might be alerted by the firing and become involved in the mock attack. Heydrich solved the problem immediately. He had the military units removed from the Hochlinden sector.

The three attack groups would be alerted and brought into action by telephone messages or, in the event of a telephone fault, by telex. The Gleiwitz section needed only the phrase 'Grandmother has died' to send them into the attack. The Pitschen and Hochlinden detachments were to receive three messages. The first would alert them, the second would prepare them and the third (the single word 'Agatha') would launch them. By one of those pieces of bungling that seemed to be characteristic of SD operations, Hochlinden did not receive the first warning message when it was telephoned on the morning of 24 August. As a consequence when the second telephoned message was received the commander panicked and moved his unit out, anticipating – wrongly as it happened – that 'Agatha' would follow almost immediately. It did not. That was the evening that the Führer changed his mind and decided not to invade Poland on 26 August, but on 1 September.

Within hours the 'Polish' troop from Hochlinden was in position, fully dressed in their foreign uniforms, ready to open fire upon the

Customs post. Their duties had been explained to them and the men of the SD, tense and expectant lay waiting in the damp undergrowth for the 'off'. Back in their hotel there was panic among the men who would form the 'German police group' and who were still in their rooms. Berlin had called and the operation was cancelled. It was explained to the furious Heydrich that the 'Polish' detachment was already lying expectantly in a field of standing crops waiting for darkness to fall. He realised that the whole plan might be compromised because the group had moved too quickly and demanded that a message be passed to them. It was explained to the Gruppenführer that the Hochlinden group was out of telephone or wireless contact. The only means of passing a message was by courier. Send a messenger was the order. Heydrich's command was obeyed immediately and to the letter. A dispatch rider went out.

Any Poles who witnessed the scene must have been as surprised as the SD group must have been embarrassed, when a German Army motor-cyclist roared his machine into a field and handed over a message to a figure, camouflaged with foliage, prone in the cabbages. The crestfallen Hochlinden group got up, moved back into the woods and returned to their hotel. Their commander was recalled to Berlin where he was shouted at by Heydrich and posted immediately to an area where his wild enthusiasm would not have such politically embarrassing results. The one positive gain from the whole farcical episode was the realisation that the attack needed fewer men than had been thought necessary. A regrouping reduced the original company-sized unit to that of a platoon, that is about forty men.

If one aspect of the Hochlinden action had contained elements of pure farce there was another which had a terrible and sinister significance. This was the appearance of a small section of men of whose existence the SD rank and file had been in total ignorance. If operation 'Hindenburg' can be seen as an operation carried out by a secret force then this new, mysterious unit was an enigma within that secret. The task of this anonymous detachment was to supply the bodies which would be found at those places where the attacks had taken place. The corpses, dressed either in Polish uniform or in civilian clothes, but all of them having Polish documents, money and bus tickets, would furnish visible and physical proof that the Poles had been the aggressors.

At senior SD level there had been long, heated and difficult discussions as to why the bodies were needed and how they were to be obtained. In view of the reputation for brutality and murder which the SS gained and, in view of its condemnation by the Nuremberg tribunal as a criminal organisation, it is with disbelief that one reads of how many of its senior officers objected to the use of dead bodies to 'dress' an attack. There was more outspoken criticism of the alternative plan to supply live criminals who would be shot at the various attack areas. The strong objections of the SS officers crumbled at the chilling words 'It is the Führer's order.' Further resistance was pointless. Hitler had commanded and, stifling their own feelings, the protesting commanders obeyed.

Subsequent developments concerning the macabre proposal assumed an almost surrealist aspect, largely because of the German love of order and routine. Bureaucratic procedures were not merely important – they were vital, and the various bureaucrats defended their mysteries with amazing tenacity. That these men, some of very low rank, were prepared to refuse the demands of very senior SS officers is amazing. Even more amazing is that most of them succeeded in their objections.

The intention to supply bodies of recently deceased concentration-camp victims was impracticable for several reasons, chiefly because bodies putrefy quickly and the autumn of 1939 was unusually hot. All inmates of concentration camps were registered and a strict check was kept on them at all times. A dead man would be entered in the camp's hospital register and when he died would be entered in the mortuary ledger. When the body left the camp, it would be recorded in the main ledger as being struck off strength and the reason for release from the camp entered correctly. It was a very well-kept set of books, up to date and absolutely accurate. The commandant of the camp and his staff were adamant. They were sorry, but they could not hand over dead bodies just like that. Records were records and not even for the SD were they prepared to fake the entries. Just think of how inefficient they would look if the next of kin of a corpse turned up demanding the body and they had to confess that they had no idea of what had happened to it.

There had to be documentation. To put a dead body from a concentration camp into a local mortuary would require documentation and precise registration. The bodies which the SD would be bringing would not of course, have any documents to show that they were German. The whole point was that they were supposed to be Poles. Without documents they could not be stored in a mortuary. Then, too, an official autopsy would have to be carried out in the coroner's office. That would reveal that the men were already dead at the time when they were supposed to have been participating in an insurgent battle. It was not possible to fabricate a cause of death for a coroner's report, not even for the SD.

Thwarted by the refusal of the SS concentration-camp authorities to let them have the bodies of the already dead, the SD then turned to live inmates and decided that the condemned to death would do nicely. The camp at Sachsenhausen contained a great number of prisoners, some of whom were murderers, most of whom were habitual prisoners. Each had a common link. They were all, in the words of Oberführer Muller of the Gestapo, 'as good as dead'. But not any condemned prisoner would be suitable. For this last service to the Fatherland only those with pronounced Slavic features could be considered. The wide choice of those who had been pronounced 'as good as dead' was reduced by selection to twelve. These were then removed from Sachsenhausen after another maniacal argument about registering, de-registering, keeping the records straight and the need to supply accurate returns. With the promise that those not required would be returned, the twelve men were removed. Only four were selected and the eight not chosen were returned to Sachsenhausen. There they were held in solitary confinement for months before returning to normal camp routine. The unlucky four were held, also in solitary confinement, until the time when they, the 'tinned beef', to use the code-name given to them, would be needed.

Discussions at senior SD level then determined that only in Hochlinden would there be more than one body. At Gleiwitz, it was decided, a single body, dressed in Polish uniform should be sufficient and at Pitschen there was no need of a body at all. The Gleiwitz victim was not one of the concentration-camp inmates, but a local man known for his pro-Polish views. He was taken quietly into custody and held incommunicado at the Gleiwitz police station. Significantly his detainment was not recorded. The story that would be spread to cover his disappearance would be that he had suddenly left the area. When his dead body was found at the radio-station, local people, aware of his Polish sympathies, would lend credence to the official story of the 'Polish' attack.

During the last week of peace that Europe was to know for the next six years, the various elements of 'Hindenburg' stood ready. In the afternoon of 31 August, the code-words were sent out to the waiting detachments. Action was for that night.

The time chosen for the Gleiwitz raid was 20.00. Dusk would have fallen by that time and rural communities retire indoors very early. By 20.00 it could be confidently expected that most local people would be at home, listening to the radio. The raiders when they struck would have a captive audience of audio witnesses to the provocation. The power of radio to influence people was immense. In those days before the Second World War the naïve belief was still current that a thing read in the newspaper or heard on the wireless must be true.

On that evening of 31 August three operations were initiated that would, by the following day, have helped to plunge Europe into war. Let us follow the course of action of each of them.

The code-message which sent Naujocks' Gleiwitz radio group into action, 'Grandmother has died', was passed to the Sturmbannführer late in the afternoon. He explained to his men, for the first time, the mission that they would be undertaking. There would be no difficulty, he told them, in entering the radio-station, the guards on the main door were comrades, SD men. Shots would be fired into the air to intimidate the staff on duty – who were not to be harmed. The radio technician accompanying the group would then cut into the programme being broadcast. The Polish-speaking announcer would read the inflammatory messages to the accompaniment of shots, shouts and curses in Polish. Naujocks' group, all disguised as Polish soldiers, would occupy the studio for about ten minutes and would then move out, leaving behind them, in the transmitting-room, objects identifiable as being of Polish origin. There would be a truck drive back to Gleiwitz and the unit would break up and return to the Fencing School. The fact that the scenario would include a dead body was introduced during the briefing. The sudden appearance in the studio of a corpse, or worse still of a man who would become very suddenly a corpse, was a factor which it was thought might upset the members of the group who would be unprepared for such a brutal act. It should be remembered, if this attitude on the part of the SD seems unusual, that they had been policemen who knew the dangers of being accessories after the fact and of guilt by association.

Naujocks checked to ensure that none of his men was carrying documents or artefacts that would identify them as German, and the Gleiwitz detail moved off. The operation went as planned, until the time came for the 'Polish' announcer to interrupt the broadcast. To the consternation of the Sturmbannführer and his men they found that Gleiwitz had no broadcasting facilities. There followed a wild search for a microphone. The only one that could be found was up an aerial, erected for meteorological purposes to pick up the sound of thunder. The technician rigged a transmitting device and the fuming SD commander was told that the 'Polish' speech could be made. This went out to a counterpoint of gunfire. The Naujocks unit left the studio after seventeen minutes, four of which had been spent in sending out the message. They passed the secret commando with their 'tinned beef', the local man. Drugged, then dressed in Polish uniform, he was carried into the brightly lit studio. There he was shot.

The local constabulary, not privy to the plot, were alerted by a telephone message to say that the radio-station was under attack. The Gleiwitz police were soon on the scene, but not soon enough to catch the raiders. The body was photographed and the unprocessed plates went by special messenger flight to Berlin. The pictures would appear next morning as pictorial proof of Polish provocation. The raid on the radio-station at Gleiwitz had been a success of sorts, but it was a success known to only the local inhabitants. Only the farmers and the peasants living near the radio-station heard the interruption, heard the speech in Polish and the sounds of shooting.

Poor Naujocks! When he reported by telephone to Heydrich that the mission had been successfully completed he was called a liar. Heydrich

declared that his own radio had been tuned to Gleiwitz the whole evening and that he had heard nothing – no shouts, no shots, no speeches.
The last farcical element was that nobody had realised that Gleiwitz, as
a relay station, had a low power output, or that its programmes went
out on the same wave-length as that of the Breslau station. The whole
purpose of the raid was that it should be heard by millions of listeners,
but the powerful Breslau transmitter had blanketed out Gleiwitz so
completely that apart from a few peasants the entire episode had gone
unheard.

The Hochlinden unit had gained experience from the mistake it had
made in its premature move. Now the 'Polish' platoon would make only
a charge from German territory. Also the earlier experience showed that
there was no need for the detachment to leave so soon after receipt of
the code-word. On D-Day minus 1, when the single word 'Agatha' was
received, at 20.00, the lorries did not leave the farm until several hours
had passed. At 23.45 they turned off the country road and onto a track
which led towards the Customs post. Headlights and sidelights were
switched off. Slowly the trucks rolled along the bumpy track through
the autumn darkness and halted at the edge of the Rauden woods which
line the frontier. Later that same evening the group, dressed as German
Frontier Police, was carried to a small hill about a mile north of the
border and there lay down to wait for H-Hour, 04.00.

There was no sound in the dark wood where the 'Polish' platoon lay.
Towards 03.00 the men donned the foreign uniforms. At the final
briefing they were warned that until the operation had been completed
they were to speak only Polish. At H-Hour they were to advance upon
the Customs building singing songs and shouting slogans in Polish and
firing their guns into the air. Surprisingly, their weapons were loaded
with ball ammunition. Once inside the post they were to destroy it. A
little before first light the platoon moved out of the woods, through the
fields and halted only 200 yards from the building. At 04.00 exactly, the
commander stood up, fired his pistol in the air and led his men into the
charge. To meet the 'Polish' attack the few men on duty, all of them SD
men dressed as policemen and all aware of what was happening, fired a
few token shots of resistance into the air and then surrendered. Their
return fire was that of blank cartridges. The destruction of the post
began.

The 'Polish' platoon left the wrecked building, passing the bodies of
the 'tinned beef' which were lying in the open near some bushes. The
rest of the incident unfolded as planned. The 'German Frontier Police'
advanced firing blank rounds and captured the 'Poles'. The prisoners
were then marched through the streets of Hochlinden and taken away
in trucks, proof to the local people of the authenticity of the attack. Back
at the Customs post the 'tinned beef' were butchered and then laid out
as if they had been shot during the raid. They were then photographed.

To add a touch of realism the dead were posed according to the wounds they had received. Some lay stomach down, others were facing upwards. The faces of the latter, being visible and possibly identifiable, were smashed in with blows from rifle butts. The undeveloped photographs, still in the camera, were rushed to Berlin and the dead, having served their purpose, were taken away and secretly buried.

The third raid took place at the gamekeeper's house at Pitschen. This went according to plan and, indeed, why should it not have done. The house was away from the village, isolated and in a deep wood which extends across the border. The raid was only a demonstration – there was to be no 'tinned beef' planted in this episode.

Towards 19.00 on 31 August, the Pitschen detachment was alerted. An order was placed by its commander for eighty pints of tea with rum, and, having consumed part of their fortifying drink, the group set out for the gamekeeper's house. At the assembly area the men changed into Polish civilian dress and marched to the house singing Polish songs. Once arrived they fired shots into the air and smashed up the kitchen. By 22.00 the group, having resumed their own clothes, were back in Pitschen drinking tea and rum, celebrating their victory as defenders of the Fatherland. At the gamekeeper's house the local mayor and his police were soon searching for clues. These were few except for some fragments of Polish clothing and bits of paper bearing Polish words. It was little enough, but it was sufficient to proclaim this as an assault upon the sovereign territory of the Reich. Operation 'Hindenburg' was over. The SD men who had carried out the attacks were moved back to the Fencing School and then returned to their own units.

As the men of the Hochlinden and the Pitschen detachments headed northwards towards Berlin in the early morning of 1 September, their trucks passed on the road the long columns of guns, tanks and men heading eastward towards Poland. 'Hindenburg' had been so successful that Hitler was able to declare in the Reichstag that same day, 'Polish troops of the Regular Army have been firing on our territory during the night. Since 05.45 we have been returning that fire.' The Führer had got his war.

As a propaganda exercise it was probably successful. The Government of the Third Reich produced a White Book which set out in detail the aggressive acts of which the Poles stood accused. Among the illustrations were the photographs which had been taken at Gleiwitz and Hochlinden, showing the dead bodies of men dressed in Polish uniforms. The immediate casualties of war were in this case, not just truth, but the concentration-camp victims and the pro-Polish sympathiser, all of whom had been murdered by the SD. They were the first of all who were to die in that war. There were the usual commissions of inquiry which visited all three sites and carried out investigations which proved, without a shadow of doubt, that the Poles had made the attacks, that Polish soldiers had been killed during those attacks and that the aggression had been unprovoked.

Reflecting upon operation 'Hindenburg', certain questions arise, the most important being: were all the charades and the dressing-up necessary if the Hochlinden Customs post could not be seen from the nearest Polish and German villages? If the guards on the door were all SD personnel and since it was night time, why was there a need to dress up a whole platoon of men as Poles? Why did they have to charge into action and why was there the play-acting with the 'German Frontier Police', pretending to attack and capture them? It seems unlikely that this elaborate performance was put on for the few people in Hochlinden who saw the so-called prisoners being bundled into trucks. Then, too, why did there have to be the elaborate performance at the gamekeeper's house? Again, the night was dark, the house was empty and the area was isolated. The group of 'Polish ruffians' did not need to dress themselves in the ill-fitting clothes which had been supplied from SD sources. What German traveller out on the dark road at that time of night and seeing a rowdy group of Poles surrounding a house would have bothered to investigate whether the men wore badly-cut Polish clothes or off-the-peg suits. In any case the house had been chosen for the excellent reason that it was isolated and that few people passed it.

At Gleiwitz, with the exception of the two duty staff in the studio, all the characters were involved in the plot. Surely it would have been less bother had two or three men driven up to the doors, carried out the pistol shooting in the studio and made the appropriate noises as the broadcast was being made? Perhaps the answer lies in the fact that Heydrich and his senior commanders had seen too many spy films and read too many spy thrillers. It can only be that they thought that their elaborate charades were the way in which agents and undercover men *were supposed* to operate and so the leaders of the SD played out their parts believing as they did so that this eccentric behaviour was the norm in clandestine activities.

As the men of the SD detachment headed northwards back to Berlin, other men of a special force had been at work opening the way for the invading German Army. The speed with which the divisions moved into Polish Silesia and the fact that the great engineering complexes in the west of that country which were a main objective fell almost undamaged into German hands, is due to the actions of men of a special unit which was later to become the Brandenburg formation.

It is not possible to give any account of the actions in which those men of von Hippel's groups were involved, for neither the War Diaries nor the post-battle reports written by their company commanders survived the war. It is known only that the Abwehr posts in three German military Districts, Breslau, Königsberg and Vienna, sent in commando detachments and that the enterprises of these groups were successful. That of the Breslau and Vienna groups may, perhaps, be considered to have been the most important, because their task was to prevent the destruction of the Polish Silesian coal- and iron-mines until the German Army arrived.

In 1939, the territory of western Poland formed a blunt salient projecting into German Silesia. It can be appreciated that such a salient, containing complexes of mines and mills and held moreover by an Army inferior in strength to its adversary, would be a primary objective in a war.

For the Germans the reduction of the Polish salient would secure the greatest part of Poland's heavy industry as well as a great deal of her western territory, and such a prize was irresistible. Equally clearly can it be appreciated that the Polish authorities, aware of the strategic disability they faced, and appreciating that the salient could not be held, would seek by sabotage to deny its industrial advantages to the Germans. It was to prevent sabotage that Brandenburgers from Breslau infiltrated the threatened factories while from the south Polish-speaking Sudeten Germans also infiltrated important plants and factories. The Abwehr post in Königsberg did not have an economic target to defend, but a military objective to capture. The mission of the Brandenburg battle group which went out from East Prussia was to seize the bridges across the Vistula and to hold them until relieved.

Long before the SD groups had arrived to undertake their mock attacks, Brandenburg detachments from the Breslau and Vienna posts had gained employment in vital factories, had reconnoitred the shop floor areas, had brought in weapons and were awaiting the orders that would activate them. In the absence of written reports it can only be assumed that on 30 August the night-shift in those factories would have been given the code-word to prepare for action, within hours of receipt of the 'Stand to' order, and the German attack upon Poland was under way. One can imagine the short but sharp fire fights which began at first light on that morning of 1 September and which continued all day as Polish soldiers fought desperately to destroy the factories and von Hippel's men fought no less desperately to prevent this. The Brandenburg defence was successful and German motor cycle spearheads, roaring through the dust clouds, took over the plants which, although damaged by bullets and hand-grenades, were still active. The Brandenburgers then slipped back into their protective anonymity.

There was no official recognition for the successes they had achieved in their vital tasks. They were not named in the triumphant communiqués and the fanfared Orders of the Day. There were sentences whose meaning was kept deliberately vague so as not to alert Germany's foes – or friends – to the existence of these very special and highly secret units. The few men of von Hippel's command had achieved so much, but there is a bitter end to the story of this first operation and it is one which shows very clearly German bureaucratic thought. Recommendations for the award of Iron Crosses to the Breslau groups for this daring undertaking were rejected on the ground that at the time of the action no state of armed conflict existed between Poland and Germany. It was an attitude of mind with which the men of Brandenburg were to become very familiar during the years of war that lay ahead.

3

THE BLUFF THAT WORKED

Brandenburg in Holland, May 1940

The outcome of the Polish campaign demonstrated the value of von Hippel's units. The 'German' Company was expanded and a second Company was formed on 15 October 1939, the day on which the unit was formally established. The racial composition of No. 2 Company was chiefly Roumanian Volksdeutsche from the Banat and Siebenburgen districts. To them were added Baltic Germans and then some men who had lived in Palestine. By January 1940, the two-Company formation needed a headquarters group to administer it, but the lowest unit allowed to have such an administrative Section was a battalion; a minimum of four Companies was required. This qualification was circumvented and soon the 'Bau-Lehr Battalion z.b.V. Nr 800' had been formed and placed under von Hippel's command. The unit's depot was in Brandenburg/Havel.

Although we cannot detail the rise of Brandenburg, certain facts about this unit, unique in the German Army, are known. By the time that it had acquired regimental status, Brandenburg was a strong and closely-knit formation with the most wide-ranging skills, not least of which was mastery of a wide variety of languages. There was not an area of Europe with which some group of Brandenburgers was not familiar, nor a language that they could not speak. For example, in No. 1 Company of the 1st Battalion were men who could speak Estonian, Latvian, Lithuanian, Finnish or Russian. The men of No. 2 Company were chiefly those who had lived in the former German African colonies and who were proficient not only in the native languages and dialects of those areas, but also in English and Portuguese. The Volksdeutsche of No. 3 Company were from Czechoslovakia and spoke the languages and dialects of that country. In No. 4 Company the men had been drawn from Eastern Europe and had command of Polish, West Russian, Ukrainian and Ruthenian as well as the local dialects peculiar to those regions. The wide variety of tongues spoken and understood in the 1st Battalion could be matched by the men of the other battalions and somewhere within the Regiment, or so it was claimed, could be found at least one soldier with knowledge of such rare languages as Tibetan or Pushtu.

Early in 1940 at Brandenburg/Havel men of the 'German' Company and of No. 2 Company had begun a training schedule which would

bring them to a peak of fighting effectiveness for the campaigns which
lay ahead. Much of the specialist training was carried out on a large
country estate near Brandenburg and at the Army Engineer Training
School. There the future raiders were taught fieldcraft: how to move
silently through trees and to live from the food which the great forests
provided. Manoeuvres were conducted using live ammunition and
grenades; parachute training was given at Spandau, and instruction in
the handling of small boats, kayaks, and assault craft on the rivers and
lakes of the province. In addition to purely military training, great
emphasis was laid on initiative tests – such as obtaining the finger-
prints of senior police officials. These tasks were introduced as a relief
from the rigours of fieldcraft and outdoor training. Of greater significance was the instruction given in the production of explosives from
such simple and basic commodities as icing sugar, flour and potash.
Methods of silent killing with a garotte or knife were practised together
with marksmanship and ski training. In short, nothing was omitted
from the curriculum that would enable the Brandenburg soldier, in
enemy territory and if necessary alone, to live off the country, survive in
the most severe weather, carry out his appointed tasks and get back to
his parent unit.

After such training a Brandenburg man could move and kill quickly
and noiselessly. He was a competent saboteur and a survivor. With
soldiers like this to spearhead future battles, and to grasp the military
initiative and gain vital objectives, it was confidently hoped that the
costly blood-baths of the Great War might be avoided and that offensives and campaigns would be completed within weeks of their
opening. The German Army was a first-class instrument, but to enable
it to achieve those fast and sweeping advances by which victory would
be gained, Brandenburg units would first have to open the doors to the
enemy heartland through which the Divisions and Corps would flood,
conducting that Blitzkrieg war for which they had been prepared.

With the campaign in Poland concluded victoriously and armed with a
non-aggression pact between his country and the Soviet Union, Adolf
Hitler could feel confident that he had secured his eastern flank.
Vaunting ambition now demanded that he seek a military decision in
the West; a campaign that would conquer France and Great Britain who
had rejected his overtures for a settlement. The German supreme Commander was determined to strike for that decision either in the late
autumn or the winter of 1939, but the OKH rejected, as premature his
demands for an offensive. It was necessary, said the High Command,
that the Army be built up and trained.

Hitler accepted the postponements with bad grace, but was com-
forted by the fact that even if the offensive could not be opened when

he wanted it, at least the preparations were in hand. Orders for Operation 'Gelb', the war in the West, were issued on 9 October. Autumn passed, and the first winter of the war, a long and hard one, the most bitter for half a century. The impatient Hitler awaited the coming of campaigning weather and the chance to begin the battles against the Western Allies for which he longed. First, however, there were certain difficulties in the North to be resolved. Germany attacked Denmark and Norway. In that first operation of 1940, Danish-speaking members of Brandenburg, disguised as Danish soldiers, seized the bridge across the Grosse Belt over which the invading ground forces had to pass to reach their objectives in the north of the Kingdom. During the opening phases of the offensive, other groups from Brandenburg fought in Norway, posing as Norwegian soldiers.

In the campaigns against Poland, Denmark and Norway, Brandenburg men had disguised themselves in enemy uniforms in order to gain a tactical advantage, and it might be thought that such a ruse was forbidden under international law. This is not so and it does not contravene Article 23 of the Geneva Convention. Post-war trials, notably the Nuremberg Process, have since confirmed that it is lawful for a soldier to disguise himself in the uniform of his enemy and in that disguise to approach objectives which he intends to attack. What he may not do is to carry out an armed assault while still wearing disguise. Before he opens fire he must first discard the enemy clothing and must be clearly seen to be wearing the uniform of his own Army. A similar situation has always been accepted in naval warfare. The true identity of a ship may be concealed both by structural alteration or by flying the enemy's flag, but before action begins the false ensign must be hauled down and the correct one flown. International law also lays down that soldiers captured while wearing enemy uniform may not be tried as spies if the purpose of their mission was merely to gain information. The firing of weapons while wearing that uniform, however, renders them liable to trial and to execution if they are found guilty.

In the case of Brandenburg, the decision as to whether the unit undertaking an operation should wear disguise was taken by an officer of Abwehr II and he decided whether the disguise was to be complete or partial. Partial disguise meant the wearing of a few pieces of clothing, such as an overcoat a cap or helmet, which would confuse for only a very brief period. A full disguise meant that all visible uniform, equipment and arms were enemy ones. The details of the operation were then passed to the Field Group, the sub-unit which would carry it out. The number of men and the composition of that Field Group depended upon the size and importance of the target. Such missions as those which will be described in this book, were usually carried out by battle groups of less than platoon strength. There was no fixed establishment, but there were constant elements. Each group was made up of men who were fluent in the enemy's language and explosives experts were included in the group composition. It was also the practice to name a detachment after the man who was to command it for that particular mission.

The war against the Anglo-French Allies opened while German forces were still fighting in Norway. Operation 'Gelb' began at 05.35 on the morning of 10 May, when one hundred and thirty-five German divisions struck across the frontiers of Holland, Belgium and France against a superior force of Allied divisions. Hitler was confident that his battle-tested army was strong enough to attack and overcome its enemies in the West. The Anglo-French showed no aggressive intentions towards Germany. Their whole strategy seemed to be defensive and Hitler was aware, through Abwehr Intelligence sources, that neither Power, whether individually or in tandem, could withstand the fast, dynamic style of war for which the Wehrmacht had been prepared. Indeed, a short campaign was essential and complete victory must be its result for the Third Reich could not afford to be involved in a long and costly war. Germany must win before the full power of the Western Empires could be developed.

The serious and weighty discussions and arguments on strategy do not need to concern us too much. Simply put, the German High Command had to decide from which direction they should make their attack in the West. Should Operation 'Gelb' be a re-run of the 1914 Schlieffen Plan? In this the German armies had marched through Belgium and then, in a giant left wheel, had descended like a sickle stroke upon Paris. The Schlieffen Plan had allowed the German armies to advance quickly across fairly flat country, but this was the obvious invasion route, the one which armies throughout history had followed when invading France. To the planners at OKH it was clear that if the Low Countries were the most obvious route, those would be the areas in which the Western Allies would deploy their strongest forces.

Running along the length of eastern France was the strong and modern defensive system of the Maginot Line and it was quite clear to the OKH that the very presence of that line forbad any attack being made through eastern/central or eastern/southern France. Keen German eyes noted that the strong forts of the Maginot Line ended at the French Ardennes and that there were no strong fortifications in the Belgium Ardennes, for Belgian military commanders had considered, as had the French High Command, that the terrain there was too rugged to permit the passage of a modern invading army. It was to prove a costly mis-appreciation of the enemy's capabilities, for on the German Staff there was an officer who held the contrary opinion. Von Manstein, who would become one of the outstanding German commanders of the

Second World War, believed that the terrain, despite the lack of roads, presented no insurmountable obstacles. Indeed, they would have to be overcome for the Ardennes was the only point at which the Germans could penetrate the Allied line quickly and exploit its weakness. The chief advantage of von Manstein's plan was that as the attack would be made from the east – a totally unexpected direction – it would catch the Allies off-balance. The bulk of the Anglo-French armies would be facing northwards towards Belgium and Manstein's plan would bring the German Panzer mass into their unprotected rear.

Manstein's plan would undoubtedly commit the main German force to bad roads through hilly and wooded country and should the attack fail, heavy losses would be suffered. On the other hand it offered the promise of a quick victory in the first phase of the campaign in the West; the destruction of the Allied armies in Flanders. It was a gamble, but one with a great promise of success. Hitler accepted the revolutionary theory as soon as it was put to him. He saw, as Manstein had seen, that the German initiative would throw his opponents into disarray. The Supreme Command emphasised that the Anglo-French must be given no chance of obtaining the initiative. The keys to success would lie in fast movement by Panzer formations which would strike deep into the enemy, and the employment of the Stuka dive-bomber as long-range artillery.

In this account of some of the special forces that went into action on D-Day of Operation 'Gelb', we will concentrate on the German Sixth Army within whose establishment were included the Brandenburg detachments and the Para Engineers. Although Sixth Army did not have to penetrate the Ardennes the barriers to its advance were no less daunting. Facing this Army were a number of water obstacles and the fortress of Eben Emael. Included in Sixth Army's Operations Order was the sentence that its forces were to '. . . advance on the line Venlo–Aachen, to cross the Meuse quickly and to pass through the Belgian defence system without delay . . .'

The most significant phrase in the long and detailed orders was that the forces had to pass through the Belgian defence systems without delay. It is the account of the Brandenburg detachments' seizure of intact bridges in Holland which opens this story, followed by the glider-borne assault by a Para group upon the fortress of Eben Emael. Both operations were vital to the success of Sixth Army's stated task, '. . . to pass . . . without delay'.

Although certain army divisions also carried out operations to capture tactically important bridges along their own front, the role of the Brandenburg in the first, vital hours of the campaign was the key one. It may be claimed, with accuracy, that of all the principal targets selected and fought for in the opening attacks of 10 May, only one was not included in the Brandenburg portfolio. That single exception was the airborne assault upon Eben Emael.

The Brandenburg were given four principal missions: all were bridges which had to be seized intact. The first of these was the Meuse bridge at Massyk, which was entrusted to the men of No. 3 Company. The second was for a group from No. 2 Company to seize and hold the Gennep bridge until German troop-trains had crossed into Holland. The third, to be executed by a detachment from No. 4 Company, had as its objective the taking out of the bridges across the Juliana Canal at Berg, Uromon, Obicht and Stein. Part of the Brandenburg battalion's headquarters group together with a reinforcement of a platoon of Brandenburgers, was to be attached to 24th Infantry Division for the fourth, major operation. The task of that detachment was to speed the advance of the division by taking out enemy defensive positions in front of the Siegfried Line and along the Luxembourg frontier.

Before the new campaign opened, Brandenburg detachments, fluent in the languages of the countries which they were to attack, had been preparing themselves in the frontier areas. Reconnaissance patrols, some made up of small sections, others consisting of single individuals, had slipped across the border to report on the positions and numbers of sentries, the location and strength of field fortifications and the villages in which enemy reinforcements and garrisons were quartered. From February onwards the number and size of these penetrations increased until a complete Intelligence picture of enemy dispositions and strengths had been built up.

The plan for Operation 'Gelb' foresaw the use of airborne troops in a number of operations against strategically important targets, several of which were located in the west of Holland. In order that the Paras should not have to carry on an unequal fight for too long it was vital that they be relieved by conventional forces within the shortest possible time. It was the necessity to relieve the paratroops who would have landed in the west of Holland that gave impetus to the Brandenburg operation against the Gennep railway bridge.

The 450-yard long bridge near the Dutch town of Gennep carries the railway line from Goch in Germany across the River Meuse and into the west of Holland. It stood more than two miles from the Dutch-German frontier, and it had to be taken before the Dutch could destroy it. The Brandenburg assault team would have to be inside the neutral Netherlands before the campaign had officially opened, so that they could capture the bridge before zero hour. Behind the group of Brandenburg men who would seize the bridge were two fully-loaded troop-trains ready to exploit the capture and to push on towards the main Dutch defences; the Peel position. The troop-trains were timed to begin their move precisely at zero hour.

The intensive training which the men of No. 2 Company had been given was of a diverse nature so that none of the soldiers was aware of the target or the importance of its seizure to the success of the Supreme Command battle plan. The training had lasted from February, when the agents were first brought to a camp in Asperden, until the evening of 9 May, when they set out on their mission. In Asperden camp there were several Dutch Nazis who were to go with No. 2 Company's detachment. Not until the night before the opening of Operation 'Gelb' did the Company Commander disclose the objective and the method by which it would be achieved.

Half an hour before midnight on the night of 9 May a small section of Brandenburgers slipped across the frontier disguised as Dutch military policemen. The group leader was a Corporal who spoke fluent Dutch and who had crossed the border several times to carry out reconnaissance. He led his group into the flat land between the River Niers and the railway embankment until they reached the road which connects the villages of Heien and Gennep. This road was frequently patrolled, but the Brandenburg unit crossed it without incident and moved silently towards the flat and marshy meadows which line the banks of the Meuse. In bushes at the foot of the railway embankment the men hid themselves, shivering in the cold night air and waiting for dawn. Although the Netherlands Army had gone to full alert as early as 22.00 on 9 May, there were no patrols in the Gennep area. Furthermore, the Dutch had received confirmation that the invasion would take place on the 10th, and this information had led to demolitions at certain places along the frontier with Germany. But at the Gennep railway bridge all was quiet.

Just before dawn the two troop-trains moved slowly across the frontier. As they approached the Gennep bridge the Dutch sentry at a paper factory shouted a warning and fired a shot in the air. This went unheard in the noise of the locomotives. For the Germans the crucial time was approaching. There were long minutes of tension when the first train, a partly armoured one, ran on to the wrong set of tracks. The Dutch had switched the points and both trains had to be reversed before they could be sent along the right rails. As the first train, now well inside Dutch territory, drew near the bridge, a Dutch military policeman telephoned the guardhouse on the eastern bank. His warning that Gennep railway station was under attack was not understood. While he was talking a group of six men appeared at the end of the bridge. The first two were dressed as Dutch military policemen, but the identity of the other four was not immediately apparent for they were wearing raincoats. At the bridge's eastern end the three Dutch sentries, now alarmed and suspicious, covered the six strangers with their rifles. The fact that two of the strange group wore the uniform of their own Army unsettled them. As they hesitated they were overpowered by the men – all Brandenburgers – who seized them together with the other member of the guard who had gone to answer the telephone.

The Germans now controlled the eastern end of the bridge. It was time to bluff the guards on the western side of the river. One of the detachment, speaking fluent Dutch, telephoned the western guardhouse. Two Dutch military policemen and four German prisoners of war, he told the guard commander, were being brought across at the order of the military commander. The 'prisoners and escort' detachment now set out for the western bank leaving another Brandenburg group to hold the eastern end of the bridge. At the bridge's middle section the two Brandenburg soldiers, disguised as Dutch MPs, handed over the four 'prisoners' and went back to the eastern end of the bridge. The Dutch sentries on the middle section carried out a most perfunctory search of the four 'prisoners' whom they had taken into custody and marched them away to a stone hut. The only guard left on duty was suddenly aware of a train approaching from Germany. He telephoned a warning to the western bank guardroom. The 51-year-old sergeant on duty there was uncertain and hesitant. He gave no orders to blow the bridge and as the single sentry at the middle section stood waiting for instructions to press the detonator, the train drew alongside him, soldiers leaped down and seized the detonating equipment. For the Dutch it was a tragedy. Where the middle section sentry was placed was the only point from which the bridge could have been blown. The sergeant's hesitancy and the sentry's inaction had allowed the bridge to pass into German hands and without loss of life.

A small group of Dutch soldiers on the western bank of the Meuse tried to establish some sort of defence and opened fire with a single gun, but the weapon jammed after the first round. In the confusion which followed, the 'prisoners of war' overpowered their guards with weapons they had concealed about them and which the perfunctory search had not revealed and went into action against the Dutch defenders. Caught between the fire of the Brandenburg 'prisoners' and that of the troops in the armoured train, the Netherlands soldiers surrendered and watched in dismay as the trains, filled with excited German soldiers of 481st Regiment, crossed dryshod into Holland and drove at speed through the Peel defence line.

So much was happening in that dawn of 10 May. Along the frontier with Luxembourg German pioneers were waiting to cross and remove the Duchy's flimsy defences for the Panzer mass to pass through. Waves of JU 52s, filled with paratroops, were flying westwards towards the Hague while, as we have seen, Brandenburg units wearing disguise were making their way through the water-meadows. In that first dawn light the huge shapes of gliders could be seen silhouetted against the lightening sky as they swooped down upon a Belgian fortress whose guns dominated the ground around the village of Eben Emael. Five minutes after the gliders touched down the German armies crossed the frontier. The whole movement of the forces in Operation 'Gelb' had been keyed to fit the airlanding by the gliders for upon the success of that operation by a special force, depended the timetable of the War in the West.

4

VERTICAL ENVELOPMENT

Eben Emael, May 1940

The fortress at Eben Emael, built upon granite, was set upon a ridge some 150 feet above the surrounding countryside. It was protected to the east and to the north-east by natural water defences; the river Meuse and the Albert Canal. To the south-west and to the south there were artificial defences of anti-tank ditches and barbed wire. The fortress was the strongest part of the Liège defence system and the heavy guns of its main armament dominated the area.

This fortress, this barrier to any advance by the Sixth Army, was the objective for a special force and only they could take it. Eben Emael was impregnable to gunfire. Conventional infantry attackers would first have to cross the Albert Canal and climb the high bank to reach the plateau on which the main defences stood. These forts and blockhouses, all mutually supporting, would have to be attacked one by one, until the whole complex was in German hands. The Belgians, of course, would react violently to such assaults and by a determined defence could not only inflict horrifying casualties, but more importantly, would delay the timetable of the advance until the military initiative had passed to the Allies.

To take out such a special target required picked men using unusual weapons. Germany had both. In a modern refinement of the hollow-charge grenade the Army had a weapon capable of destroying the armoured cupolas of Eben Emael. If a horizontal attack by conventional infantry advancing across open ground could not succeed, a vertical assault by paratroops or glider-borne soldiers armed with their hollow-charge grenades might be a practical if radical solution.

Thus far we have found the weapons that will destroy the guns and the way in which the explosives can be brought to the scene of the action. But what of the men who were to carry out the operation? Shortly after the outbreak of war the Luftwaffe took on to establishment the 7th Fallschirmjäger Division and it was the highly-trained para-troops of that formation who were to carry out the mission.

From conferences and discussions among the commanders of the Paratroop Division it was soon established that a landing by parachute offered scant chance of success. Troops air-dropped by parachute were often dispersed over a fairly wide area on landing and the target zone of Eben Emael was only 1,000 yards long by 900 yards wide at its maximum point. Nor was parachute design so sophisticated that the troopers could manoeuvre themselves as precisely as they can today. The prospect of the widely separated assault troops having first to concentrate before conducting the assault was daunting. Victory at Eben Emael would depend upon a concentration of forces and fast action. Dispersal would lose the surprise factor that was all important.

The alternative to dropping parachute troops was to land gliders carrying the soldiers directly into the fortress area. This solution prompted a new question. Did Germany have glider pilots so skilful and proficient that in almost total darkness they could not only locate the small, triangular site of Eben Emael, but could land at precise points within its small area? The answer was that there were some Luftwaffe and civilian pilots whose skill was internationally recognised and who could pass on those skills. For other flyers to reach that level of expertise would need long and hard training, but at the end there would be a large number of proficient men ready to meet the unusual challenges which the operation would demand.

The final point was that a night landing was impossible; a minimum of light was essential. Thus the glider landings could not take place during the night nor at the onset of night, but either in full daylight or at first light. The entire operation plan of the German Army was thus tied to the landings by Para Assault Detachment Koch and, more specifically, to the success that the troops at Eben Emael would achieve.

Under conditions of the greatest secrecy the glider pilots were taken to Hildesheim where dummy forts had been set up and upon which they practised the techniques of landing on small target areas. It was soon found that landing distances were too long. When the operation took place there would be eleven gliders all landing more or less simultaneously. It was essential for the pilots to achieve the minimum landing distance if collisions between the machines were to be avoided. Experiments showed that barbed wire wrapped round the slide under the aircraft's belly could reduce the landing run to an acceptable length.

At the same time as the pilots were improving their skills at Hildesheim the paratroops had progressed from rehearsing rapid exits from gliders to the use of hollow-charge grenades, practising on fortifications in the former Czech defence line, which were similar in design to the constructions at Eben Emael. Finally, in the early spring of 1940, the two groups, glider pilots and paratroops, undertook joint exercises, practising by night and by day until their individual skills had been blended to perfection. The pilots were all able to land their machines, even in half light, to within twenty yards of a designated point while the paras took only seconds to burst out of the wooden gliders and to go straight into action. By the time that this stage of perfection had been reached, Operation 'Gelb' was in the final stages of preparation. The day and time for the new campaign had been fixed: 05.30 on 10 May. Five minutes before that time the gliders would have made their silent landings upon Belgium and the War in the West would have begun.

In the opening hours of the campaign it was important not to alarm the Belgians. So as to give no hint of the impending attack it was planned that the JU 52s which were towing the gliders would maintain radio silence. They would not be directed towards the target by radio so a means of ensuring correct direction had to be improvised. The route to the frontier would be lit by a chain of beacons forming a flare-path which would guide the pilots as they flew very high through the dark May night towards the border. While still over German territory and at 7,000 feet the JUs would cast off their tow-ropes and the wooden gliders, each filled with a troop of paras, would glide towards the fort, some twenty miles away. The troops would begin their tasks and five minutes later the great mass of Armies, Corps and Divisions of the German Army would advance. Behind the gliders and in front of the Army would come the assault waves of the Luftwaffe. At H-Hour plus 15, Stukas would swoop, bomb and destroy the enemy while transport aircraft would drop dummy figures of parachutists to cover the real landings and to create the maximum confusion.

We must now remove our concentration from Eben Emael and see the attack upon it as part of a larger airborne operation whose principal task it was to '. . . enable Sixth Army to pass . . . without delay'. Accepting that the assault upon Eben Emael would be successful, the corollary was the capture of certain bridges across the Canal at Veldwezelt, at Vroenhoven and at Canne. These bridges, as well as the fortress of Eben Emael, were the objectives of the para assault detachment commanded by Hauptmann Koch. All attacks would be glider-borne and all would take place simultaneously. To each of the four assault groups a code-name was given: 'Iron', 'Steel' and 'Concrete'. To Oberleutnant Witzig's Eben Emael commando was given the code-name 'Granite'.

The bridges would be captured by rapid assault before they could be blown and the concurrent seizure of the fort would prevent its guns from bombarding the bridges or from firing upon the units of Sixth Army as they swept across the Meuse and the Albert Canal. Para Assault Detachment Koch was made up of 11 officers, 427 NCOs and men. This total included forty-two glider pilots who, in addition to their specialist flying skills, had been trained in infantry warfare so that they could take part in the ground fighting. Koch's orders to Oberleutnant Witzig, Commander of 'Granite' detachment, were simple and direct. They concluded with the words '. . . (your group will) put out of action the armoured cupolas, casemates and anti-aircraft positions (of the Fort). You are to destroy the enemy's resistance and to defend the gains you have made, until relieved . . .'

'Until relieved'. That was the crucial phrase of the operations order. The glider-borne men would be equipped with demolition charges to destroy the cupolas, and flame-throwers to beat down opposition, but they had no heavy weapons, nothing that would enable them to withstand the many and heavy infantry or tank attacks which the Belgians would certainly launch against them. The 'Granite' men would be completely isolated.

Those groups which were to attack the bridges would receive the reinforcement of heavy machine-gun units who would parachute in at H-Hour plus 40, but Witzig's detachment could receive no support from paratroop drops, nor would there be any more space for gliders to land on the roof of Eben Emael. 'Granite' would have to rely on its own efforts and those of the Stukas.

'Until relieved'. Witzig's group would, it was anticipated, fight like demons against an enemy garrison of more than two thousand men, but hold they must until they were relieved. The distance from the frontier was not great – it was only twenty miles from the border to the Meuse – so relief should be possible within four hours. H-Hour was 05.30. Therefore, by noon of D-Day, if all went well, Witzig's detachment could expect to be *en route* back to Germany, its mission completed.

All through the night of 9 May German armies closed up to the frontier. The infantry masses lay silent and blacked out in the forward zones. Behind them, from concentration points throughout western Germany, convoys of trucks rolled along the autobahns, headlights blazing, making no attempt to conceal their identity or the direction in which they were heading. Three massive Army Groups were concentrated along the western border. At 05.00 detachments of Brandenburg would move out through the darkness, across the dewy, misty low-lying meadows, to undertake their secret moves which would speed the advance. Behind them in the east, dawn would soon break.

The telephone call to Witzig in the evening of 9 May, brought 'Granite' to full alert. His unit was billeted in the Hilden barracks near Düsseldorf, where its incognito had been preserved under the bland name, 'No 17 Reserve Squadron'. Soon, with a heavy escort of Military Police, a convoy of vehicles bearing the Para Assault Detachment Koch headed for two airfields outside Cologne where they entered a pre-operational headquarters in the suburbs of that city. There was to be a final briefing, then the gliders would be loaded. Reveille on D-Day would be at 02.45 and take-off would be just over an hour later.

But now let us see, as the soldiers of Witzig's 'Granite' detachment were seeing on that evening, the objectives that they would be attacking at dawn. On a low table in front of them is a model of the fortifications at Eben Emael as well as a collection of aerial photographs of the complex and the area surrounding it. What the troopers of 'Granite' see is a very modern piece of military engineering. A 12-foot wall surrounds a small piece of land, roughly diamond shaped, out of which project cupolas and other defensive works. In addition to the four artillery casemates with triple armament, there are two twin gun turrets and a single emplacement carrying two large-calibre pieces. There are also seven anti-aircraft machine-gun positions. The complex is surrounded by an anti-tank ditch running round its landward side. In the 12-foot wall are six pillboxes and an extra-mural position to the south-east, on the canal side.

The grassy, diamond-shaped area is the roof of the complex. To the relief of the paratroopers there are neither trenches, nor obstructions, nor barbed wire defences on that roof. It is clear that for whatever form of assault the defenders are prepared, an attack from the skies is not one of them. Nevertheless the Belgians have ensured that even if the fort were to be cut off from the outside world it would still be defensible. Connecting tunnels enable troops to reinforce a danger point or to concentrate to mount a counter-attack.

From the position and number of the guns on the model, it is clear that the artillery armament has two functions. One group of guns are long-range pieces and the others are for local defence. The long-range batteries are positioned and armed so that their guns could dominate either the ground around Maastricht to the north, or around the area of Vise to the south. On the accompanying drawing the numbers shown are those given by the Germans to the individual defensive positions marked on a captured Belgian drawing. The positions are not numbered in any sort of order nor in order of importance to the mission. Some of them have descriptions in French, some are cupolas and others blockhouses. To avoid confusion they are all described here as being objectives and the numbers which I have used in the text are those that appear on the drawing.

Objectives 12 and 18, in the west and south-west of the diamond-shaped area, each carry a battery of three 7.5cm guns whose fire can be directed northwards. Forts 9 and 26, also fitted with triple 7.5s, are aimed southwards. Also included in the long-range artillery group are Objectives 23 and 31, retractable turrets each fitted with twin 7.5s. Objective 24 mounts twin 12cm guns which can be traversed to bombard targets at any point of the compass. That comprises the whole of the long-range armament.

The short-range pieces are intended for local defence, to enable forts to protect one another. Those short-range guns also protect the domed blockhouses set around the perimeter wall. Each of these little forts holds an anti-tank gun, machine-guns and a searchlight. Objective 35, situated extra-murally to the south-east of the complex, is sited, as was Objective 17, nearly at water level facing the Albert Canal. The other two objectives, 13 and 19, hold machine-guns and searchlights. Objective 29 is a battery of anti-aircraft guns.

To the paratroops of 'Granite', studying the target area as a whole, the task must have seemed impossible. Witzig's Command was made up of only two officers, Witzig and Delica, and eighty-three rank and file. Eleven men of that total were the pilots of the gliders who, upon landing, would support the ground attacks. Arms to be carried, in addition to personal weapons, were six light machine-guns, sixteen medium machine-guns, fifty-eight carbines and four flame-throwers. A total weight of 2½ tons of every sort of explosive was to be distributed among the eleven gliders, and the group would also have a wireless set. The eleven gliders would all land within seconds of each other, on the small roof of Eben Emael. The dangers of collision would be enormous. Supposing the landings to have been accomplished without accident, each Troop had to take out one or more objectives. The most important – to be taken first – were those positions whose guns fired to the north and which could, therefore, bombard the bridges across the River Meuse.

The eighty-five men of 'Granite' were expected to land and to neutralise opposition within Eben Emael very quickly. They were all members of the Para Assault Engineers; assault troops, storm detachments who spearheaded the most desperate attacks. These men were the cream of the cream of the fighting men and to lead such men only the finest officers, the best graduates of the Military Engineers Academy, were selected. Witzig was the best of them.

Reveille sounded at 02.45 on 10 May and first parade was forty-five minutes later – in full equipment. In the lighted halls of several aerodromes in the Rhineland, small groups of men from the Para Assault Detachment Koch, gathered for the last time around the models and photographs which they had been studying for weeks. A short talk by their Commander put them at last in the picture. Their objectives were named and the vital importance of their mission was stressed. Within the hour, they were told, they would undertake an operation that would open the road for the German armies in the West and the success of which could bring victory within weeks.

The German Parachute troops have an anthem, *Rot scheint die Sonne* (The dawn sun shines red); in the German armed forces there has always been great stress laid upon the use of songs to raise unit morale. As their strong, young voices filled the cold halls of the departure 'dromes, did the paratroops, I wonder, consider the words which told of death in the red light of sunrise?

At the gliders they were checked aboard, settled down and waited, uncomfortable in their bulky clothing. Then the sound of the JUs' idling engines changed to a high-pitched note as the throttles were opened to gain full power for take-off. Away on the apron surrounding the grassy field dispatching officers checked their watches, raised Very pistols and fired white flares into the dark sky. It was exactly 04.30. The first towing plane moved forward. The rope strained and tightened. Then the glider was dragged across the grass behind the lumbering JU 52, wobbled, jerked and took to the air. Operation 'Gelb' had begun.

High into the sky rose the aircraft, wing lights indicating their positions to other pilots. Once the towing machines and their gliders had formed up the armada took course westwards. Pilots who looked down from the cramped confines of their cabins saw below them a line of flame pointing towards the objective. As the JUs climbed higher the fires of the flare-path became smaller and were remembered by one pilot as being like a long necklace of sparkling rubies. The glider-borne troops had no such view. All they knew was that it was bitterly cold in the wooden flying boxes and that, as usual, there was the sick-making motion as the machines pitched and swayed.

In Witzig's glider there was a sudden shock. The tow-rope had snapped. The armada had reached a point in the flight where a glider had insufficient height to carry it as far as Eben Emael, but it might be possible for the pilot to coax it back to an airfield on the east bank of the Rhine. It was unfortunate for 'Granite' that the Commanding Officer's glider also held the Reserve Troop – men who would be used to exploit success or restore lost momentum. Serious though the loss of Witzig's glider was, it was not disastrous. The paras had been trained to carry out each of the many tasks that were required. Only minutes later there was another incident. A second glider, carrying No. 2 Troop, was released prematurely and had to force-land at Düren. These losses reduced dramatically the strength of 'Granite'. The other machines of the armada sailed on; the mission could not be aborted because of two 'downed' aircraft. The plan was for the gliders to be towed to just over 7,000 feet and at a given point, while still over German territory, for them to be released. The aircraft, even though heavily laden, could cover easily the twenty miles to the objective. The reason for their being cast off so far from the target was so that the noise of aircraft engines would not warn the Belgians that the attack was under way. Precisely to the second the towing-lines were cast off.

For the first seconds after release from the tug there was an uncomfortable yawing as the wooden gliders swayed and swung in the thin cold air. Quickly, the pilot gained trim and then came the slow glide towards the objective ending in the familiar tightening of the stomach muscles as at last, close to the target, the nose of the glider pointed downwards and the machine descended to the ground. The approach of the nine remaining gliders had not gone totally unobserved. A sentry at Eben Emael had seen, silhouetted against the lightening sky, the huge, winged shapes as they plunged downwards. His hand pressed the alarm button and within seconds the young lieutenant commanding Objective 29, the multiple anti-aircraft machine-gun post, had his guns in action firing into the fuselage of one machine as it swooped silently down. As the tracers flicked through the sky the question uppermost in the minds of the pilot must have been, 'Are those bursts of fire the prelude to massive Belgian retaliation?' Apparently they were not. There was no other opposition to be seen. For the paras came the jolt as the fuselages struck the earth and then the alarming speed of the machine as it skidded across the grass. The scene must have been a bewildering one to those Belgians who witnessed it. Within seconds nine huge, black, silent aircraft had come out of the night and were now racing across the roof of the fort, swinging violently from side to side, seemingly all about to collide with the casemates and turrets which projected above the ground.

The barbed wire, which had been wrapped round the slides of the gliders, effectively reduced the length of the landing run and the machines were soon at rest, tipped to one side. Within seconds the paras had broken out of the craft and were standing, the first soldiers of the invading army, on Belgian soil. It was a glorious sun-filled dawn. As the paras went through the well-rehearsed moves they knew that far to the east Reichenau's Sixth Army, was beginning the advance towards them. If that Army was to be spared casualties the forts had to be taken and quickly. Time was now the important factor.

In the following hectic hour much was to happen and most of it occurred all at once. There can be no attempt to describe the fighting in a chronological account. The battle was everywhere. What you must see, as the increasing daylight makes objects clear, giving them both shape and colour, are all the troops bursting out of the wooden flying machines which have brought them to this place. You must see them as, apparently haphazardly, but in fact highly-trained, they erupt from the gliders and race towards their objectives. Across the length and breadth of the grassy triangle little groups of green-smocked men, ten or eleven strong, are running, staggering under the weight of explosive charges, carrying machine-guns or flame-throwers. Fifty-five men have only minutes in which to achieve their tasks. Speed, skill and determination will assist them and you must share the feelings, experience the emotions, smell the stink of burnt powder and the crisp nose biting tang of cordite on the fresh morning air. See, then, as the NCO in charge of an MG34 throws himself down on the wet grass, raises the butt of the machine-gun, presses it firmly into his shoulder and opens fire. Beside him, his No. 2 on the gun, opening boxes of ammunition, hurries to load new belts as the chattering mechanism takes the cartridges into the breach, fires them and extracts the empty cases nearly 400 times in a minute. Machine-gun groups of all the troops cover the assault of the demolition teams as they race towards the cupolas and domes, shining now in the first rays of the sun.

There were surprises for the para groups. Several of the strong defensive positions, particularly Objectives 15 and 16, were dummy installations, and many cupolas had no local protection against ground attack. These factors would make the task easier.

Let us now consider some of the troops and their objectives: Glider No. 1 was under the command of the only remaining officer, Leutnant Delica. It will be remembered that the glider carrying Oberleutnant Witzig and the rest of the Reserve Troop had broken its tow-rope and had landed near Cologne. Command of 'Granite' should have passed to Delica, but was actually taken over by Hauptfeldwebel Wenzel until Witzig was able to link up with his men, some hours later.

Delica and his No. 1 Troop had been given the task of attacking and destroying Objective 18, one of the triple cupolas in the south-western corner of Eben Emael. The guns of No. 18 were trained northwards. This was one of the two prime targets whose destruction was vital. Delica raced across the ground, anticipating with each step, that the Belgian gunners would open fire upon him. There was no fire. Calmly he took his time and placed a 25lb charge very carefully on the barrel of the nearest gun in the triple turret. A sharp tug on the detonating cord, a ten-second pause and then a crashing explosion which destroyed the barrel. While the thunder of the detonation was still reverberating a 110lb charge was hefted on to No. 18's armoured observation dome. The armour shattered. One of the two principal targets had been taken out within minutes.

The glider which had come down at Düren was carrying No. 2 Troop, and their tasks were taken over by the men in Glider 5.

The attack by the troop in Glider 3, was made against Objective 12. This, too, was a prime target; the second of the triple turrets whose guns fired northwards. The Commander of No. 3 Troop, Feldwebel Arens, placed a light charge on the first gun and destroyed its barrel, before a second and heavier grenade smashed the other weapons in the turret. The second prime target was dead; its guns could not now menace the Meuse bridges.

The pilot of Glider 4 had bad luck. The barbed wire wrapped around the slide of his machine was so effective that it stopped the glider while it was still a hundred yards from Objective 19. As the assault troops raced unopposed across the short grass they noticed with relief that the shutters over the gun embrasures were still closed. Surprise had been complete. The Belgians had been taken unawares. Indeed, the first indication the defenders of Objective 19 must have had of the German attack was the crashing detonation of a 2lb charge inside the periscope well. This explosion, in effect, blinded the Commander of No. 19. He could not control the fire of his main armament but he could bring into play the automatic weapons which formed part of his Command Group. There were bursts of fire from a machine-gun bunker. Two paras wriggled their way forward dragging along with them a 25lb charge and placed it firmly against the pillbox wall. Ten seconds later the bunker was destroyed and inside its ruins lay the dead and dying defenders. Under covering fire from their Troop machine-guns and bursts of fire from flame-throwers, two other paras dashed forward and hefted a 110lb charge on to the cupola of No. 19. The fierce explosion smashed the armour plate as if it had been a chocolate egg. The principal task of No. 4 Troop had been completed. Inside the machine-gun pillbox which they had destroyed, men of the Troop set up a Command Post and used the shattered concrete walls as protection against the artillery fire which was now crashing down from the Belgian defenders of Objective 23. This was a complication in the battle plan. It had not been foreseen that 23 would need to be attacked; its guns had seemed to be set too low to sweep the roof of the fort. This belief was now seen to be wrong, its fire was strong and destructive. The guns had to be neutralised. The men of No. 4 Troop began to work out a plan of attack.

The Troop in Glider 5 was switched from the original objective and ordered to take out No. 26, another triple turret whose guns dominated the ground to the south. The first explosion of a well-placed charge damaged the ventilating system and the Belgian gun crews had to abandon their turret or die of suffocation. They withdrew into the corridors and waited for the air to clear. The guns ceased firing and the paras, thinking that they had gained an easy victory, moved on to take Objective 4, a fortress in the perimeter wall.

Down in the underground galleries of No. 26 the smoke cleared slowly, but the air became clear enough to breathe. The Belgian crews returned to their post and opened fire with the one undamaged gun. The Lieutenant in charge of the turret ordered that the shells be set with a minimum fuse so that they burst immediately outside the turret. The intention was to spray the area with red-hot splinters catching the German troops in the open and without cover.

The men of No. 5 Troop now found themselves under fire from a target they thought they had destroyed. Abandoning the attack upon Objective 4 the paras went in again, racing through the shrapnel bursts from Objective 26. Once again the explosion of a massive charge was heard and that signalled the end of 26. Down in the crippled turret the Belgian crew lay dead or wounded. The battery had fallen.

The targets for the troop in Glider 8 were 25, a barrack hut, and 31, a twin turret carrying 7.5cm guns. Glider 8 was the machine which had been struck along its fuselage by the machine-gun bullets of the AA position past which it had flown only seconds before touchdown. It landed under fire, and the Belgian machine-guns kept up their fire as the glider skidded along the ground. Bullets swept the machine as it raced across the grass. It halted at last. The paras burst out of the fuselage and raced to engage their targets leaving to their comrades of Glider 9 to take out the troublesome Belgian machine-gun posts.

Not far from the barrack block which was the first objective, two machine-gunners from No. 8 Troop lay on the grass and poured a stream of bullets into the wooden hut. This kept the Belgian troops pinned down and while they were thus immobile, other paras rushed to place their charges on the armoured turret of Objective 31. Although neither of the two 110lb charges succeeded in smashing the cupola, their force jammed it so that the guns could not be depressed or elevated. This did not stop the Belgians from firing from an exit tunnel. A 25lb charge heaved in by the paratroopers brought down the tunnel wall and buried many of the gun crew under heavy concrete blocks. Then the attack went in against Objective 25 and in a quick burst of fire and movement the barrack block was taken.

Objective No. 13 was the target of Glider 9's Troop; a casemate whose machine-guns had an arc of fire extending from 180° to 360°. That semi-circle of fire from three pillboxes protected two forts to the west of the diamond, part of the area to the north-west and other positions in the south-western half of the perimeter.

No. 9 Troop's glider came to a halt about sixty yards from its objective and the paras erupted from the fuselage. There was no defensive fire from the garrison. Perhaps this assault might produce a rapid and successful result, but then it was seen that the turret was surrounded by barbed wire. There was a frustrating wait while a runner went to fetch cutters. Strand by strand the paras cut through the obstruction, all the time anticipating a stream of bullets to pour into them as they lay defenceless on the ground. There was still no response from the defenders, but clearly this inaction on the part of the Belgians could not continue. What the Germans feared became true. Even as they cut the last strand of wire the garrison of Objective 13, had raced through the underground corridors and had reached the armoured turret. A steel shutter was flung open and through it projected the snout of a machine-gun. Before the Belgian soldier manning the piece could open fire a paratrooper armed with a flame-thrower pressed the trigger on his weapon. A plume of yellow fire arced towards the embrasure and covered the turret in a sheet of burning phosphorus. Under cover of the flames other paras placed and detonated an explosive charge on the embrasure, which dominated the southern area, while the remainder smashed the observation dome with a 110lb charge. The victorious paras of No. 9 Glider raced on to their second objective, No. 29.

This post had opened fire upon the gliders as they landed. Its armament was a bank of four machine-guns set up for an anti-aircraft role. As such it ought to have been rated as a main target for it could have inflicted terrible damage on the flimsy gliders. Indeed there was evidence of what it could do. As we have seen, Objective 29 was under the command of a very determined young lieutenant who, alerted to the gliders' approach by the sentry, reacted swiftly and ordered his men to open fire. Bursts of bullets swept the gliders as they landed, but a small para battle group, firing as they went, and flinging grenades ahead of them, stormed the gun position and shot down the crews, all of whom died at their posts. Not stopping to disable the guns, the paras raced on to other targets. In Objective 29 the machine-guns lay silent. But not for long. Streaming out of the underground galleries and passages came more Belgian troops whose fire swept the open ground. Once again a small German battle group went into action. The paras finally overran 29, killed the second gun detachment and this time destroyed the guns. Then a few light charges dropped into the galleries compelled the survivors of the machine-gun company to surrender.

It will be recalled that the troop in Glider No. 4 had come under fire from Objective 23, a position which it had not been planned to attack became of the low-lying position of its main armament. The men from that glider, together with Leutnant Delica's Troop, saw the cupola rise out of the ground and open fire with its main armament upon the men of the glider force moving between the various objectives. Quickly a heavy charge was placed and detonated, but it seemed to have little effect. The twin 7.5cm guns opened fire again, blanketing the triangular area of the fort with high-explosive shells. No. 23 now represented an acute danger. The hollow-charge grenades had proved ineffectual so it was decided to call in the Stukas. The unit radio set was sent for. There is an axiom in all armies: the more desperate the situation the less well the radio functions. The set at Eben Emael worked perfectly on this occasion and by 09.30 the dive-bombers were over the target, screaming down almost vertically upon the armoured dome. Not a single bomb hit the target, but the defenders quickly retracted the dome and it was not raised again during the remainder of the fighting.

There remained only one untaken principal target. Objective No. 24 was a twin turret with 12cm guns. The troops of Gliders 6 and 7 combined to take on this, the largest of all the turrets. The eighteen men split up. Covering fire was laid down while the 18ft armoured dome was attacked from two sides. The paras placed their charges and ran. The explosions were almost synchronised, but even the massive force of two 110lb charges could not smash the thick armoured shell. The alternative was to destroy the gun barrels. A legend has grown up of 2lb charges being stuffed up each of the two 12cm barrels, but I can find no corroboration of this story; a 25lb charge placed on the barrel would be as effective. The question of how it was done is academic. The most important thing to the Germans was that the guns were destroyed.

Well within an hour of landing, it was clear that 'Granite' attack had succeeded. There was still some resistance, but the main objectives had been taken. There was still artillery fire coming down on the paras, some of it from guns outside the fortress, but shelling from weapons within the Eben Emael complex had only nuisance value. The Belgians could not now interfere with the passage of Sixth Army which should, if the timetable was being adhered to, be within only a few hours of relieving the paras. The confident hopes of the men on Eben Emael, that relief was nigh, were not to be realised however. The Belgians had blown up three bridges across the Meuse and by skilfully directed artillery fire were stopping any forward movement. The Sixth Army was halted, while Engineer units forced their way through the congested roads to reach the river and begin erecting pontoon bridges. Behind the leading assault divisions the roads, as far back as the German border, were choked with vehicles, but the men of Para Assault Detachment Koch were unaware of this. They did not know that, in effect, they were cut off; isolated from the main body of the Army, but had they known it it would not have affected their decision to hold until relieved.

On Eben Emael, the objectives neutralised, it was time to mop up the few pockets of resistance. It was particularly necessary to gain and retain a hold on Objective 4, the main gate to the fortress, for it was through that gate that the relieving force of 51st Armoured Engineer Battalion would arrive. The other important task was to gain access to the upper of the two levels of underground passages below the cupolas and casemates and to drive the Belgians from that combat level down into the lower passages, the accommodation level. Delica sent out patrols to penetrate the combat level of passages. The hollow charges which had taken out Objective 18 had blown a huge hole in the side of the structure. Through this gap the men of Delica's first patrol passed on their reconnaissance. The feelings of these men can be imagined as they slid stealthily through the breach and into the smoke-filled space below the cupola. A hollow charge had been exploded on the dome and the scene at the point of the explosion was a frightful one.

The principle of the hollow-charge grenade is that the explosive force is concentrated into a thin stream of power which literally burns its way through steel or concrete. The 110lb charge could penetrate up to 25cm of armour plate and even though the armour at Eben Emael was 28cm thick and could, therefore, resist a single charge, penetration could be achieved using two charges in succession. Even using only one charge produced casualties and damage from the large fragments of armour plate from the cupola roof which were flung off by the explosion. The results of the successful penetration were even more frightful for the jet of power destroyed or burned everything in its path and concussed those who were not killed outright. The German patrol made their way through blood and shattered bodies, awestruck by the devastation wrought upon the crews and upon the three 7.5cm guns which had formed the armament of No. 18.

The lights in the galleries flickered as the power supply faltered, now becoming brighter now dimmer. There were seconds when the lights failed altogether and the patrol stood in the smoke-filled darkness, listening for the sounds of the Belgian enemy and waiting for the lights to come on again. During their cautious advance, the patrol had met no one and had seen nothing save rubble and dead bodies, but as the first man of the patrol turned a corner he was met with a shout and a burst of gunfire. He ducked back into cover quickly, but in that brief moment he saw that the Belgians had put up a barricade in the corridor. The way forward was blocked. Patrols searching in other parts of the corridors also reported Belgian barricades below each objective. It seemed that the enemy was determined that if he could not man the guns, he would certainly deny them to the paras.

The capture of the objectives was not the end of the operation. In accordance with Koch's battle orders, the ground had to be held until they were relieved. The period immediately following a hard fight is one of tiredness and anti-climax. It is precisely at this time that a strong counter-attack or even a heavy barrage can affect adversely the best troops. Just in time to prevent this, a glider swooped down across the Albert Canal and from it stepped Witzig, the Commanding Officer of 'Granite' force. His arrival revitalised the flagging men. His first action was to order the spreading of the German war flag across one of the cupolas as a signal to the Luftwaffe and, more particularly to let his para comrades know that the fort was in German hands.

The recent frustrations of the young commander may well be imagined. The glider in which he and the Reserve Troop had been flying had had to come down short of the target. He knew the directing officers of other Luftwaffe units were under pressure on this the first morning of Operation 'Gelb', but Witzig insisted on being supplied with a fresh JU 52 and a new glider. Impressed by the confidence and insistence of this subaltern, machines were made ready and Witzig's Troop was brought to battle. There was no need of secrecy now, nor was any anti-aircraft fire directed at the glider as it came down in a shallow dive to land in the fortress area. The time was 08.30 and except for a few minor hitches the operation had gone as planned and had been completed more or less on time.

Witzig's first glance took in the fact that the Belgians were still resisting in places; at least one gun was still bombarding the landing area, and there was a certain amount of machine-gun fire and sniper activity. The young CO called for reports. From these it was clear that enemy activity was confined chiefly to the northern part of the diamond and that the Belgians were probably moving troops up to carry out an infantry attack. This belief was confirmed when brown-uniformed figures debouched from the woods on the north-west side of the fortress and advanced up the slope towards the German positions. The thick undergrowth on the north-western slope favoured the attackers who worked their way forward skilfully, but the attack had little impetus and the Belgian infantry was unsupported either by tanks or by artillery. German machine-guns brought the attack to a halt. With this immediate task resolved, Witzig sent out patrols to determine the position of the enemy forces outside the defensive complex. Patrols in the galleries were now using hollow-charge grenades to bring down the ceilings and to cut off the defenders from their comrades in the other forts. Such patrols were not without danger and one three-man group, checking the upper level of galleries between Objectives 12 and 3, was intercepted and destroyed.

Late in the afternoon another series of probes by Belgian infantry showed that they had been reinforced, but the assaults, although repeated, were not aggressively conducted. Nevertheless, under that pressure the men of 'Granite' were pushed back inside the walls of the fort. From outside there came heavy and well-directed Belgian artillery fire which swept the fortress area. At one time the barrage was so intense and so prolonged that Witzig, feeling the safety of his men to be of paramount importance, now that Eben Emael had been neutralised, considered withdrawing the survivors of his little force from the exposed and dangerous salient which they held.

The long day began at last to die. In the intervals between bursts of Belgian shelling ears were cocked for the sound of German guns. There was an occasional noise of shellfire but it was distant and came no nearer despite the passing of the hours. It was now clear to all the paras that there had been a hold-up in the Army's advance, but there was also confidence that relief would come in the morning.

In his Command Post, set up in a broken pillbox, 'Granite's commanding officer drew up his plans for the coming night. Chief among these was that under cover of darkness fighting patrols would attack those objectives which might seem to be still capable of offering resistance. In obedience to these orders throughout the hours of darkness there were crashing explosions as the demolitions continued. The Belgian garrison could do nothing to oppose the destruction of their fort. They were penned in the lower galleries, all exits from the fort being guarded by German machine-gun teams.

There remained one objective which had not been attacked. No. 17 was set at water level facing the Albert Canal. In this position its machine-gunners could destroy any German attempt to cross the canal by assault craft. Witzig was informed that elements of the 51st Armoured Engineer Battalion were to undertake an assault at dawn, and Objective 17 had to be destroyed before that crossing took place. This was easier said than done. The only way in which explosives could be brought against the machine-gun embrasures was by hanging them over the edge of the fortress wall.

Meanwhile, during the night of 10/11 May a determined effort by the 'ditched' men of No. 2 Troop, whose glider had come down at Düren, brought them through the Belgian defences and into the fortress. It was a wild night. Belgian artillerymen, as if they knew that their time was running out, fired salvo after salvo at the Para Engineers in their little perimeter. Tracer fire from machine-guns laced the darkness. Far away to the north and to the west there were huge fires, the results of Stuka attacks, and everywhere the dark feeling of uncertainty.

The breakthrough by No. 2 Troop gave a slight but confident indication of the general progress of the battle. This handful of men had fought its way through Belgian infantry groups, dispersing many and capturing others. What they had done, other units might do. The canal crossing at dawn, by assault detachments of the 51st Engineer Battalion was costly but successful. The men of the assault group, urged on by their commanding officer, had launched their attack to hold the attention of the defenders of Eben Emael, while the bulk of their formation crossed a bridge near St Servaas.

The link-up between 'Granite' and the assault groups of 51st Battalion took place at 07.00 and both groups immediately went into action to sweep the Belgians from the northern part of the diamond and to clear the road outside Objective 4, so as to allow the motorised column of 51st Battalion formally to relieve the exhausted paras. The link-up with the main body of that battalion came shortly before noon. The motorised battalion had fought its way across the Meuse at 14.00 on the 10th and then southwards, past Fort St Peter. Its advanced guard had made contact with the most northern group of 'Granite' Group by 07.00 on the 11th, as had the survivors of the canal crossing. The operation was over. Well, not quite. There was still sniper fire coming in. Here and there shells were falling, some of them being fired by pieces within Eben Emael, but it was token resistance. Across the Meuse and the Albert Canal the divisions of Reichenau's Army were now flooding westwards. The task of the Para Assault Detachment Koch had been achieved. The intention to build and to hold a bridgehead facing west had succeeded.

In the midst of this war of new tactics, new weapons and new components of warfare, came a sudden reminder of the glamour and the chivalry of war – a formality curiously old-fashioned in the age of blitzkrieg and petrol. It was the formal offer of surrender. At noon on 11 May, a bugle sounded down in the corridors of the fort. The call to parley had sounded; was repeated and then rang out for a third time. A white flag was waved and into the sunlight stepped a soldier carrying that flag, accompanied by two officers and a bugler. The senior Belgian officer saluted the leader of the German group and offered to surrender the fort. Now, it was all over.

The capture of Eben Emael raised the question of how well the other groups had carried out their allotted tasks. The answer is that the bridges at Veldwezelt and Vroenhoven had been taken intact. At Canne the bridge, although damaged, was useable. The whole operation by Koch's assault group had been an outstanding success; the crowning achievement being the seizure of the fortress complex. If one includes the two glider loads of men who arrived late, the total of paras involved in the operation was eighty-five. Six of these fell in action, twenty more were wounded. For this small loss the gateway had been opened and a bridgehead built. There would be Knights' Crosses for the officers and Iron Crosses, First Class for the men. But more important than the thought of any decoration to the men of 'Granite', as their trucks carried them eastwards during the late afternoon of 11 May, was the prospect of hot food, a hot bath and a long, long sleep.

Throughout the next fortnight, as the German battle plan unfolded, the pace of the advances was so fast that there was no call for special forces. Then, late in May, the need arose again for the Brandenburg to go into action.

5

INTERDICTION

Brandenburg in Belgium, May/June 1940

The Gennep bridge operation had been a success. Eben Emael had been a success. With very few exceptions all the missions which the German paras and special forces had undertaken to open the way for their invading armies had been successful. Through the gaps that they had created and across the bridges which they had captured poured a great mass of German armour and infantry flooding across western Europe. Holland was forced to capitulate within days and within a fortnight it was clear that Operation 'Gelb' was a victory. The Allied armies in Flanders had been forced back to a coastal area between Calais and Ostend, with the centre of the bridgehead around Dunkirk. These troops were cut off from the mass of the French armies south of the River Somme and were facing annihilation. The northern end of the shallow Allied perimeter was the small town of Nieuport. Here another Brandenburg operation was mounted, this time to prevent a repetition of a military incident which took place during the First World War.

In the first months of that war the Belgians, who were in the coastal sector, holding the extreme left flank of the Allied armies, had deliberately flooded the Nieuport area. By opening the sluices they had inundated the land and halted the German advance. The Brandenburg operation of 27 May 1940 was intended to prevent history repeating itself and speed was important if it was to succeed. But there was no available Brandenburg detachment ready for action; they had all been stood down and sent on leave after the first missions had been completed. A Brandenburg officer, Leutnant Grabert, on leave in Germany, was alerted, formed a party of twelve men and ordered them to concentrate in Ghent, where the mission was explained to them. The task was to prevent the opening of the Yser sluices by seizing the pump control houses on the south bank of the river at the foot of the Nieuport-Ostend road bridge. Belgian military greatcoats and caps had been collected and the disguised Brandenburgers were to travel from Ostend in a captured Belgian Army bus southwards to Nieuport and get as close to the bridge as possible.

In the confusion which prevailed on the Allied side during those critical days, it was not out of the way for a bus-load of what looked like Belgian infantrymen to be travelling through western Flanders. The bus was not challenged as it swung through the fighting area and headed

71

towards Ostend. That town was filled with a mass of Belgian soldiers milling about, apparently leaderless. The crowds of men thronging the streets forced the bus to a crawl and it was soon noticed that most of the soldiers were not carrying weapons. This was a situation unusual enough to need an explanation. A Brandenburger spoke in rapid and idiomatic French to a group outside Ostend railway station. The news he received was startling. The Belgian Army had surrendered. Where were the nearest British troops? Near Nieuport, on the far side of the Yser and in about Company strength. No, the bridge had not been blown although charges had been laid.

It was important for the Brandenburgers to cover the ground between Ostend and Nieuport as fast as possible to carry out their orders. It is no great distance from Ostend to Nieuport – no more than fifteen miles – but it took hours to cover the distance, and it was early evening before the Germans got through the last crowds of refugees and soldiers and bumped their way over bomb and shell damage into the target area – the Nieuport bridge.

Behind the spearhead of the special force, the divisions of the German XXVI Corps, which formed the shaft of the spear, were driving southwards to strike at the left flank of the Dunkirk perimeter. A Brandenburg success at Nieuport would permit XXVI Corps to attack the British Expeditionary Force which was being evacuated from the flat and sandy beaches. The British garrison at Nieuport was indeed a small one: patrols from 12th Lancers, some gunners converted to infantry and small detachments from a number of County Regiments of 12th Brigade (4th Infantry Division). In Gregory Blaxland's *Destination Dunkirk*, he states that a German motorcycle patrol approached the Yser bridge at 11.00 on 27 May. The patrol clashed with armoured cars of 12th Lancers, during which a German soldier who had tried to fire his pistol through the gun port of an armoured car had been shot dead. That single, German corpse, at the middle of the bridge was commented upon in post-battle reports written by the Brandenburgers who had believed themselves the first German soldiers to arrive at the bridge.

It was about 19.00 as the twelve-man group at last approached their target and came immediately under fire from British posts on the far side of the river. The Brandenburg driver skidded the bus off the road and put it broadside on to the bridge and the Germans leapt from the vehicle and took off their Belgian uniforms. There was no time to carry out a reconnaissance, but a single glance showed that at the approaches to the bridge, now only fifty yards away, there was dead ground. The group reformed there, safe from the machine-gun bullets which whistled and cracked over their heads. A simple plan of action was quickly worked out, there was no time for anything elaborate.

When it was quite dark Leutnant Grabert and Unteroffizier Janovsky were to belly-crawl onto the bridge and cross it, feeling for and cutting any wires leading to explosive charges. On the far side of the Yser they would open fire with their automatic weapons and this would be the signal for the remaining members of the detachment to storm forward. When they reached the southern side of the bridge they would shout orders and fire from different positions so as to give the impression of an attack in strength. This deception would, Grabert hoped, bluff the British into believing that his twelve-man group was a reconnaissance detachment behind which there would be reinforcements. It was a desperate gamble.

A post-battle report describes how white Very lights were fired into the dark night sky and British tracer bullets whipped across the length of the bridge. At Grabert's signal the corporal and the officer crawled from the fold of dead ground, each carrying insulated wire-cutters and an MP 38. They slid slowly along the bridge, the Lieutenant on the left side of the road and Janovsky on the right. Hugging the ground, they wriggled forward feeling for the wires leading to the charges. To their dismay the explosives were fixed to the structure of the bridge. To reach the charges they would have to crawl along the pavement. To do this they needed to know at what height the British machine-guns were firing. A helmet raised cautiously on a pair of wire-cutters was hit when it was about a foot above the ground. There would be barely half an inch clearance between the whipping bullets and their prone bodies.

Keeping as flat as possible they slid from the road onto the raised sidewalk. The light of a waning Very light showed the positions of the first leads. Those were cut to render this particular charge harmless. The British seemed not to have noticed the Brandenburgers. A single press of a plunger could still detonate the as yet uncut charges.

Slowly they advanced. Each time a Very light exploded they froze into immobility, waiting through long, long seconds until the brilliant magnesium flare began to die. Then, in the more intense darkness produced as a contrast to the brilliant white light, they moved forward again. A slight, but perceptible, rise as the road neared the centre of the bridge sufficed to bring the bullets cracking only fractions of an inch above their bodies, but the road began to dip again as it approached the far bank of the Yser. Now the two-man team was in full view of the British defenders, and they rolled closer into the shadows of the structure of the bridge as yet another Very light flared and threatened to expose them. The light died. A few more paces were crawled. A slow, exploring hand found the leads to another charge. A quick snip with the wire-cutters and that charge was dead. Each had now cut three. With any luck they had neutralised all the explosive charges and the bridge could not now be destroyed.

It was time to bring the other Brandenburg men across and to set up a small defensive perimeter to hold the Yser bridge against counter-attack and then to capture the sluice houses. At the foot of the bridge, sheltered by a girder, Grabert and Janovsky open fire upon the house opposite them. Janovsky fired off magazine after magazine from his machine-pistol and Grabert flung a succession of grenades at the British machine-gunners in the houses. At the sound of the German weapons being fired the remaining Brandenburg men stormed across the bridge. Less than half a minute had elapsed since Janovsky had opened fire and in those few seconds the whole detachment had crossed the bridge and was preparing to storm the British positions. The men rushed about firing their machine-pistols from different positions and succeeded in confusing the British machine-gunners. In the area around the foot of the bridge, hand-grenade explosions lit up the night and the rattle of small arms indicated how the battle was progressing. One British position after another was bombed, stormed and destroyed. Resistance was soon broken. As the small groups of defenders were forced back from the pump houses, three Brandenburgs checked them for demolition charges and ensured that the sluices had not been opened. The Germans then regrouped around the houses on the bank of the river and took up defensive positions. No counter-attack came. The Brandenburgers had won. The bridge and control of the sluices was now in their hands. Patrols which went out to check the area found no sign of the British.

Farther south there were sounds of firing; the last gestures of defiance from British rearguards before they too slipped away to a new defence line near the evacuation beaches. With the Brandenburg success on the Yser it was no longer possible for the Allies to flood the area along the Flanders coast and thereby obstruct the German advance southwards to Dunkirk.

The short battle was over and there had been casualties on the German side. For his part in the operation Janovsky was decorated with the Iron Cross, but Grabert received nothing. The recommendation for his award was turned down on the grounds that the leads to the explosive charges had been cut, but not removed completely from the detonators. It was the standard response from pedantic staff officers to Brandenburg heroism.

Only a few weeks later the war in the west was over. The Dutch had been beaten. The Belgians had surrendered. The French Army had been smashed, first in Flanders and then south of the River Somme. The British Expeditionary Force had suffered defeat and had been withdrawn from the Continent. Hitler was now the master in the west as well as in the east. Now was the time for him to plan the subduing of the United Kingdom which showed itself still reluctant to admit that it had lost the war. Plans were prepared for Operation 'Sealion', a cross-Channel assault, and to ensure that once Great Britain had been occupied, it was brought swiftly and totally into the German New Order for Europe, a special SD force was set up which would administer the occupation of that off-shore island whose defeat was now only a matter of weeks away. Hitler was master of Continental Europe in that lovely summer of 1940.

6

BARBAROSSA

*Brandenburg in the Opening Phases of the
War against the Soviet Union, 1941*

The campaign against Russia, Operation 'Barbarossa', opened at dawn on 22 June 1941, but before the sun rose on that fateful day, before the new war had begun, groups of Brandenburg soldiers were already in position on or near Soviet territory, ready to undertake the commando- like missions that would assist the advance of their Army. From the masses of equipment captured by the Finns during their winter war with Russia, the Abwehr had obtained Russian overcoats, Red Army transport and weapons, all of which could be used in clandestine operations. There were hundreds of objectives along the Russian frontier: bridges, tunnels, airfields, and road junctions which needed to be taken. Possession of them was vital to the German advance. These tactical objectives would be captured by Brandenburg men dressed and equipped as Red Army soldiers.

The seizure of some of these objectives would require little more than a short drive into Soviet territory, the men disguised in Red Army greatcoats and riding in a Russian truck. Farther afield Brandenburg operators would have to land by parachute or gliders. The account which follows is typical of the short-range missions which Brandenburg agents undertook at this stage of the campaign.

The War had already run two days before the call came which brought the first of the Brandenburg companies into action. Guderian had sent his Panzer Group 2 smashing through the Soviet front and his tanks were beginning to spread out across the flat country of the Pripet Marsh. An armoured column had been given the task of seizing and holding a river bridge and its embankment across the swampy area. The objective could not be taken by frontal assault. To capture it would require skill and guile. Brandenburg was called for.

Not long after dawn on Thursday 26 June, the officers of the Special Company arrived at Corps Headquarters and were briefed. It was vital that the bridge be taken; it was the only one for miles up or down-stream which could take the weight of the German tanks. To under-stand the importance of the operation it must be stressed that there were few good roads or suitable bridges in Russia and even fewer in the great expanse of almost impassable ground that was the Pripet Marsh. Possession of road junctions or crossing-points was essential to the momentum of the Panzer advance. Failure to gain the objective would delay, for precious hours or even days, the advance of Guderian's Panzer Group and the eastward advance of the German Fourth Army.

The Brandenburg company lay in the vast woods on the German side of the frontier, ready for a call to action. Within two hours of that call being received the group was *en route* to the operational area. The journey across the frontier into enemy territory and then north-east-wards across Galicia and Belorussia, was a dusty and bone-shattering experience. The men were flung from side to side in the primitive Red Army trucks as they bounced from one pothole to another. The whole width of the highway was choked with vehicles. At the height of its power, the German Army was moving forward, seemingly irresistible.

Despite the urgency of the alarm call, the Brandenburg Commander did not want to attract attention by insisting that his convoy be given traffic priority; Russian agents might be anywhere. It was better to arrive at the rendezvous and to go into action with insufficient rest than to have a mission endangered through a breach of security. Thus it was not until well into the early hours of Friday, 27 June, that the convoy arrived in the concentration area of the Panzer regiment which would support the Brandenburg mission. At the briefing that morning the Abwehr officer was given full details of the Panzer regiment's task. The lieutenant appreciated the difficulties of his mission. Obviously, no German tank must be seen anywhere near the embankment which led towards the bridge. The German armour would have to hide while he took the bridge before it could debouch onto the causeway and begin the advance to the bridge. Too premature a move would warn the Red Army engineers who would demolish the structure.

The Brandenburg detachment would have to bluff its way forward, seize the bridge and hold it until relieved. How long would that be? The Panzer Commander calculated the distance between the point at which his vehicles would debouch on to the embankment and the far end of the bridge. The average speed of a Panzer III was less than 16mph. There would be, the Panzerman calculated, a period of about fifteen minutes during which the Abwehr group would be alone and holding the captured objective. For fifteen minutes they would have to prevent the mass of Soviet soldiers which surrounded them from destroying the bridge. If the Brandenburgers were able to capture it and were able to prevent its destruction, the Red Army officers would fling in attack after attack to recapture it and would sacrifice all their men, if need be, in that endeavour. The Soviet officers knew that failure to blow the structure would bring them in front of a firing-squad. Against the Red masses and their determined commanders the small German group could pit only their resolution and the element of surprise.

As with most Brandenburg operations the plan was very simple. Two truck-loads of men, dressed in Russian greatcoats and helmets and shouting that German tank columns were near, were to drive along the embankment towards the bridge. The first truck would cross it, the second would break down before it reached that far. The men of the lead truck, showing signs of panic, would shout orders that the bridge should not be blown until their comrades had reached them. In the first few minutes of their arrival with orders and countermands producing chaos there should be a chance for them to locate the firing-point from which the Red Army Engineers would blow the charges. The 'broken-down' truck would then limp slowly onto the bridge and as it reached the roadway, all the Brandenburgers would throw off their Red Army coats and show their German uniforms, hoping by surprise to overcome any resistance and seize both the bridge and the firing-point.

It was quite usual for even junior Brandenburg officers to dictate the time and mode of their attack and the young lieutenant held firm to his decision not to start the operation until the sun was low in the west and shining in the eyes of the Russian sentries. His two trucks would be silhouetted against the lowering sun which would blind the enemy, but which would illuminate the ground ahead for him.

All was made ready. German machine-pistols were stowed on the bottom of the trucks and Russian rifles were carried. Equipment, taken from the bodies of dead Russians was put on. As a final touch the young lieutenant, a fluent Russian-speaker and with a Leningrad accent, took the cap and shoulder-straps from a fallen NKVD officer and by this sub-terfuge was converted instantly to a member of the dread secret police. Another element of the German plan was that artillery would bombard the embankment road as if firing at the two Brandenburg trucks. This fire would include a near miss from one shell and that would seem to cause damage to the second truck, which would move slowly as if hit. A Panzer Company assault group would assemble in dead ground near the western end of the embankment leading to the bridge and would prepare to drive forward at top speed as soon as the second truck had limped across to the eastern side. To drown the noise of the Panzer engines, German guns would lay heavy fire around and behind the bridge. To further distract the Soviet defenders a flight of Stukas would make a mock bombing raid, but would deliberately drop their bombs wide of the target. They would not machine-gun the bridge in case a stray bullet should set off a detonating charge and bring all the ground operation to naught.

It was a long, hot day. German infantry patrols kept up their pressure against the Soviet troops, forcing them to withdraw towards and finally on to the embankment. So far as Brandenburg was concerned these retreating Red Army men were a perfect cover for their own operations. The greater the number of troops on the road retreating towards the bridge, the easier it would be for the trucks of the commando group to

pass unnoticed. A steady stream of men flooded along the embankment, their ranks breaking whenever the German artillery bombarded
them.

The Stukas, the black Hussars of the air, flew in, made a great deal of
noise in their mock raid and then retired westwards again. Under cover
of the air attack the Brandenburg group boarded their trucks, crashed
through the concealing undergrowth and, pursued by shellbursts,
roared towards the embankment. Swaying from side to side the trucks
were driven at speed onto its broken surface. Standing among his
disguised men stood the lieutenant, dressed in his NKVD uniform and
waving his arms to clear a way through the mob of retreating soldiers.
At a snail's pace they pushed their way through the masses of men now
crowding onto the bridge. At one point a Red Army officer who tried to
stop the commando trucks with the demand that they carry his
wounded men, had to be threatened with a pistol before he would clear
the way.

Then, as planned, shells began to fall near the second truck which
slowed even more as if it had been damaged. This created an unfore-
seen problem. As the vehicle slowed the soldiers tried desperately to
haul themselves aboard and had to be beaten off with rifle butts. Then
the first lorry was on the bridge. It crossed and reached the Red Army
Engineer detachment charged with the demolition. The Abwehr
lieutenant shouted for the officer in charge of the Engineers and began
to hector him, demanding that the bridge be spared. The argument
between the two officers held the attention of the Soviet troops so that
they did not notice the other Brandenburg men searching for and
removing the explosive charges on the eastern bank. The two officers,
still locked in argument, moved towards a small hollow where the
firing-point was concealed. The second truck was now only a few
hundred yards away. With a loud cry of 'Brandenburg' the German
lieutenant flung off the NKVD cap and opened his coat to show the
German tunic beneath it. There was a flurry of shots and he fell dead.
Close-quarter fighting then took place around the firing-point. A
Brandenburg sergeant flung himself across the detonator and cut the
wires. The device was now harmless. The next task was to hold both
ends of the bridge until the Panzers arrived.

The commando group set up their machine-guns and brought them
into action. Bursts of machine-gun fire cut down the Russians on the
bridge at its eastern end. Men of the second truck formed a small
bridgehead on the western side and opened fire upon the bewildered
men plodding along the embankmented highway. Soviet officers
quickly assessed the situation. Their training had taught them always to
attack and they sent forward their men in human waves attacking both
ends of the bridge simultaneously. The struggle grew in intensity. Soon
mortars and artillery were brought up to destroy the two Brandenburg

groups. A small patrol from the detachment at the eastern end of the bridge was sent back to make contact with the group at the western end. The patrols met, joined forces and together began to rip out the remaining explosive charges and to cut the wires leading to the detonating point.

Half an hour passed and the sun had almost set, but there was still no sight or sound of the relieving Panzer column. The explanation? The lead tank had broken down and was blocking the road. The offending vehicle could not be tipped over or towed back, nor could it be by-passed because the road was too narrow and a belt of sturdy oaks prevented another tank from manoeuvring alongside. Pioneers were brought forward and worked at full speed to cut down the trees until there was space for a second vehicle to move up and carry out the unblocking task. The Panzer III turned turtle as it fell down the steep embankment. The road was clear. The second Panzer emerged from cover and was soon smothered in a barrage of Russian artillery shells. It was hit and halted, burning and exploding on the road. A third vehicle advanced and was hit. A fourth was hit and stopped. The situation was critical. Unless the Russian guns could be silenced the tanks could not advance. The Luftwaffe liaison officer with the Panzer regiment called for Stuka support. None was available for an hour. The Panzer crews laid down a smoke-screen, but it dispersed quickly in the strong evening wind.

In the two bridgeheads there was acute concern. Ammunition was running low and casualties were increasing; the groups would soon be overrun. Then came good news to the waiting tank men. A Stuka attack ordered on another target had been aborted and the squadron was on its way to the bridge. It was last light before the aircraft dived to release their bombs on the Soviet gun positions. Covered by the confusion of the air assault the tank group moved out and thundered up the embankment in an all-out charge. Half a mile was covered; then a mile had been gained. The Russian guns opened up again. The lead tank was hit, but remained a 'runner'. The second was untouched; the third suffered a direct hit on its track. It swung on its remaining track so as not to block the road completely. The fourth vehicle, waiting on the embankment until the manoeuvre had been completed, was then hit and set on fire. Of the whole Company, there now remained only three vehicles.

The first two Panzers drove through and scattered the Russian infantry groups still plodding along the highway; the third broke down. The two survivors of the Panzer Company reached and crossed the bridge to take up defensive positions on the eastern side. They were not alone for long. Under cover of darkness, tanks of another hastily-formed assault group thundered through the Soviet barrage and reached the bridge. During the night the remainder of the Panzer regiment closed up. Very few of the tank crews saw the tired Brandenburgers pick up their dead, stow them in a truck and set off back to the camp site from which they had set out. The Brandenburg detachment had held the bridge not for fifteen minutes, but for two hours, and if it was the Panzer crews who received the medals and the praise in the OKW communiqués, this was only to be expected; a secret unit cannot be mentioned by name in broadcast reports. There was, in any case, little time for self-pity. New missions were being planned. The war had to go on, medals or no medals.

7
DEEP PENETRATION
Brandenburg in Africa and
the Parachute Engineer Battalion in Tunisia

The continent of Africa was one theatre of operations which, even before the outbreak of war, might have been thought ideal for the infiltration of Abwehr agents. Their use, however, seems not to have been considered until a German expeditionary Corps had been dispatched to Africa and had already undertaken several offensives.

The German Army had come to North Africa in the spring of 1941, in support of Italy, the failing Axis partner, whose forces had been all but destroyed by a small British army under General Wavell. So swift had been the pace of the British counter-stroke, that by February 1941, most of Mussolini's African Empire had been taken and Tripoli, his last African possession, was threatened with capture. It was at this point that OKW put into operation its contingency plan and dispatched a group which was to become known as the Afrika Korps. Its commander was Erwin Rommel.

As this move into Africa had been so quickly conceived and executed, Canaris had had no time to prepare for the employment of his agents there. Within Brandenburg were men who had lived or worked in tropical lands. Most of them were from families that had colonised the former German possessions of East and South West Africa. There were also Palestinian Germans and others from South Africa. Volunteers were called for and these former emigrés came forward in such numbers that within weeks more than sixty had been sifted, interviewed, selected and accepted. To the number of those chosen for the 'Afrika Kompanie' were added communications experts. Command of the Company was given to Oberleutnant von Koenen, a man of wide experience with a great knowledge of Africa. He divided the Company into two half-Companies and sent them to Tripoli where the first half-Company arrived in October 1941. The second detachment sailed four months later. Most of the men in 'Afrika Kompanie' not only spoke English more or less fluently, but also had command of Arabic and Swahili as main languages, backed up by several of the African dialects.

It was intended that the Brandenburg detachments be used for reconnaissance operations: to penetrate a short distance into the British lines and glean information about the conditions awaiting the Panzer Army. This idea of short, sharp missions was changed during June 1942, when it seemed as if Rommel had defeated the British Eighth Army and was about to drive on to the Nile. A new and vital task was now passed to von Koenen's Company; a typical Brandenburg operation. His groups were to infiltrate the British front line and advance as far as the Nile and the Suez Canal, where they would seize and hold the bridges so as to prevent their destruction. The prerequisites for this special commando undertaking were never met. Rommel's Panzerarmee Afrika lacked the strength to smash through to the Nile. Allied resistance at El Alamein during the month of July, forced Rommel to essay an outflanking thrust at Alam el Halfa in September. This attempted right hook was flung back in disorder and just over a month later, on a bright moonlit night in late October, Eighth Army put in its own offensive and the thunder of a thousand guns beat out the signal that the end of Axis endeavours in Africa was at hand.

This chapter deals with two other reconnaissance operations under-taken by small groups from von Koenen's Company: the first, to locate the British supply route from West Africa to the Red Sea; the second, to infiltrate Abwehr agents into Cairo.

As an explanation of the background to the first operation it will be appreciated that supply and reinforcement were vital to the European forces which were fighting a war in Africa. For the Axis, reinforcements and supplies came by the short sea route from Sicily to Tripoli, during which the Italian and German ships were attacked by the Royal Navy and by Royal Air Force aircraft operating out of Malta. On the other side, supplies to the predominantly British Army came from the Home-land, the Empire or from America. Some of the convoys bringing in the tanks, guns and men to defeat Rommel sailed through the Mediter-ranean; that is to say, by the short sea route, but most made the long haul down the West African coast, around the Cape, up the eastern side of the continent and into the Red Sea.

The Germans were convinced that Allied convoys on the long haul, sailed only as far as West Africa where the ships congregated in the Gulf of Guinea before unloading their cargoes in the port of Lagos. From there, according to German Intelligence, supplies were carried overland to Port Sudan in Egypt. Thus, between West Africa and Egypt, so the Germans thought, ran the chief supply route to the British Desert Army. It was to establish exactly the location of that road that the Branden-burgers were sent out on the mission. If the reports from the long-range patrols confirmed that the road existed, a strong German force would be sent to cut the artery and the flow of vehicles and weapons to the British.

The Brandenburg reconnaissance operation would involve the soldiers in a round trip of nearly three thousand miles, of which the greatest part would be through the Sahara desert. The patrols would first go southwards from Tripoli to the province of Chad in French Equatorial Africa through which the road was believed to run. This, the major part of the trek, would be through enemy countries so that the group would wear British uniforms and would travel in captured British Army vehicles. These would form a road convoy with all the appearance of a Long Range Desert Group patrol. Twelve 15cwt trucks, twelve half-tracks fitted with 2pdr guns, four jeeps carrying multiple anti-aircraft machine-guns, a Staff car, wireless truck, water truck, petrol tanker, ration trucks and a workshop vehicle would form the motorised column. One accompaniment which more than anything else would help to maintain the adopted identity of a British detachment was a captured Spitfire, which would fly in from Italy on the first day and which would be used to carry out long-range reconnaissance ahead of the group.

In the last week of June the column set out for Marzuq in the deep south of Libya, where there was an isolated garrison maintaining the Italian presence. There was a longish halt to service the vehicles thoroughly before the drive continued to Gatrun. Here the Branden-burgers set up a base camp staffed by the Signals group and the crews of two half-trucks to provide local defence against attack by Arab marauders. At Gatrun the whole detachment set to work and laid out an airstrip for the Spitfire. The group waited and waited, but by the end of the fourth day the aircraft had still not arrived. Unwilling to delay the operation, von Leipzig, Commanding Officer of the reconnaissance detachment, decided to press on. This decision now placed upon his small group a heavier burden than that which they had expected to carry. It had been planned that the Spitfire would carry out reconnais-sance from the air. Now, this would have to be carried out by ground patrols and they would have to search a wider area than had been planned. Von Leipzig divided his detachment into three. The largest of these he himself led. The area which this group had to reconnoitre was the Toummo mountains. Having established the type of terrain *en route* to the mountains and whether Allied troops held the area, von Leipzig's group would then match towards the Tassili plateau across which, it was thought, ran the British supply route.

A sergeant commanded a second and smaller group which had as its objective the Tibesti mountains to the south-east of Gatrun, to deter-mine whether these were held by the Allies. Leutnant Becker, the Commander of the third group, was ordered to strike westwards towards the Algerian frontier and carry out reconnaissance inside that French colony. Having completed their tasks the groups would rendez-vous and return to base camp.

Consider the journeys that these three small groups were about to undertake. They would penetrate areas of Africa, terrible in their cruelty of climate and terrain; regions in which the presence of human life was rare and that of white men even more so. Through the forbid-ding, arid and desolate wastes of the great Sahara they would march, without the prospect of reinforcement or support, across quicksands, shale, rock and jebel, facing hostile even savage, tribes, until each group had gathered its quota of Intelligence. Then, united again, they had to get home. During this return trip and in order to save petrol, the number of 'runner' vehicles would be reduced almost daily. Trucks would be abandoned by the side of the track, drained of every drop of petrol, water and oil for later use. The mission would be a daunting task for young Oberleutnant von Leipzig and his men, not one of whom had travelled in that region or had experience of the great Sahara.

The groups achieved their several missions, regrouped and returned to Gatrun. The information gained was radioed to Rommel, but the Field Marshal had more immediate concerns than the results of a reconnaissance carried out a thousand miles away. He was fighting and losing the battle at Alam el Halfa. To him the knowledge that the Toummo and the Tibesti mountains were held by strong French forces, was academic. At that time the details of the route along which Eighth Army received supplies was less important than knowing what the British already had and what they could put into the present battle. Panzerarmee Afrika was certainly not so strong in numbers and equipment that it could spare the divisions and vehicles which von Leipzig estimated would be required to drive the French from the mountains. While the reconnaissance had been a brilliant success, both in planning and in execution, it brought no practical benefit.

While the operation described above was still in its planning stage, other groups of Brandenburgers were preparing to launch Operation 'Salam', the dropping off of Abwehr agents behind the British lines.

As early as the spring of 1941, when Rommel and his Afrika Korps were still new to the desert, OKW ordered Abwehr to form a special commando to infiltrate Intelligence agents or radio-operators into the rear areas of Eighth Army. There had been previous attempts, at least one of which had proved tragic: the agents had gone off into the 'blue' and had vanished completely. They are still missing. Operation 'Salam' was the latest of the series of 'drops' and was to be planned meticulously, in order to avoid a repeat of the tragedy.

The British commanded both the air and the sea, so it would not be possible to parachute the Abwehr men in or land them from a small craft. They would have to take the overland route across the desert. This would mean a round trip of more than four thousand miles for those who would escort the agents. To guide the group through terrain that boasted few landmarks, a man of outstanding ability and knowledge of the desert was needed. The Germans knew such a man: Hauptmann Count Almasy who, through years spent in North Africa, had achieved an international reputation as a desert traveller. He would act as guide to the Abwehr party whose military commander was Hauptmann von Steffens. Like Almasy, he had lived in Africa for years and was fluent, as were a number of his men, in Arabic. Both Almasy and von Steffens spoke English fluently. They were both supremely confident men. Indeed, when an OKW officer asked the Count how he would bring his agents behind the British lines, Almasy's answer was typical of him. 'We shall', he replied, 'drive straight through the desert to reach the Nile and we shall set them down there.'

Almasy planned to take the whole group to the Yapsa Pass, near Assiut on the Nile. On the summit of the pass the agents would be 'dropped' and would drive to the nearest railway station in a military truck. From the station they would travel by train direct to Cairo, there to establish contact with anti-British elements and set up a radio-transmitter. Von Steffens' troop would then return to Panzer Army.

On the outward journey the group would travel in a convoy of five trucks and make for the Dyalo oasis; a point on the Kufra track, some 160 miles south of Ajedabia. At intervals along the road to the dropping-off point, three of the heavy trucks would be left by the side of the track to conserve petrol and to serve as fuel and ration dumps for the return trip. On the way home the commando would not need more than one truck, so the three abandoned trucks, stripped of fuel and provisions, could be destroyed.

It was, of course, understood that since Assiut was on a direct line to Cairo, the whole area around the dropping-off point was in British hands and Eighth Army also controlled the all-weather road to the Egyptian capital. The Abwehr group, therefore, would travel dressed in Luftwaffe tropical uniform which resembled very closely the khaki drill of the British Army. Furthermore, each truck was to be marked with the German straight-sided cross, although this identifying insignia would be hidden under a layer of sand and dust and would be recognised only by close scrutiny. With the last preparations completed the 'Salam' commando set out, but within a few miles were brought to a halt. Von Steffens' truck had stuck fast in the sand and the Germans had not brought any sand channels with them. The strenuous efforts required to push and dig the vehicle clear of the soft, clinging sand had their effect. Von Steffens suffered a heart attack and had to be rushed to a field hospital. Then colic struck and the group was held fast in the grip of that agonising complaint. Finally, on 11 May, the commando set out again, this time with such success that not only was Almasy able to lead them to a pass in the mountains which he had reconnoitred a decade earlier, but he found there the water supply which had been stored at the time of his original expedition. By now the group was well within British military territory, but as yet there had been no sign of Eighth Army troops. This good fortune of being able to pass through the great desert waste without check was not to last. Once on the military road, which had been built to connect the principal cities of Egypt, the Abwehr group soon encountered the first of a series of control posts and military patrols. The Sudanese troops on duty at the first check-point were stopping all traffic and checking all documents. Both Abwehr trucks carried a white shield, an identification mark used by Eighth Army to indicate that the truck bearing it was allowed through check-points without control. The Brandenburgers were confident that the white shield would grant them immunity, but as a precaution the first truck did stop next to the Sudanese sentry. Now was the testing time. With a casual air which belied his feelings the Brandenburg driver leaned out of the cab, spoke in Arabic to the sentry, presented the vehicle documents, pointed to the white shield and ordered the road-block to be removed. Without scrutinising the papers the sentries complied with the order and the two trucks passed through heading for the summit of the Yapsa pass. There the two Abwehr agents changed into civilian clothes and, equipped with their radios, made for Assiut. Soon they would be on a train and heading for Cairo.

The return journey for Almasy and the Brandenburg group was not without incident. They picked up the three abandoned trucks, filled the tanks of their own vehicles, distributed the supplies and then blew up the three-tonners. They then drove on until they had used all the spare fuel and were down to what remained in the vehicle tanks. Now something alarming happened. While crossing a stretch of desolate sand the compasses were affected by magnetic interference, but the fact that the group was off course was not immediately realised. When Almasy appreciated that they were lost he halted and waited for nightfall. By astro-navigation he worked out their position and, carefully husbanding the food, drove on hoping for something to turn up. Something did: a number of stationary British supply trucks, loaded with food, water and fuel, left as dumps for the men and vehicles of British long-range desert patrols.

On 4 June Almasy sent the signal announcing his return. Operation 'Salam' had been undertaken and completed – but it had all been in vain. British Intelligence officers had learned in advance of the plan to plant Abwehr agents in Cairo and had not only captured them there but had 'turned' them against the Germans. The British had, in fact, intended to locate the German group with the aid of aircraft, and have them captured by ground patrols, but faults in liaison on the British side had allowed Almasy to drop his agents and to return to base. The operation was a failure, but the skill and determination of Almasy and the Brandenburg group are worthy of recognition by being included in this book on Special Forces.

The offensive launched by the Eighth Army at Alamein forced the Axis armies to retreat, first from Egypt, then out of Libya and finally across the frontier into Tunisia, a colony of the neutral Vichy French Empire. It was believed in London and in Washington that the French North African Empire could be invaded by an Anglo-American force, and that only minimal opposition would come from the French forces stationed there. A speedy occupation of the French colonies would trap Rommel's Panzerarmee Afrika between the British Eighth Army storming northwards out of Tripoli and the Allied Army invading Tunisia from the west. The war in Africa would thus be brought to a successful conclusion. Confident in this belief, during November 1942, British and American troops were landed at various ports along the southern Mediterranean coast between Oran and Bone, whence a composite group known as 'Blade Force' drove eastwards to capture Bizerta and Tunis, the two principal cities and ports of Tunisia.

Hitler's reaction to the Allied move was both swift and violent. Within days German paratroops had been flown in and had taken over the airfields in and around the capital. Tanks were flown across the Mediterranean in Messerschmitt transport gliders, and further reinforcements, including Tiger tanks, followed by sea convoy. The armoured cars and tanks of 'Blade Force' were driving towards the flimsy perimeter held by paratroops who had now been strengthened by the Para Engineer Battalion commanded by Major Witzig, the hero of Eben Emael.

In October Witzig's battalion had been warned to stand by for overseas service in the Western Desert, but nothing had happened until Sunday, 15 November. On that date the battalion headquarters, a signals platoon and No. 1 Platoon of No. 1 Company flew to Africa in a six-engined seaplane. On the following day, with only the advance guard present out of the whole battalion, Witzig formed a small battle group and advanced westwards. His orders were to gain ground; to give the German forces in Tunisia the greatest possible perimeter. The Para Engineer Battalion's advance party had brought no vehicles except six motorcycle combinations. Witzig commandeered a couple of civilian lorries and around the nucleus of his Para group and the two trucks, assembled a force made up of 2cm Flak gunners, a battery of 10.5cm guns, a Company of Panzer IV and an Italian anti-tank Company mounted in half-tracks. With this small battle group the Para Engineer officer struck westwards.

On the morning of 17 November, a British armoured car patrol from Blade Force was sighted by Battle Group Witzig, but no contact was made. In the afternoon of that day the Axis group, *en route* for Sedjenane, met opposition at Jebel Abiod, some 80 miles from Bizerta. In bright sunlight the vehicles of the Axis column were climbing the winding road towards the little town into which, a few hours earlier, a British force had arrived, had deployed and was waiting. The British group: three Rifle Companies of 6th Battalion, The Queen's Own Royal West Kent Regiment, a troop of 25pdrs and some machine-gunners

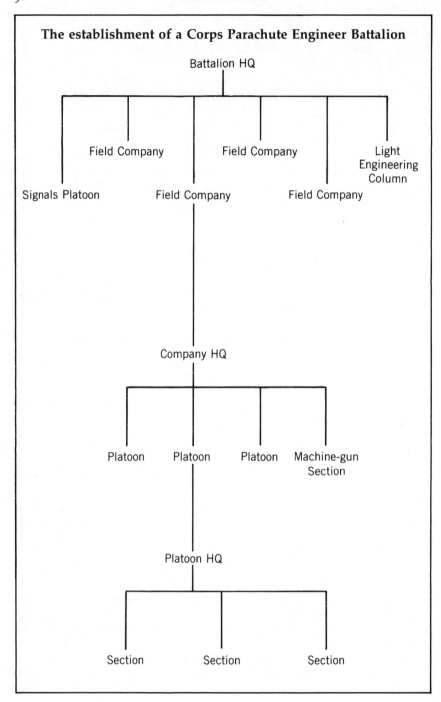

The establishment of a Corps Parachute Engineer Battalion

Battalion HQ

Field Company　　　Field Company　　　Light Engineering Column

Signals Platoon　　　Field Company　　　Field Company

Company HQ

Platoon　　　Platoon　　　Platoon　　　Machine-gun Section

Platoon HQ

Section　　　Section　　　Section

from 5th Battalion, The Northamptonshire Regiment, held the ground through which Witzig's battle group had to pass. The German/Italian columns, unaware that the town was in British hands, drove steadily uphill, hidden at times by the curves in the road, but finally coming into full view of the West Kent garrison. The feelings of some of the British detachment are expressed by a private soldier of 6th Battalion. 'I had a rotten feeling. These were the first Germans I had ever seen. Their column, compact and moving deliberately towards us, seemed very confident, assured of victory and very powerful. For all we knew the group might be the advance guard of some Panzer Division. We were miles away from any of our own troops, quite isolated. Jerry's planes flew about all over the place. We didn't see one of ours. Speaking for myself, when I saw that mass of tanks, guns and trucks I thought there were only two ways out, death or imprisonment.'

The British fire discipline was firm. Not until the range had come down to less than two hundred yards did the 25pdrs open fire. The first salvoes smashed eight German tanks and enveloped the unlimbered German guns with high explosives. The paratroopers sprang from the soft-skin trucks, deployed and went to ground taking up firing positions. Their fire had no effect, not did that of their Flak guns. The British defence was solid. The German thrust westwards had been halted and, except for such minor advances and withdrawals as occurred during the weeks and months of the war in Tunisia, the point reached by Witzig's battle group in that mid-November encounter formed the perimeter of the battle line which the Germans held to the west of Tunis.

The German/Italian battle group dug in in front of Jebel Abiod and held it against British attacks throughout those first critical days. On the only occasion when Witzig's men were relieved, by an Italian paratroop battalion, the first thrust which the Italians made was driven back with heavy loss and the German paras had to be rushed back to their former positions. Slowly the situation improved as more and more Axis troops strengthened the line. The flow of reinforcements was sufficient for Witzig's specialist companies, which by this time had arrived in Tunisia, to be withdrawn from Jebel Abiod to form a special counterattack reserve. This force was also trained in the tactics of deep penetration and the small, skilled groups went out in the cold and rainy November nights, slipping past the British sentries and deep into the rear areas. Accounts by men of the Para Engineers record active service life in the Tunisian hills during those bitter days and nights.

'I had always believed North Africa to be a hot and sandy desert and was surprised to see bare hills and to experience the damp and bitter cold of those open slopes. The usual patrols which we undertook behind the British lines lasted for three nights, two of which were spent in enemy territory. We went out in skeleton order, armed with machine-pistols and each of us portering two Teller mines as well as other explosive devices. The patrol leader carried the fuses. Rations were hard tack and sardines. We practically lived on sardines. There were also food concentrates and sometimes Benzedrine tablets to keep us awake. These were not popular for they brought on a terrible thirst which was hard to quench in that inhospitable terrain.

'We relied to a very great deal upon Arab guides to take us through the lines. The natives welcomed us at that time as troops who had come to liberate us from the French. We were billeted in farms behind the front and moved up the line so that by mid-afternoon we reached the area just behind the forward zone.

'This was both our form-up line and our start-line. There we also picked up the Teller mines and the other explosives as well as extra ammunition, wire-cutters and the like. Finally, we were issued with rations, filled our water-bottles and were given a hot meal. For what remained of the daylight hours we slept or otherwise kept under cover. We soon learned that this was essential, for any movement on our side of the line was seen by enemy artillery observers or aircraft who would bring down a hurricane of shells upon us. The British would fire for hours, banging away but causing little damage. What was there to damage but cactus and gorse bushes?

'Quite often the Arab guides for whom we had been waiting would come from the direction of the British lines and we always wondered whether they were acting for both sides. Some would simply ride over to us on donkey back while others would drive sheep and goats across No Man's Land, seeming to be harmless shepherds. At last light we would set off, each man briefed on the intention, the targets and the routes that we were to follow; out and back, for we naturally did not return by the same route as that by which we had left.

'It was easy to cross the British front-line positions in those early days. The discipline of the Tommies was not always good. Many smoked while they were on guard and the glow of the lighted tip could be seen for some distance. It was winter time with long dark nights, heavy cloud and sometimes fog so that it was not really difficult to cross the British trench line. Once we were through the firing-line came the difficult part, for the area behind the forward zone was often filled with parties of men marching up to the line, with men collecting rations or ammunition, digging holes or carrying out some other duty. All these we took good care to avoid. The rear area behind this first zone, was usually clear and we could even march along the roads without fear of being halted or questioned, but we took no unnecessary risks and skirted around villages, for often these contained military garrisons.

'We would march all night and shortly before first light our Arab guides would take us up into the hills. We would lie-up all day alone and sleep under bushes because we found the huts and caves to be infested with vermin. At last light we would set off to the target area.

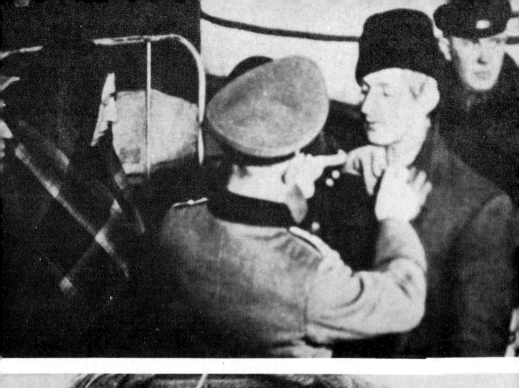

Top Operations in the east: SD men disguise themselves as Russian or Polish civilians in order to mix with the local population. It was in just such a way that SD units had carried out the raids in August 1939 which precipitated the Second World War.
Centre Men of a Brandenburg detachment dressed in Red Army uniform and in a Soviet truck en route to a mission behind the Russian lines during the autumn of 1941.
Right Newly-captured Red Army prisoners being interrogated by men of the Brandenburg Regiment's 1st Battalion.

Left A signals detachment of the Brandenburg Regiment during anti-partisan operations in Russia during 1942. The wireless set is coordinating the movements by companies of the 1st Battalion in its sweep through the 'bandit'-infested area.
Right Two men of the Brandenburg von Koenen detachment — one in Arab guise — during a mission in Africa.
Below Soldiers of Para Engineer Battalion Witzig marching through Tunis in the days shortly after their arrival in North Africa, November 1942. Note the high proportion of automatic weapons carried.
Bottom The first German paratroops in Tunisia setting out to extend the perimeter around the ports of Tunis and Bizerta, November 1942.

Above Brandenburg soldiers from the von Koenen detachment rest in a wadi after one of their missions in Tunisia during the winter of 1942/3.
Left Witzig presents Iron Crosses to men of his unit in Tunisia.
Below He gives a valedictory address at the funeral of Oberleutnant Hans Hard of the Para Corps Engineer Battalion in Tunisia, February 1943.
Right Sturmbannfuhrer Otto Skorzeny, the SS officer who rescued Mussolini and then went on to lead the special forces of the Third Reich.

Above The glider in which Skorzeny flew to the Gran Sasso to rescue Benito Mussolini, the imprisoned Italian Fascist dictator.
Below Skorzeny, the burly figure on the left of this photo- graph, escorts Mussolini from the hotel on the Gran Sasso.
Bottom The Fiesler Storch being prepared for the escap flight. Mussolini and Skorzeny are already aboard; Gerlac the pilot, is about to climb into the machine.

Above Tito (fifth from left) talking to the men and women of his partisan forces who had captured the town of Jajce. This place then became the headquarters of the partisan forces until early 1944, when it was recaptured by the Germans and Tito was forced to move into the cave at Drvar.

Left Tito and one of his commanders rest outside a cave that was used temporarily after his flight from Jajce. Tito had been slightly wounded during the fighting in and around that town.

Above Officers of the 7th SS Mountain Division 'Prinz Eugen' confer shortly before the attack upon Tito's headquarters. **Below left** Men of SS Para Battalion 500 wait to emplane at the outset of Operation 'Rosselsprung'. **Below right** The midday drop of paratroops as photographed by a Yugoslav partisan from a post high on a hill outside Drvar.

Minelaying was a simple matter. A shallow hole would be dug and the Teller mine would be laid in it. It would then be covered with loose earth. We would plant the mines around a blind corner or in a narrow defile. In that way any vehicle blown up created a traffic problem. And, of course, we would often lay dummy mines, just heaping up the earth as if a Teller had been laid. We seldom waited to see the results of our activities although sometimes after the mines had been laid and we were resting on a hillside we might hear a detonation and would wonder what the truck had been carrying.

'There was one time when I had just finished laying a mine and a truck came round the corner. I went to ground. Only the right wheel of the vehicle went over the Teller and the explosion took it off. Most of the force of the detonation went up in the open air so that the driver was not killed but only badly shaken. In the back of the truck we found rations and cigarettes and loaded ourselves up with as much as we could carry. As I have already said, we practically lived on sardines so the chance to eat British Army rations was one gladly taken'.

The nervousness caused to the Allied High Command by these deep penetrations is evidenced by a tragic incident which followed one patrol. Determined to drive even deeper into the British rear areas part of No. 3 Company was trained and briefed for a night drop to destroy important bridges and airfields in the Souk el Arba and Souk el Ahras regions. Oberst Harlinghausen, the Luftwaffe Commander in Tunisia, attended the briefing and stressed the importance of preventing an Allied build-up which would give the Anglo-American forces the strength to make a general assault upon the German perimeter, to the west of Tunis. The paras from No. 3 Company jumped on a dark and windswept December night, but the unskilled pilots of their transports failed to locate the targets. The paras landed miles away from their objectives and were badly dispersed. Aggressive British patrolling had soon rounded them up. German reports state that captured men of No. 3 Company were court-martialled and shot in retaliation for Hitler's infamous order that commandos taken prisoner would be executed. Whether this is true or not, it is certainly the case that drops were stopped immediately on the orders of Feldmarschall Kesselring.

The British First Army in Tunisia, was weaker and had less experience fighting in bad terrain than the veteran Eighth Army commanded by Montgomery. The First Army was fighting in the Tunisian mountains and its principal supply routes were limited to a poor road network and a few railway lines snaking their way through those bare and hostile mountain ranges. It would be easy for the Germans to disrupt the flow of supplies by blowing up bridges and cratering mountain roads. Brandenburg units were selected to carry out the task.

The first operation was undertaken on 26 December when two groups set out, each travelling in three gliders, and each charged with the destruction of certain railway bridges. One major objective was the Sidi bou Sakr bridge in the central part of Tunisia; a second was a road and rail bridge to the north-east of Kasserine. No detailed account of these raids exists, but from war diaries and reports it is clear that on both occasions the raiders had very bad luck.

The flight of the group which was to attack Sidi bou Sakr was quite unremarkable; the JUs flew over the Allied front lines and were not fired on – the trip was quiet and peaceful. The pilots of the tug aircraft navigating superbly by dead reckoning, cast off the gliders only a few miles short of the target and saw them swoop down through the dark night towards the even darker bulk of the bridge. Undeterred by the inky blackness the glider pilots headed for the banks of the river, which was spanned by the Sidi bou Bakr bridge, and set the wooden machines down. The fully-loaded gliders ploughed through the dust of the river bank. The landings had been classic and the machines came to a halt only a few yards away from the huge railway bridge. Even before the gliders had halted they were lashed by streams of machine-gun bullets. The concrete pillboxes protecting the bridge were manned by soldiers of a French cavalry reconnaissance regiment which had moved into the area only days earlier. Arab agents had failed to pass on this vital information.

The first bursts of fire caused severe casualties, but the paratroops were trained to react instantly and were soon engaging the French garrison. In the short but bitter fire fight which followed, most of the Brandenburgers were killed, wounded or captured. The very few survivors fought their way through the French encirclement and made their way back to the German lines. The Sidi bou Bakr landing had been a total disaster.

The second of the two airborne detachments fared even worse. The towing machines had come under intense fire even before they had crossed the British line. The inexperienced pilot of the JU 52 immediately cast off the glider whose pilot was not skilled enough to undertake the necessary emergency action. The machine crash-landed in a wadi – a dried-up river bed – miles from the objective. This was no soft landing; the wadi was filled with huge boulders and the flimsy machine crashed and ricochetted from one to another. The wings were torn off and the fuselage began to break up as the glider tore its way along the wadi bed. By the time that it had come to a halt most of the men were either dead or badly wounded. The senior officer of the party was prepared to abort the mission and strike out for the German lines, but a council of war decided that a patrol should be sent out with the object of locating the target. Soon after the patrol had set out they were alerted by sounds of firing. Turning back the men saw the flash and flicker of tracers criss-crossing the night sky. Firing was being concentrated upon the glider. The firing then stopped. It was clear what had happened. The

Brandenburg detachment had been located and its resistance had been beaten down. The paras were either killed or taken prisoner.

The sergeant commanding the patrol brought his small group home after nearly two weeks of travelling, mainly by night. The failure of the operations did not halt German attempts to take out the bridges, and dive-bombers were sent in to carry out the work of destruction which the Brandenburgers had been unable to achieve. The Stukas also failed to demolish the bridges and Allied war material continued to pour across them.

The quantities of supplies which the Allies had built up were so great that they were able to re-equip completely the French Colonial Army and the French Army in the North African colonies. The Axis armies, by comparison, were starved of everything they needed and were being compressed into a bridgehead whose area was reduced almost daily by new Allied advances.

By the beginning of 1943 the strength of Witzig's Para Engineer Battalion, like that of all the German forces in the Tunisian bridgehead, had fallen to a dangerously low level. Its overtired men had been in action almost continuously since November and their patrols were becoming fewer and were not penetrating so deeply into the Allied lines. The patrols brought back depressing news of growing Allied strength. The strain and the steady erosion by wounds and sickness were taking their toll and only the arrival during February of the survivors of Ramcke's battalion, which had fought at El Alamein, brought Witzig's battalion back up to something approaching effective strength. By mid February the Allies' constricting ring of steel around the Axis bridgehead demanded that the Germans again attempt to gain ground, this time to accommodate the withdrawal of Rommel's army in front of the Eighth Army. To maintain initiative of a sort, Hans von Arnim, who had been given command of the Axis armies in Tunisia, launched an operation to capture Medjez el Bab, with the dual intention of weakening First Army and of gaining ground to the west of Tunis. The role of Witzig's battalion in this offensive was to pass through the hills and to cut off the Allied forces around Mateur. These encircled units would be driven on to the guns of German formations coming in from the east, and through the gap which would have been created, fast, mobile units would pour in to widen the perimeter.

During the opening days of the operation the Para Engineer Battalion, moving chiefly by night to avoid the vigilant Spitfires and Hurricanes which ruled the daylight sky, found increasingly that the roads were blocked by British tank detachments. The Germans were also saddened to note that the Arabs had sensed that the Allies were gaining the upper hand and were betraying the German positions to the Anglo-American troops, or else were leading German troops into ambushes.

A battle group from Witzig's formation, frustrated by British tanks at every cross-roads, attacked the Churchills at close-quarters. On one mission, armed only with hand-grenades and Teller mines, the Para Engineers moved swiftly through the night to strike at a British laager. A small section of paras passed the sentries and placed mines in the tank tracks. The main body of commandos then withdrew leaving a couple of paras standing on the rear deck of two of the Churchills. As the German squad melted into the darkness the intrepid pair dropped satchels of explosives into the open turrets. The Churchills brewed up. The tank crews, brutally awakened, rushed to get their vehicles away from the burning tanks. As the heavy machines rolled slowly forward they set off the Teller mines in their tracks. Detonation followed detonation and soon seven vehicles had blown up and were burning. The paras made off in the dark, pausing only to lay a belt of mines across the track to slow down any pursuit.

Meanwhile, at other sectors along the line Para Engineer battle groups had been fighting as infantry and had mounted a series of unsuccessful attacks to drive back the British troops in the Sidi bou Keone sector. The failure of the specialist paras was a reflection of the overall German weakness; Allied strength was too great. The Axis High Command's offensive to capture Medjez el Bab had failed, as had the intention to extend the perimeter. When the operation was halted there remained only the original bridgehead holding a beleaguered garrison; one which could never be reinforced or supplied with the arms and equipment it needed. No help would ever come to nourish the Axis armies for the Anglo-American forces now had air superiority over both land and sea and many of the flocks of JU 52s which attempted the short flight from Sicily were shot out of the skies.

German unit strengths continued to fall and reached a level at which the formations were but a shadow of their former strength. The wastage in sick and wounded could be made good when the convalescents returned to their parent units, but the dead would never be replaced. No replacements would ever come for those who had fallen in battle and as the fatal losses continued the burden of fighting fell upon fewer and fewer men. As an example, by mid April the strength of the Para Engineer Battalion had sunk to two officers, four NCOs and twenty-seven men. It had begun the campaign with more than eight hundred all ranks.

Down in the south, Rommel had also launched an offensive in a final bid to destroy the Anglo-American armies in Tunisia. The strategic intention of this attack was to strike First Army in the back and force it to retreat into Algeria, but Rommel's vast strategic concept was watered down to become a two-part operation with only tactical possibilities.

Brandenburg had a part to play in Rommel's offensive: groups were to carry out reconnaissance in front of Panzerarmee Afrika, demoralise the enemy and create chaos in the US rear areas. Driving through pouring rain and across trackless mountains, one Brandenburg patrol found a gap in the Allied line. To exploit this gap might bring about, if not victory in Tunisia, at least a respite, a breathing-space. If German units could be brought forward and ferried through this opening in the Anglo-US front, the enemy battle line from Kasserine to Bone might be rolled up. But it was not to be. The Brandenburgers had no radio and could only get back to Rommel's headquarters by road. By the time that they had arrived with this Intelligence, General Anderson, commanding First Army, had plugged the gap with reinforcements rushed down from other sectors of the line.

The fate of the Brandenburg groups during what remained of the African campaign was one common to all crack units and special formations: they were used as storm troops in conventional infantry battles. In the last week of the campaign when German transport aircraft were running the gauntlet of swarms of Allied fighters to airdrop, of all things, illustrated magazines, Party propaganda exhortations and, quite inexplicably, wooden crosses to mark the graves of the fallen, men of the Brandenburg companies worked frantically to salvage from the chaos which marked the death throes of the Axis armies, the specialists and equipment which could be used to continue the fight on the mainland of Europe.

The last drive by the British, American and French armies came during the first week of May 1943, and to meet the onslaught on his sector of the front, Witzig deployed the remnants of his battalion. The first Allied attacks were flung back. According to him: 'American infantry were not skilful or aggressive, but relied upon artillery to blast a path through our positions. After each barrage they would come forward again, moving nonchalantly, confident that our resistance had been totally destroyed. It was easy to pin them down and then to drive them back, but we left them avenues of escape. With our reduced numbers we could not have spared men to act as escorts even if we had taken them prisoner. So we let the Amis escape. Nor were their tank units very determined. The crews seemed to think that their role was to act as locally-employed, short-range SP guns. If one of our two-man close-combat teams knocked out one or two of a whole wave of US tanks, this was sufficient to destroy the cohesion of the attack and to cause the American tank men to behave in a panic-stricken manner. They would mill around firing indiscriminately at anything. If we only had with us at the end the men who had landed with us in November, we could have smashed them completely.'

By 6 May it was clear that the end of the war in Africa was close and the men of the Para Engineers were authorised to make their way back

to Italy. Other units would hold the line while they and other specialist units escaped. On Hitler's direct order, Witzig was flown out of
the bridgehead and his men set about preparing to escape from the
North African shore. The battalion had by this time grown in strength
to ninety-one men. From hospitals and camps the Para Engineer convalescents and wounded had returned, determined to be with their unit if
it came to a last battle. Those ninety-one men were divided into escape
parties, each commanded by an NCO. Some managed to find places on
the last aircraft to fly out of Tunis and Bizerta. Others found rowing-
boats or rubber dinghies and struck out across the Mediterranean for
the island of Sicily. Most of these were picked up by an Italian hospital
ship or were captured by RAF rescue launches. Inevitably many
perished by drowning.

A last ship – an army ferry – sailed late one night from the shores of
Tunisia towards Sicily; a few irreplaceable specialist detachments were
aboard. The remaining Brandenburgers, for whom there was no room,
stayed behind and amid the wrack and ruin of the German-Italian
defeat, sat in an olive grove and, by the light of a bonfire sang the songs
of their army and of their homeland, waiting for the inevitable Allied
patrol to come and take them prisoner.

For the Para Engineer battalion which had fought in Africa the war
was over, but in Germany a new battalion was formed around a cadre
which had escaped from Tunisia. This new unit was fleshed out with
replacements from the Corps depot and muscled with men, convalescing in Germany and Austria from wounds received during the battles in
Tunisia. The new battalion fought until the end of the war, serving now
on the Western Front, now in the East. Wherever it was put in its men
restored ruptured front lines, knitted up broken sectors of the battle
front and to the very end confounded their opponents by their special
skills.

8

SKORZENY

The Mussolini Rescue Mission

The struggle for control of the Intelligence services of the Third Reich was between Admiral Canaris and the SS General Heydrich. It was a long and bitter battle, but one which the Admiral lost because he lacked the ruthlessness of the SS. Then fate intervened. An assassination attempt upon Heydrich on 27 May 1942 succeeded when he died of blood-poisoning on 4 June. It would seem that Canaris was once again in control, but the SS did not give in so easily and Himmler, the Reichsführer SS, took upon himself the task of leading the RSHA. He filled the subordinate posts with his protégés and all of them worked to accomplish the task which Heydrich had begun – the unification of the Intelligence and counter-Intelligence systems, but without his flair and imagination.

In the summer of 1943 an event occurred which was to produce an SS rival to Canaris, a man who may have lacked the intelligence of Heydrich, but who had flair and panache. This SS officer reaped the harvest of the conflict between Abwehr and SD and went on to become the leader of most of the special forces raised in Germany during the latter half of the Second World War. The collapse of Fascist Italy, the imprisonment of Mussolini and the determination of Adolf Hitler to liberate the fallen dictator were the events which set the scene for the arrival on stage of Otto Skorzeny.

On 25 July 1943, the King of Italy removed Mussolini from the post of Prime Minister and placed him under arrest. From a group of dynamic young officers of the Army, the Luftwaffe and the SS, Hitler selected the man who would carry out the rescue mission. The choice was Major Skorzeny of the SS, who, accompanied by twenty Luftwaffe paratroops and equipment which included explosives, laughing-gas and forged British banknotes, arrived at Practica di Mare aerodrome, south of Rome, where fifty SS men of Skorzeny's own detachment had already arrived. Radio messages intercepted by the German communications experts soon located the area in which the Duce was being held and inquiries established that in the Gran Sasso there was a large hotel, the Albergo Rifugio, set upon the summit of the mountain peak. It was accessible only by funicular railway. Skorzeny's battle plan ruled out any frontal assault from the valley to the crest of the Gran Sasso. The alternative was a glider landing on the summit concurrent with which would be an attack upon the funicular terminal in the valley to prevent the arrival of Italian reinforcements.

Twelve fully-manned DFS 230 gliders took off from Practica di Mare at 12.30 on 12 September. Four of the twelve dropped out *en route* and failed to reach the target area. The loss was disconcerting, but worse was to come. As the gliders made their descent Skorzeny saw that the landing site which he had selected from a high-altitude photograph, was not a flat Alpine meadow but a small triangular piece of very steep ground, probably a ski run, which ended abruptly at the edge of a precipice. The gliders would have to crash-land close to the hotel.

One after the other the machines touched down and raced along the boulder-strewn ground, their braking 'chutes streaming behind them. Skorzeny's machine halted only fifteen or twenty yards from the hotel's main door. He raced up the slope and into the foyer, kicked an Italian radio-operator and his set out of action, found and liberated the Italian leader. From touch down to liberation had taken less than four minutes. The next step was to bring the Fascist leader to Hitler's headquarters. It has never been clearly established why Skorzeny did not use the funicular down into the valley whence he could have organised a fast motor convoy to the aerodrome. Instead, his flamboyant gesture was a masterpiece of propaganda: he flew Mussolini from the Gran Sasso in a light Fieseler Storch.

The danger of a take-off from the small meadow was increased when Skorzeny insisted on accompanying the Italian leader and the pilot. The Storch was not built to carry such a load. In vain the pilot pointed out this fact, and how short was the runway. The SS officer was adamant. The men boarded the plane, the engine was revved to produce maximum power. The brake was released suddenly and the Storch shot forward along the boulder-strewn runway, careered over the edge of the cliff and vanished from sight. For a few frightening seconds the light plane plunged towards the valley floor, but the pilot regained control and landed at Practica di Mare whence Mussolini, still escorted by Skorzeny, was flown to Hitler's headquarters.

Skorzeny's first mission as the leader of a commando-type operation had been a complete success. Although much of the real planning had been carried out by the Luftwaffe paratroops, it was the SS who featured in the radio broadcasts and newsreels and Skorzeny came to be, and has remained, identified in the public mind as sole architect, planner and executant of the operation. The leaders of the SD were confident that in him they had found the answer to Brandenburg which the SS had been seeking and, furthermore, that any troops which Skorzeny led would become the German equivalent of the British Commandos. The young SS Major was empowered to raise No. 502 Special Services Battalion and then had placed under his authority the newly formed 500th Parachute Battalion. It was the beginning of a career during which Skorzeny formed a number of other special groups. Among these were anti-partisan formations to which he gave the name Jagdverbände. The battalion-sized Jagdverbände were based in various places in Europe and each was named for the area in which it worked. Thus there was an Eastern, a South-Eastern and a Western Jagdverbände. This scheme of Skorzeny's was, in reality, little more than a return to the first principles of Brandenburg, but what Skorzeny's men lacked in language and territorial knowledge they more than made up for in their anti-partisan abilities.

Although Skorzeny is associated chiefly with the rescue of Mussolini and with the use of American-speaking German soldiers during the Battle of the Bulge, he was also responsible for keeping the Hungarian Government loyal to Hitler by the simple expedient of capturing the buildings in which the Magyar ministers had their offices. Skorzeny was known as the 'Most dangerous man in Europe', not for what he achieved but because of what he *might* have achieved.

9

EXCISION

The SS Parachute Battalion Attack on Tito's Headquarters, 1944

It will be understood that the year 1944 brought no pleasure of anticipation to those who were directing the war effort of the Third Reich. The opening days were filled with reports of fresh disasters, the nights were made hideous with air raids, and it was certain that during the course of the year, even heavier blows would be rained upon Germany and her allies.

The Eastern Front remained the principal theatre of operations. There, a Russian offensive, which had begun at Kursk in July 1943, had rolled without pause throughout the autumn and into the winter. In the West in the spring of 1944 there was no land warfare, but the armed forces were alert against the day, which must surely come, when the Anglo-American armies would invade. Indeed, Weichold, the writer of the report on 'German Naval Defence against the Allied invasion of Normandy', claimed that he and the Naval Staff had expected a landing in 1943. When the invasion came it was clear that unless a miracle happened Germany would be crushed like a rotten nut between the Eastern and the Western fronts.

In the Mediterranean theatre, Allied armies had pushed forward from the landing beaches around Salerno and were nearing Rome. True, Monte Cassino blocked the advance, but in the spring of 1944 on the Allied side of the line, there were troop movements under way which would free the first capital city in Europe from its Axis occupiers. There was another front in the south of Europe on which the Axis forces were under pressure: the Balkan battlefield of Yugoslavia. It is an offensive in that embattled country which is dealt with here.

The Kingdom of Yugoslavia had been attacked and defeated during the spring of 1941. Remnants of the defeated army continued the struggle against the occupying Powers: Germany and Italy. These early groups were the Chetniks, usually, but not exclusively, Royalist officers and men. With the opening of the German war against the Soviet Union in June 1941, detachments of Communists also began guerrilla operations against the Germans.

When one considers the formation and growth of the partisans in Yugoslavia, and the operations undertaken by them, the name of one man is pre-eminent: that of the veteran Communist 'Tito'. The dynamism of his control, the power which was soon in his hands and his tightly-knit, disciplined organisation convinced the British that he would prove a more useful ally than the Chetniks. The support which had hitherto been given unstintingly to the Royalist forces was withdrawn and placed instead at Tito's disposal.

Much of Tito's Yugoslav Liberation Army was eventually uniformed in British battledress, was armed and provided for by the British who had maintained a Military Mission with the partisans from the earliest days. Not until much later in the war was the British Mission joined by an American and then by a Soviet group. By 1943, the partisans of the Yugoslav People's Liberation Army, now a disciplined and well-organised body, had reconquered nearly one third of the country. This claim must be qualified by the statement that nowhere did the guerrillas control main roads, principal railways or cities. But they ruled the rural areas totally and utterly. For the men of the Axis occupying forces, service in Yugoslavia was no comfortable life among the flesh-pots, but a nerve-tearing existence of uncertainty in a primitive outpost.

The Liberation Army had become by 1943 a powerful force numbering more than a quarter of a million men and women soldiers. This host was organised into eleven Army Corps controlling thirty-seven divisions, together with twenty-two independent brigades, twenty-five independent battalions and more than a hundred other detachments. These latter, together with the independent units, were urban guerrillas, waiting for the time when they could strike a blow in the cities against the occupying forces. The rise in the strength of the partisan army produced a corresponding increase in the number and type of Axis divisions to combat them. The first formations to be employed in Yugoslavia in the early days of the occupation had been second- or even third-line troops; the mere presence of German soldiers sufficing to maintain order. As guerrilla activity grew, the types of German formation changed, and SS Mountain Divisions, made up of Bosnian volunteers, as well as Croatian militia regiments were raised and deployed. First-class divisions of the German Army also had to be sent to Yugoslavia to hold down the rebels, thus removing those élite troops from the Russian Front where their skill and ability were sorely missed.

From the earliest days of the occupation the Axis forces in Yugoslavia had conducted offensives in an endeavour to destroy the partisan movement. The first had been mounted as early as September 1941, and was followed in January and February 1942 by a second and greater encircling operation. There is in anti-partisan operations a law of diminishing returns. There comes a point at which the occupying Power is too weak in manpower to encircle all partisan-held areas, and this was the situation which faced the Germans at the end of the third offensive in November 1942, and again in February 1943 when the fourth abortive offensive closed. The German and Italian formations, aided by locally-raised, anti-Communist militias, fought desperately to hold the initiative, but by July 1943 British aid to Tito's armies was flowing on a massive scale and if that were not enough, shortly there-after Italy signed an armistice with the Allies. There followed a rush by both the Germans and the partisans to secure the weapons with which the war-weary Italians had been armed. Aided by the Italians the partisans were frequently the first on the spot and Tito's arsenals were soon filled with every type of firearm, but particularly mountain artillery guns. The guerrillas now had the capability of fighting a major campaign backed by heavy weapons.

To the German Supreme Commander in the South East, Feld-marschall Löhr, it was only too apparent that he lacked men and *matériel* to gain total victory in the field over the partisan masses. What was needed was the destruction of the brain and heart of the entire move-ment. Tito, the undisputed leader of the partisans, the personification of the will to fight, had to be killed or captured. But while that plan was being worked upon, the fifth offensive, which had opened during May and which had dragged on throughout the summer of 1943, would have to be revived if only to chivvy the partisans and force them to change the location of their headquarters. As a direct result of the fifth offen-sive, Tito was obliged to abandon his headquarters in Jajce and move westwards into Bosnia to the small town of Drvar. It will be understood that these offensives were costly in manpower and time, to both sides. So far as the partisans were concerned, the German drives through the high mountains necessitated the frequent removal of their field head-quarters to safe areas. Such moves disrupted, if only temporarily, the execution of guerrilla plans. The moving of Tito's HQ, which by 1944 embodied a large number of personnel and masses of radio equipment, required detailed planning and a vast amount of effort. Such a major move interfered with the unfolding of partisan military operations and was not lightly undertaken.

For the Germans, the inconvenience which the bandits suffered was their only real reward. To halt the flow of guerrilla orders and instruc-tions was to prevent or at least delay the concentration of hostile groups. Accordingly, offensives were planned, prepared and launched. Thousands of soldiers, hundreds of vehicles, sometimes even squadrons of Luftwaffe aircraft, were sent out to grasp a shadow; for the partisans withdrew in the face of such power, unwilling to be lured into a set-piece battle fought on German terms.

In each offensive German soldiers went up into the mountains which were partisan strongholds. There they strained with tired muscles and aching limbs to reach a peak that was almost identical with one they had already scaled that day or on previous days. It was an exhausting, frightening battlefield. Blinding hot in summer, freezing cold in winter and always with the danger of meeting, quite unexpectedly the partisan enemy who was master of the terrain. To be wounded in the hills meant having to be carried by relays of sweating, cursing comrades for twelve or more hours to a medical collecting-point. Only rarely did the Medical Corps Fieseler Storch venture to fly in to remove the wounded. The partisans were deadly accurate marksmen and could easily hit the low-flying, slow-flying machines.

To be overrun and to be taken prisoner was often, in those early days, tantamount to a death sentence, for there was no rear area into which the partisans could take their captives. A bullet was usually the end of a very brief span of captivity. To fall on the terrible battlefield of the mountains was to gain a pile of rocks. There could be no excavated grave for there was no soil. A pile of rocks and a helmet on a stick. A lonely grave, far away from the cemeteries in which other comrades lay side by side.

The success of military operations depends to a very great degree upon Intelligence and in Yugoslavia such information was easy to come by for both armies. On the German side there were indiscretions in the presence of Yugoslav servants and waiters, confidently thought by the Germans to have no knowledge of German or to be too unsophisticated to evaluate what they heard. The information gleaned from table-talk and more importantly, pillow-talk, gave the partisan Intelligence officers a great insight into German plans. Conversely the anti-Communist feelings of many Yugoslavs and the racial hatreds which existed in the country were exploited by the Germans to obtain the information they needed to destroy the guerrillas.

From Brandenburg sources it was learned that the time was nearly ripe to begin a new offensive, the sixth. The moving of Tito's head-quarters had reduced the level of partisan military activity; the costly failure of the guerrilla offensive to regain Serbia had lowered partisan morale. The Brandenburg officers argued that a blow struck now – early 1944 – would produce a favourable result. This, too, was the conclusion drawn by other German Intelligence officers.

Reports coming in to the headquarters of the Supreme Commander South East, all urged that action be taken. Löhr decided. Orders went out for a sixth offensive to be launched. That the intent was to destroy Tito himself, is recorded in the War Diary of the OKW Operations Staff. It was with that purpose that Operation 'Rösselsprung' (Knight's Move) was directed. Responsibility for the conduct of the offensive was given to Second Panzer Army who, in turn, passed the orders to the unit in the field, XV Mountain Corps. From a translation of the Corps Order outlining the offensive, it can be seen that the calibre and type of troops involved in 'Rösselsprung' was of a superior grade. There was to be no mistake in the execution of this operation.

'*Corps Order. 21.5.1944*

'1. Located in the area of Drvar in western Bosnia is the Supreme Communist Command with supply depots and headquarters (Tito's headquarters with the Allied Military Missions); in Petrovac (supply centre and aerodrome). In the whole area there are about 12,000 men with heavy weapons (incl. artillery and anti-tank guns) as well as possibly a few tanks in the Petrovac area. The roads in the area are heavily mined and have roadblocks. Strong resistance is to be expected from 1st (Proletarian) Division in the area west and south-west of Mrkonjicgrad and from the 6th (Lika) Division in the area east of the upper reaches of the Unac river.

'2. The enemy will be attacked in an encircling operation using paratroops and our Air Force with the aim of destroying the enemy leadership, supply bases and headquarters in the area Drvar–Petrovac and all enemy groups found in the area. The operation will be commanded by XV Mountain Corps. The operation will be known as 'Rösselsprung'. The success of the operation will be of the greatest significance for the conduct of the war in the interior of the country as well as in the coastal areas. Decisiveness, cool leadership and self-sacrifice by each individual soldier are the prerequisites for total success.

'3. The 7th SS Mountain Division 'Prinz Eugen' with a regimental group and an assault battalion of Panzer Grenadiers under command, will smash through the enemy resistance east of the Sana river and will then advance on a broad front between the Sana and the Unac in and immediately north of the wooded hills. There they will hunt down the enemy bands and will take out the supply bases as well as prevent the flight eastwards of the beaten enemy groups and headquarters, near Drvar. The assault battalion battle group with Tank Company No. 202 under command will drive from Banja Luka towards Klujc (first bound) and will seize the crossing place at present controlled by the partisans. The regimental group of 7th SS will drive from Jajce along the railways and roads via Savici and will have as their first bound, the area south of the Sana wells and the railway station at Mlinista. Reinforced Reconnaissance Battalion 105 with an SS Tank Company under command will destroy the enemy bands in Livanskopolje, will then go on to take out the supply bases in that area and, by driving via Grahovo towards Drvar, will prevent the escape southwards of the bandit groups, headquarters and military missions. Reconnaissance Group 369 of the 105th Reconnaissance Battalion will drive from Livno to Glamocko Polje and then to Drvar in a south-easterly direction to intercept the withdrawing enemy. Livno must be securely occupied.

'All Groups will be accompanied by Engineer detachments.

'4. The 373rd Division accompanied by a regimental group (Battle Group Willam) will move out on D-Day at 05.00 from the area of Srb and will advance at best speed via Trubar to Drvar and there relieve, at whatever cost and on the same day, SS Paratroop Battalion 500 in Drvar. Once contact has been gained the SS battalion will come under the command of Battle Group Willam. All military missions and command posts in the Drvar area are to be destroyed. While Drvar is held secure elements will thrust from the Drvar area towards Petrovac. Battle Group Willam is to be made as strong as possible (artillery, heavy weapons, Engineers).

'Another battle group of the Division, possibly of battalion strength, is to leave Lapac on D-Day, at 05.00 and to proceed by Kulen Vakuf to Vrtoce. It is important to seize the Vrtoce cross-roads as quickly as possible and then, depending upon circumstances, to open the Bihac-Vrtoce road by driving in a north-westerly direction.

'5. Motorised Regiment 92 with Reconnaissance Battalion 54 and a regimental Group of the 2nd Croatian Jäger Brigade under command, will leave the area of Bihac on D-Day at 05.00 and drive through Krupa in a south-easterly direction, in order to capture Petrovac. The bandits and headquarters in that place are to be destroyed; the aerodrome and the supply bases are to be taken. The advance of this battle group is of decisive importance. Motorised Grenadier Regiment No. 92 will fight through and clear the Petrovac areas and will then move towards Drvar, will prevent the enemy on the Drvar road from moving northwards and will link up with the SS Parachute Battalion and the Battle Group Willam.

'6. The 1st Brandenburg Regiment with Croatian battle detachments under command will drive from Knin towards Grahovo and will then thrust along a line Prekaja–Drvar.

'7. SS Para Battalion 500 will drop on D-Day after Stukas have attacked Drvar, with the task of destroying completely and utterly Tito's Main Headquarters. The Commander of our Air Forces in Croatia will order attacks, immediately preceding the landing, upon all identified enemy groups and headquarters, on security areas and anti-aircraft gun positions. Thereby the enemy will be forced to take cover from the air assault. Until D-Day minus 1 the SS Para Battalion will be located as follows. Rybka Group (Parachutists) with headquarters. No. 2 and 3 Companies and a platoon of No. 4 Company in Nagy Betskerek (314 men). The men of No. 4 Company, No. 1 Company, 40 men of the Benesch Detachment, 6 men from the Abwehr as well as the Luftwaffe Liaison Troop (320 men) in Zagreb. The second wave of parachutists will be made up of the remainder of No. 2 Company and the Para Training Company. This group of 220 men will be located in Banja Luka. The SS Para Battalion 500 will be under the command of the Luftwaffe GOC in Croatia from the time that the unit emplanes. From jumping time the SS unit will come under the command of XV Mountain Corps. Once contact has been made with one of the relieving battle groups (from other Divisions) Para Battalion 500 will come directly under its command.

'8 to 10. Signals and communications: Rations: Reporting areas and times.

'11. From D-Day on, Corps HQ will be located in Bihac.'

D-Day for the operation was 25 May; by a singular coincidence, the birthday of Marshal Tito. H-Hour was set for 07.00 at which time the airborne landings would take place. Two hours in advance of the airborne's H-Hour, the various battle groups from the encircling units would have crossed their own start-lines.

The German Command knew that any attempt to deploy troops on the ground in an attack on Tito's headquarters would meet with stiff resistance from the partisans. Only from the air could a swift surprise attack be launched. The problems attendant on the dropping of a lightly-armed force within a heavily-guarded perimeter were formidable, but the Germans did have total air superiority and this was a fearful handicap to the partisans. In the early days they had had only rifles and then machine-guns as anti-aircraft weapons. Later in the war British supplies had included light anti-aircraft guns, but in the rapid move to Drvar these been left behind. At the time of 'Rösselsprung' the partisans had the protection of RAF fighters. These were 'scrambled' too late to be of use against the airborne assault, but the British aircraft were deployed effectively against the vehicle columns of the German ground formations, notably those of Brandenburg.

Although the roles they played were important and will be touched upon in this narrative, we are not concerned here with either 7th SS Mountain Division 'Prinz Eugen', or with the Brandenburg formations which participated in 'Rösselsprung'. This account deals principally with the battle fought by another special force: the SS Parachute Rifle Battalion 500.

At one time it was widely believed in Anglo-American circles that the SS Para Battalion 500 was a penal unit, its undertrained men drawn from SS military prisoners and led by NCOs and officers who were themselves 'hard cases'. There is no evidence to support this evaluation and former paratroops with whom I have spoken strongly deny the accusation. They claim that the battalion was made up of volunteers, all of whom were fully trained in a paratroop role, and that the unit commanders, from sergeant upwards, were professional SS soldiers with a great deal of front-line, combat experience. This expertise grafted on to the SS ethos produced paratroops of outstanding ability, endurance and daring. Since it was to be expected that the Mountain Corps' slow-moving encircling advance on Tito's headquarters would warn the enemy, it was felt that only a paratroop landing would achieve the surprise necessary for the attack to succeed. Such a landing would hold the partisan forces pinned down until the other German units could

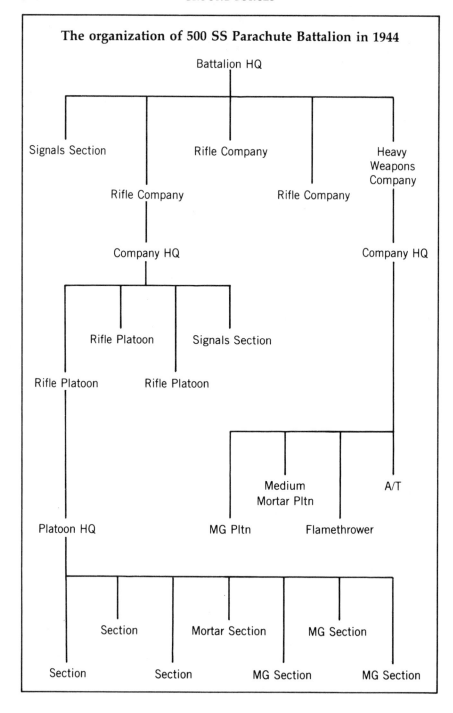

The organization of 500 SS Parachute Battalion in 1944

Battalion HQ

Signals Section

Rifle Company

Heavy Weapons Company

Rifle Company

Rifle Company

Company HQ

Company HQ

Rifle Platoon

Signals Section

Rifle Platoon

Rifle Platoon

Medium Mortar Pltn

A/T

Platoon HQ

MG Pltn

Flamethrower

Section

Mortar Section

MG Section

Section

Section

MG Section

MG Section

reach the area and relieve the SS Fallschirmjäger. It all depended upon the speed with which the link-up could be made. The assault of Battalion 500 was predicated upon a swift drop, an early and successful snatch of the partisan Marshal and a speedy deliverance from inside the guerrilla camp.

Before we go on to examine the tasks which the SS battalion had to achieve, let us consider two questions to which the planners of the operation needed to have precise and accurate answers. The first and most important was the exact location of Tito's headquarters building. The second was how to keep secret an operation of such size and importance. Reference has already been made to the ease with which Intelligence could be gained in Yugoslavia, but it was vital that 'Rössel-sprung' and particularly the role of the SS Para Battalion in that operation, be kept the most closely-guarded secret.

Brandenburg agents among the local population soon established that Tito's headquarters was in a cave in Bastasi some three miles from the centre of Drvar. The approximate position was confirmed by intercepts of partisan radio traffic, and then precise confirmation was obtained from a partisan deserter who, under interrogation, pinpointed the cave and laid out the composition of Tito's escort battalion and the guard details in the HQ area. The escort battalion was made up of three hundred and fifty men and women organised into four infantry companies supported by four light tanks. There were five guards at the mouth of the cave at any one time, each with a machine-pistol.

The small town of Drvar had been chosen as partisan headquarters for the excellent tactical reason that approach to it was difficult. High wooded hills formed a defile at the end of which lay the town. The advance of any enemy through the narrow pass could be observed and a strong defence set up to challenge the Germans. Then, too, the river Unac bends around the town and protects it by a water barrier on three sides. From a tactical viewpoint Drvar was ideal as a guerrilla base and Tito's vast headquarters complex had settled in by the end of January 1944. There were few partisan groups in the town of Drvar itself. Luftwaffe bombing raids had forced them to disperse into the hills around the town where they formed a loose perimeter. There were, however, strong and well-armed detachments on the approach roads to Drvar and dominating other tactically important areas.

On 21 May, XV Mountain Corps HQ passed to its subordinate units the Intelligence received from Second Panzer Army together with details which its own officers and agents had gathered. Corps gave the exact location of the partisan leader's headquarters, the composition of the guerrilla detachments defending the aerodrome at Petrovac and an updated Order of Battle of the enemy forces in the region.

The Intelligence which 7th SS Mountain Division 'Prinz Eugen' was able to pass on to its regiments and battalions was even more precise and detailed. From sources of its own it had located and identified three partisan Corps: I, V and VIII, but had assessed the fighting value of those units as low. This discounting of partisan combat efficiency was in direct contrast to the more sober and realistic appreciation made by the knowledgeable Brandenburg officers whose agents had been supplying information since before the time of the fifth offensive. They had compiled an accurate picture of partisan strengths and intentions. Six partisan divisions had been identified in and around Drvar together with a number of élite units including an officer cadet school.

Intelligence-gathering is a two-edged weapon which can divulge as well as gain information and, not surprisingly, accurate details of 'Rösselsprung' were soon being openly discussed by Yugoslav civilians. Otto Skorzeny, the new and aggressive leader of the German secret forces, was able to obtain precise information about the forth-coming operation from native and civilian sources within hours of his arriving in Yugoslavia. He realised that if his agents could gain such knowledge so quickly, the details must be known to the partisan High Command. His first instinct was to cancel 'Rösselsprung' on the grounds that it had been compromised, but he allowed himself to be convinced that such breaches of confidence were the norm and not the exception in Yugoslavia. Brandenburg officers told him that the partisans had known, as early as March, that the location of Tito's HQ had been betrayed. The Yugoslav who had deserted to the Branden-burgers had been recaptured by the partisans who soon knew the full extent of his disclosures.

For their part, the guerrilla Intelligence officers were able to identify the units opposing them and to forecast correctly how the ground assaults would develop, but they knew nothing about the most impor-tant element in the operation – SS Para Battalion 500 and its role. They were completely unprepared for a parachute drop and glider landing.

On 20 May, Obersturmführer Rybka, the young Commander of Parachute Rifle Battalion 500, was given a meagre outline of the role he and his men were to perform in the operation to destroy Tito. He began to draw up a provisional battle plan. He decided that the assault should be made by glider, but was then told that there were insufficient machines to carry the whole battalion plus the extra detachments which would be accompanying them. It was clear that some of his battalion would have to parachute in, but then his planning suffered another bitter blow. There were insufficient carrier planes to convey the para-troops in a single lift. There would have to be a second wave of paras, but there could be no second wave of glider landings. Gliders were a one-shot weapon.

Rybka then had to set out his priorities. The most important task was to attack the 'Citadel', Tito's headquarters cave, and either kill or capture him. The force that would carry out this part of the mission would be brought by glider as close as possible to the mouth of the cave. The next most important targets were the communications network and the foreign military missions. These, too, would be attacked by glider-borne troops. The first wave of paratroops would seize the town of Drvar, cordon it off and thereby prevent the partisan forces interfering with the glider-borne component. The second wave of paratroops would add their strength wherever required.

As more and more information was given to him, Rybka began the detailed planning of his unit's part in 'Rösselsprung'. The initial attacking force would be divided into two groups of approximately equal strength, each having a code-name. The paras of the second wave would not be divided into groups, but would be used as a back-up force.

The three hundred and fourteen paras of the first wave were divided into three groups: 'Red', 'Green' and 'Blue'. They would drop at 07.00 and would land in Drvar within twenty seconds of leaving their aircraft. Rybka would accompany 'Red' group, and estimated that his men would have seized the town within an hour. Only a skeleton force would be required to hold it; the remaining paras would be free to support, if necessary, the glider group attacking the cave. The glider-borne component was not made up entirely of men from the SS battalion, but included the 'Savadil Troop' of specialist signallers drawn from Brandenburg units, plus other groups from Brandenburg, the Luftwaffe and the 'Benesch' group – a combination of all the Bosnian units.

Tactically, the glider troops, numbering about three hundred and twenty men, were divided into six assault units, each with a specific task to complete. These groups and their missions were:

'Panther' Group	One hundred and ten men: to destroy the 'Citadel'.
'Greifer' Group	Forty men: to destroy the British Military Mission.
'Stürmer' Group	Fifty men: to destroy the Russian Military Mission.
'Brecher' Group	Fifty men: to destroy the American Military Mission.
'Draufgänger' Group	Composite force of about fifty SS men plus the 'Savadil Troop', Intelligence officers from Brandenburg and the Bosnians. To destroy the partisan line and radio communications network, gather Intelligence, and evaluate radio techniques and capture code and signal books.
'Beisser' Group	Twenty men: to seize an outpost radio-station, after which it was to assist 'Greifer' to attack the British Military Mission.

The assault by 'Panther' would be led by Rybka and his paratroops. Success of the assault would be signalled by displaying a swastika flag on the ground above the cave entrance; failure by the firing of a red flare, in which case 'Green' and 'Stürmer' groups were to disengage and move forward to support a fresh assault on the 'Citadel'.

Throughout the night of 22 May, the small groups of men who would make up the air-landing contingent began to move to their assembly areas. To hide their identity as paratroopers, some were dressed in infantry-pattern uniforms and were taken to the concentration areas in trucks which bore no unit insignia. Larger groups travelled by train – again disguised as infantrymen – and these carried the rations, equipment and weapons of the entire airborne component. Not one of these men, who only days later would be fighting a savage battle, knew the nature of their mission or its objectives. Warned of the need for absolute security, Rybka had disclosed the barest details only to his most senior officers who, in turn, kept silent until the evening of 23 May, when they briefed their men in a session which lasted into the early hours of 24 May. During that day, last-minute preparations and final briefings were completed. 'Each of us was given a photographic print of Tito so that we could identify him. His was a completely undistinguished face. I had seen hundreds looking just like him all over Croatia and Serbia. We were told that he wore a uniform with no badges of rank. So we were looking for an undistinguished Yugoslav with a plain uniform.'

Late in the evening of the 24th, the units set out for the airfields from which they would take off. The group under Rybka's immediate control, the first-wave paratroop detachment, congregated on the operational airfield at Nagy Betskerek. With him would go his Battalion HQ plus the whole of Nos. 2 and 3 Companies and a single platoon from No. 4 The remainder of No. 4 Company would form part of the glider-borne contingent, together with the whole of No. 1 Company, the detachment from the Brandenburg Regiment, the Bosnian groups and the Luftwaffe Air Landing Section. This glider-borne group was taken to the airfield at Zagreb. The men of the second wave of paratroops, together with the remainder of No. 2 Company and the Para Training Company, would take off from the airfield at Banja Luka.

During the evening reports confirmed that the glider and second-wave para detachments were in position. Everything was now ready and Rybka's coded signal to Corps received the countersign ordering the SS battalion, the divisions and regiments of the Panzer Grenadier and the SS 'Prinz Eugen' Gebirgsjäger to execute the operation as planned. Operation 'Rösselsprung' was on.

'We paratroops were now ready. Whether anybody slept that night I don't know. Certainly none of us could have slept soundly. I slept very little. It was my very first operation as a soldier as well as my first operational jump. Reveille was at 3.30 am and we were on parade an hour later, each of us fully dressed and wearing our 'chutes. Weapons were already packed in the containers. The CO came out of the airport building. We were called to attention. He marched up and down our ranks, at the salute the whole time. He halted in front of us and made the usual sort of speech with which I was to become very familiar in the future. "Don't waste ammunition, don't stop for the wounded. Press on to the objective." We came to attention and sang the paratroop song. It might sound banal but I was deeply moved. There were three hundred of us young, keen men who believed in what we were doing. Then we boarded the machines.'

Take-off was shortly after dawn, with a flight time of just over fifty-five minutes. The morning was high and bright when the JU 52s carrying the paratroops and the Henschels towing the gliders, began their run in over Drvar, which was shrouded in smoke. Stukas and Messerschmitts had been active over the target area since first light, bombing and machine-gunning against only slight opposition. The only weapons the partisans could deploy were multiple machine-guns mounted for anti-aircraft defence. The Stukas concentrated on these and soon the machine-guns crews were dead or wounded, or had scattered from the howling dive bombers and the crashing explosions.

At 06.50 the dispatchers standing at the open doors of the Junkers lined up the first of the strings of paras standing ready with their static lines attached. The dispatchers moved away from the doorway through which could be seen the dun and olive-coloured hills which surrounded Drvar. So close that they seemed to be flying wing tip to wing tip were other transport machines. The aim was to achieve the maximum concentration of paratroops on the drop zone; dispersal meant a weakening of the assault and the loss of surprise. The planes flew low and steady on their course. One second before 07.00 the dispatchers slapped the first men of each string on the shoulder. The response was instantaneous. Each man as he came to the open door flung himself horizontally through it into the rushing air, arms outstretched to absorb the shock of the canopy opening. The low height at which the transports had been flying together with the improved type of parachute with which the battalion had been issued, cut down the time that the paratroops were falling – to about twenty seconds.

'We flew so low that I was afraid there would be no time for our parachutes to open and to support our descent. We really seemed to be skimming just above the ground, that is how low it seemed. Everything happens so quickly. The ground seems to race up; there's the shock of landing, a shoulder roll, get rid of the 'chute and look for the weapons canister. The Luftwaffe is still busy above our heads and there is no doubt that the splendid support which we got from them kept the partisans' heads down while we rushed for the canisters and armed ourselves. Inevitably, there was some confusion in the first minute or two. Men are looking for their Section commanders; but pretty soon we had all been sorted out and were moving out towards our objectives. In my Section there were three missing. Two of them were dead; the third had broken his ankle.'

The landing ground was secured. Now it was time for the Henschels, still circling above Drvar, to release the DS 230 gliders. There is no doubt that the glider pilots of the Luftwaffe were highly skilled; most had identified their targets even before the tow-lines had been released, so that they were able to swing the machines and point them at their objectives. Diving steeply, the wooden gliders struck, then raced across the ground, throwing up clouds of dust. Their occupants braced themselves as the machines skidded across the rocky terrain. Wings were torn off as the pilots tried desperately to avoid the larger boulders; inevitably, some of the machines smashed into them killing or wounding the men inside.

All save one of the gliders landed close to their given objectives. The exception was the craft carrying the leader of 'Greifer' group together with his HQ. This machine had cast off more than seven miles from the objective and was last seen diving almost vertically. It crashed into the bank of a shallow mountain stream and disintegrated. There were no survivors.

A glider-borne landing is a frightening business. There is a high-pitched screaming sound as the glider ploughs across the ground; the floor of the fuselage heats up from the friction, and the occupants sit, braced and fearful, knowing that they may die in an instant. When at last the, more or less, crumpled wreck lies motionless in a cloud of dust, the immediate reaction is to sit quietly, breathe out and relax. This is the dangerous time, when glider troops are at their most vulnerable. It is vital to leave the machine immediately, for it now becomes a target for enemy fire.

Those of the SS battle groups who had survived the landing and who failed to leave their gliders quickly enough paid for their slowness with blood; the guerrillas opened fire immediately.

Landing close to the centre of the town the 'Draufgänger' group were quickly out and moving on their objective. The building housing the radio-station was prominent and large enough to contain the vast and complex equipment needed to direct partisan operations at a national level, and the many operators of the sets and the main telephone exchange. The destruction of 'line' contact is easy; a simple matter of breaking the wire. So a single high-explosive charge would destroy all the lines and break all 'line contact' between Tito and his units in Drvar. More immediately it would cut off the partisan units in the outlying villages.

While the bulk of 'Draufgänger' group fanned out to find other wire-less points, ten paras and the 'Savadil Troop' charged for the telephone building. It was easy to break down the flimsy door, but once inside they were soon involved in a furious close-quarters battle. The women partisans and their officers knew that it was a question of fight or die. With grenades, Sten guns, Schmeisser machine-pistols – even knives – they tried to hold back the paras. Into the house stormed the 'Savadil Troop' in support of the SS and then came the Bosnians, each group caught up immediately in the storm of gunfire and thundering explosions. The telephone personnel were too many, too determined and too well-armed to be defeated easily.

Reinforcements were called up. Satchel charges were laid at barricaded doors and then detonated. Advancing through the dense smoke and dust, the Germans poured into the rooms, firing from the hip. Outside, a cordon of SS troops picked off the defenders who jumped from windows. The SS men mouseholed their way through the building with explosives, firing bursts of armour-piercing bullets through ceilings seeking to destroy the guerrillas in the upper rooms. The Draufgänger men worked their way from room to room and from floor to floor until, dust covered, faces blacked by smoke, and puffing cigarettes with quick nervous inhalations, they stood victorious in the shattered building.

A quick search produced a few files, some papers – little of Intelligence value. The SS and the 'Savadil Troop' left the building, and it was destroyed by satchel charges. The Group was ready to move on.

It was now past 7 o'clock. The paras and glider troops were on the ground and moving out. Through the empty streets of Drvar they moved at the double, their shadows long on the ground, cast by a sun already hot enough to make the men sweat profusely. Only minimal opposition was encountered; a single rifle shot would crack and a man would fall. The shot would provoke a hurricane of fire from the others; an over-reaction – the product of fear.

'One of the things we had not been taught was house-to-house fighting, that is fighting in urban areas. Although Drvar was not a large place it did have houses and streets – which sheltered the bandits – and therefore qualifies for the term 'urban'. The enemy fire was random and uncoordinated. It was really the worst sort of luck to be hit by such undirected fire.

'The point man of our patrol – he was a sort of scout – was hit and fell. We were so well conditioned that before his body had hit the ground we had identified the window from which the shot had come and were blazing away at it. We were consumed with hate. A damned good, trained and specialist warrior had just been slaughtered by a ragged partisan. It was undignified. Some of us shouldered down the door and rushed up the stairs. There lying on the floor, hiding from the machine-gun fire, that the rest of the Section was still pumping in, was a scruffy old man of about 50. The rifle, a 98, one of ours, was by his side. He was dragged downstairs and bundled away – none too gently. If I had been the Section Corporal I would have shot the sniper. He was in civvies; not a badge nor a cap to show he was a partisan. We would have been justified in executing the Serb as a franc tireur. We flung grenades into the house. It was a standard operational procedure to lob them through the windows of suspect houses.

'Everything was so quiet. It was quite frightening. There were no civilians about in the streets; no dogs. Nothing. There were usually some people to be seen wandering about even in the middle of a fire fight. Then we realised. Of course, the bombing would have driven them out of the town. We heard that a platoon in front of us met some really fierce opposition, but that MG 42s and rifle grenades had soon forced the Reds back and out of the town. Opposition to us had, however, been minimal. We soon had Drvar under control, but it was about an hour before all the groups had reported in. Then we waited for further orders.

'The one thing that really bothered us was the shortage of water. It was bad enough in the morning. In the heat of the afternoon we would have sold our souls for a cool drink. We had all taken the pep pills before take-off, to give us extra energy and faster reflexes. We all knew that the tablets had unpleasant side effects but we thought that we would be able to withstand the raging thirst that they produced. It was a real torment.'

The one complete and unmoveable obstacle to the successes which SS Para Battalion 500 had achieved in only a few hours, was at the Citadel. There the glider-borne troops of 'Panther' Group, whose task it was to take out Tito's HQ, were pinned down by machine-gun fire. The speed with which the escort battalion came into action had disconcerted the Germans and this fast reaction by the partisans was stressed in the post-battle reports. To the Germans it seemed that within seconds of touch-down guerrilla machine-gunners were already pouring fire into the wrecked gliders, pausing only when they switched targets to aim at the men of 'Panther' Group as they moved into position for the assault on the cave.

Obersturmführer Rybka set up his own HQ next to one of the gliders which had landed at the entrance to the town, and his Signals detachments sent out message after message to the widely-scattered units of the Command: 'Report in, report in.'

From his position Rybka could see the groups in his immediate area. Machine-guns were being set up at street corners to command the approaches to town. A column of smoke and dust above the far end of Drvar showed where the communications building had stood until 'Savadil Troop' had blown it up. Wounded paras were being directed to a large house near the glider HQ and the medical teams were already at work. Scattered around Rybka lay the gliders, wings crumpled, fuselages buckled, but each almost at the doors of the buildings which had been their objectives. Hastily-shrouded dead bodies showed that the landings had not been made without loss. Runners came panting in. The glider group at the far end of town had completed its mission. The radio-station had been destroyed. The signals element of the battle group was heading back to HQ while the SS troopers who had accompanied the radio-men were moving on to the next phase. With the town now firmly in German hands, patrols of paras were sent to seize high ground, buildings and farms which dominated the roads leading into Drvar. The entire German effort could now be concentrated on carrying out the main intention of 'Rösselsprung'; the destruction of Tito and the partisan nerve-centre. A disturbing message came in. One stick of paratroops had landed away from the target area and had come under fire. The partisans had been too strong to resist and the paras had been forced back. They were now holding a small perimeter on the south bank of the River Unac and, having a direct line of sight on the cave, had set up MG 42s on tripods and were firing at long-range into the mouth of the cave.

Here the scene showed clearly how bitter the fighting had been. With great skill the glider pilots had brought Panther Group's six machines almost to the mouth of the cave. It should have been simple to take the few steps to the grotto, but by now (about 08.00) no living German was to be seen. There were many dead – mostly German. Some had been killed in the landings, others had been caught in the defensive fire of the partisan escort battalion as they struggled out of the fuselages. The greatest number, and they were many, had fallen while striving desperately and unsuccessfully to storm the cave. But not all the dead were German; many partisans had fallen. All were wearing British battledress and there were some whose feminine shape could not be concealed by the shapeless khaki uniform.

The very air on that sun-baked hillside was alive with the noise of battle. The flat crack of hand-grenades, the hysterical chatter of the MG 42 and, to the Germans, a worrying and sinister sound – the crump of mortar bombs. The paras had nothing similar with which to retaliate or to support their assaults.

The report from the Citadel area that the initial attacks had failed decided Rybka's next moves. A red flare burst in the sky; its message, 'Rally on HQ for an attack on the Citadel' was understood and acted upon. Quickly Rybka gave orders to his reserves. These reserves consisted of the glider-borne detachments detailed to destroy the three Military Missions. Apparently the missions, together with the entire population of Drvar had simply abandoned the town and gone into the hills. (The British and US missions had, in fact, moved to the area of Tito's headquarters two days before the German assault; a move which was to give rise to Soviet charges that the Western Allies had either known of, or even instigated 'Rösselsprung'.)

The cave and its, by now, reinforced partisan garrison was several miles from the centre of the town, but the SS battalion, urged on by its aggressive young commander, made good time. Rybka was taken to a small gulley at the bottom of the hill, in which the Commander of Panther Group had set up his tiny command post. An appreciation was quickly made and a plan drawn up; a simple fire and movement assault. The battle groups were formed up in the thick scrub which covered the forward slopes of the hill. The paras did not know, although they must have suspected, that Tito's HQ area had been prepared for defence. And so it was. Indeed the hill upon which Tito's cave was located had been, since his arrival during January, the scene of intensive defence preparations. The whole area had been carefully surveyed and field fortifications dug. Strong-points had been set up, sniper hides constructed and machine-gun posts, with interlocking fire zones, established. Thus it was against a firm defence, superior in numbers and weapons and in first-class positions on rising ground, that the paratroopers were expected to fight and to emerge victorious.

It was an unequal contest. Paratroops are limited in the number of weapons and the amount of ammunition they can carry. Moreover, they have scant opportunity of being resupplied. Thus, the small sections of SS men crawling from cover to cover up the slopes did not have the covering fire from machine-guns and machine-pistols that normally would have accompanied so vital an assault. The attack had to be accomplished very quickly and in small bounds. Short bursts of fire from machine-gunners on the flanks would be followed by a crouched dash by a group from the shelter of one huddle of rocks to another; braving sniper fire, the far-flung destruction of mortar bombs and the shrapnel of hand-grenades. Once the charging group had reached their bound they would open fire to cover the next group, who would in turn carry the advance forward another few paces. By strong fire discipline and with desperate courage the paras came closer and closer to the cave.

As they battled forward the sound of firing was heard coming from a flank. Guerrilla companies from outlying villages, alerted by the sound of gunfire and by reports of paratroops dropping from the sky and of glider descents, realised that a major assault was being made against the HQ cave and hastened to join in. Their detachments came into action piecemeal and were all infantry units. Yugoslav accounts of the fighting claim that one of a platoon of tanks outside Drvar was in action, but German post-battle reports make no mention of armoured fighting vehicles.

The first reinforcements to arrive in the Yugoslav battle line were a hundred or more officer cadets. These had been force-marched from Sipoulyani, a village on the River Unac, a short distance from Drvar, where their training school was located. They were put into action immediately and the assault by this élite body of highly-trained soldiers countered the German plan to turn the partisan flank. The main weight of the German drive then had to be swung against the cadets. In the words of one SS battle report, the fighting was 'hard and uncompromising'. One can well imagine what those sober words imply. Casualties increased on both sides, and the Germans had insufficient medical personnel. The wounded had to be left until a pause in the fighting would allow them to be carried away. The taking of prisoners was a luxury which neither side entertained.

It was now about 09.30. The sun was climbing higher in the cloudless sky and it was very hot. On the ground the opposing forces were locked in combat, so close that Rybka's call for Stuka support had to be rejected. The Luftwaffe liaison officers were forced to abort the mission when the pilots of the JU 87s, circling overhead like vultures, radioed that they could not be sure of even locating their targets, let alone hitting them, so close were the paras and the partisans on that terrible hillside.

It was at this time that the partisan commanders realised that they had the measure of their enemy. Now it was no longer a matter of merely containing the SS, the guerrillas forces could take the offensive and smash them. First they would regroup and concentrate their forces. To the west of Drvar pressure from the German ground troops was not heavy and although it was a risk to take away any guerrilla unit from the battle line, the risk was a calculated one and the decision was taken. An entire brigade from 6th Division was moved from the eastern hills and put in to face the paras in the west of the town. Within minutes of reaching the new location, the brigade went into action against the SS. This put the Para Battalion under pressure from the new brigade on its western flank and from the officer cadets on the south-western sector. The situation was serious and required desperate measures. One more strong frontal attack might succeed where the others had failed. In ordering this, Rybka, too, had to take a calculated risk. In less than three hours the second wave of paras would drop, and with that reinforcement the objective might be gained. On the other hand, during those three hours the partisans might accrue new strength. The gamble was simply whether he could depend on pressure exerted by the encircling units of XV Corps to prevent the partisan build-up. One thing was certain: he needed to regroup his Command – to call a pause in order to assess the situation. Whistle-blasts echoed across the hillside. The paras saw their NCOs waving them back.

'I wondered why we had to withdraw. It had taken us a long time and a great number of casualties to get as close as we had to that cave. Still, withdraw was the order – so we withdrew. We were grouped round a biggish rock. It was really hot and I can remember the smell of gorse in the hot sunshine. There was the usual ammunition count. Those who were running low were re-supplied. We got extra ammunition by taking it from the wounded, leaving them defenceless. I didn't like the idea of that. We had been sheltering behind that rock for about ten minutes when we heard the sound of aircraft and our second wave came in over our heads and dropped in a sort of bowl at the foot of the hill.'

Obermeier's group of two hundred and twenty men dropped in an area dominated by the machine-guns of the guerrilla troops. The landing zone was swept by mortar fire. The second-wave paras were pinned down and suffered heavy casualties before the weapons containers could be retrieved. Immediately, the group swung out and within minutes had reached battalion TAC HQ. Strengthened, revitalised by this increase in fire-power, the SS paras returned to the attack, pushing out aggressive patrols to the flanks as a counter to partisan pressure. Slowly the advance went forward. Through curtains of mortar bombs and machine-gun fire, the men pressed on towards the objective in fierce, determined rushes. It was during this midday attack that Rybka was hit and severely wounded.

It would, perhaps, be untrue to say that because of the loss of their young leader the SS attack was not pressed home as vigorously as it might have been, but it is a fact that the effort upon which such hopes had reposed, failed, as did subsequent ones. New fresh troops arrived – for the Yugoslavs. The 1st Battalion of the crack 1st Partisan Brigade was put in to replace the escort battalion and the officer cadets who had borne the heat of the battle since early morning. Under pressure from these well-trained, well-armed and, above all, fresh troops, the SS attack faltered and died. It was clear to the German commanders on the hillside that the balance had swung conclusively against them and that unless they withdrew, the whole SS Para Battalion would soon be outflanked, surrounded and destroyed. The calculated risk that Rybka had banked on had failed.

Partisan pressure had not been drawn off from around the SS battalion as its commander had hoped. If anything it had increased. Supply drops had not been entirely successful so the shortage of ammunition was of very real concern. The whole purpose of 'Rösselsprung' had gone for naught. Even if Tito were still in the cave, SS Para Battalion 500 was too weak to take him. The battalion was surrounded and there was no sign of the battle group from 373 Division, whose orders had been to relieve the paras on D-Day without fail. The afternoon was already far advanced. There had been heavy casualties including men who had gone out to rescue the wounded under fire and had themselves been wounded. The paras were thirsty, hungry and tired. They had been fighting since just after sun-up. Their food was hard tack and their water-bottles were long since empty.

Runners were sent to the outposts around Drvar with orders from battalion for the groups to rally in the town cemetery. On the hillside the SS platoons had to disengage and withdraw in good order to the rendezvous. These groups had advanced using the tactic of fire and movement; they withdrew in the same way. The MG 42s opened up. Known as 'Hitler's saws', from the sound produced by their high rate of fire, they swept the rocky upland scrub. Under cover of their fire, one section of SS men after another dropped back, to hold the line until another section had passed through. By such means the companies which had been battling all day pulled back to the foot of the hill. Other para groups held the flanks secure against the partisans in order to cover the withdrawal. As the para sections leap-frogged back down through the gorse bushes and rocks, lines of exultant Yugoslavs pursued them with *élan* and overran the machine-gun posts where the close-quarters fighting became brutal; bayonet and entrenching-tool; hand-grenade and machine-pistol. No quarter was given. It was not until almost 22.00 that the main body of the battalion reached the foot of the hill. By one of the tragedies of war, the order to withdraw did not reach one small SS unit which was dug in around a farm, half a mile or so south-west of the town. Upon that isolated outpost the Yugoslav officer cadets launched a series of violent attacks which were repulsed by the Germans whose numbers dwindled with each new assault. The last of them fell shortly before midnight, cut down by bullets and hand-grenades in a brutal skirmish in the dark rooms of the old farmhouse.

Now the night was completely dark except when tracers streamed towards the partisan positions, hand-grenades burst or Very lights soared skywards. Through the alleys and streets of Drvar the paras of other outpost detachments pulled back, fighting desperately to hold off the closely pursuing partisans; fighting, firing, turning at bay and pulling back until they too reached the battalion concentration area, the town cemetery, inside which the main body of SS 500 was gathered. In the whole of Drvar there were only two places which could have been considered as defensible. One was a ruined cellulose factory, but that was now too large an area to be held by a battalion so reduced in number. The alternative was the small cemetery which had the advantage of being surrounded by a thick stone wall. Inside that wall the survivors of the battalion and the accompanying detachments were organised for defence.

The battle had been so bitter that both sides were too exhausted to gain a clear-cut victory. Each saw the principal task as that of hanging on. The partisans fought until Tito had escaped, which he did through a door on the verandah of the living-room in the cave. The door gave on to a dried-up water course along which the Marshal and his head-quarters group made their way to Potoci, where a train took him, his Staff and the Military Missions out of the area. Before he left, Tito, ordered his troops to break off the battle and disperse, for he knew that the arrival of massive German support to the hard-pressed paras was only a matter of time. But the guerrilla commanders on the ground were determined to overrun and destroy the SS battalion, and drew up a plan for a series of attacks which would accomplish that intention.

That night the cemetery was the scene of bitter hand-to-hand fighting. The partisans of 1st Battalion, 1st Brigade, confident in the knowledge that they had engaged and held regular forces in battle, were determined to destroy the last survivors of the para battalion. The paras, for their part, fought with the desperation of men trapped in a seemingly hopeless situation. Throughout the long, cold night of 25/26 May, the fortunes of battle swung first to one side and then to the other.

'I was dug in under a cross in the cemetery. Platoon headquarters was in a tomb from which we had taken off the stone cover and turfed out the coffins. I was never so frightened in my life as I was that night. We had an outer perimeter of positions and a small inner perimeter. After every one of the bandit attacks was driven off those in the outer perimeter were relieved by a man from the inner line. That way the burden was not too hard to carry.

'It was about 1.30 in the morning. It was cold. I was sleepy and the only water was a trickle from a sort of stand-pipe inside the cemetery, near to the chapel. At intervals Very lights would be fired to see if the bandits were forming up for a new assault. One light had just gone out. Suddenly, without warning the Reds were climbing over the wall. A whole mass of our flares burst – all of them white – and in the glare the bandits were silhouetted. We shot them down but they seemed to be immune to rifle fire and kept on coming. Then some of them from behind the cover of the wall threw hand-grenades and got some light mortars into action. In that particular attack the Reds actually got inside the cemetery and held a small bridgehead. Those partisans in the bridgehead and those outside the wall tried to knock it down in order to form a corridor through which to ferry forward reinforcements of men and weapons. One of our platoons went into a counter-attack and wiped out the Reds who had crossed the wall. It was a frightening night.'

The last assault came just before dawn; a thrust from two places across the walls, but the growing light brought confidence to the paras. The arrival of reinforcements and relief could not be long delayed and with fresh heart they crushed the pre-dawn attack as they had smashed all those before it. The Yugoslav units began to fall back; their task had been completed. They had held the Germans until Tito had escaped and he was now far away. The time had come for them to melt into the hills again, but many were caught in the fury of a Luftwaffe dawn strike as they crossed the bare and open slopes. Their losses were heavy as the MEs and the JUs harried them across the rocky faces of the high ground.

Tito's prediction proved to be a correct one. Shortly after dawn the distinctive sound of an MG 42 was heard outside the cemetery perimeter and then a group of German Schwimmwagen was seen. A patrol from the 13th Regiment of the 'Prinz Eugen' Division had broken through from the east to be followed at intervals by the advance-guard of other battle groups driving in from the west and from the north. The last of these units arrived in Drvar at 16.00, by which time, operation 'Rösselsprung' was over and the Germans were in possession of the whole area; the town of Drvar, the outlying villages and the cave. For all their efforts they had gained only one of Tito's uniforms, his Jeep and a great amount of partisan propaganda material, but neither vital information nor secret documents. It is true that 'Rösselsprung' did bring about a temporary pause to partisan activities and forced Tito to move his headquarters once again; this time to the offshore island of Vis. But it had failed to kill him or to halt his operations.

So little had been achieved. The German losses recorded in the War Diary of XV Corps are: two hundred and thirteen killed in action, eight hundred and eighty-one wounded and fifty-nine missing. Yugoslav sources admit casualties of two hundred killed, four hundred wounded and seventy missing, but a German High Command communiqué estimated the partisan losses as exceeding six thousand. In 'Rösselsprung' SS Para Battalion 500 was almost wiped out. Its survivors were posted to Skorzeny's Command and were trained for a para drop on Budapest. That mission was aborted. Some members of the battalion, no more than a handful, were involved in the Battle of the Bulge. The remainder fought as infantry on the Eastern Front and went into captivity at the end of the war.

German post-battle reports were written by officer participants, by commanders of detachments and of special units. The general tenor of the reports written about 'Rösselsprung', lays great emphasis on the absolute need of total security. Many of the writers were convinced that the operation should have been aborted for it was clear that the most intimate details of it were known to the enemy. With the hindsight given by access to documents not available to the men who wrote their reports within days of the battle, it is clear that the partisans did not expect an aerial assault, although they had anticipated a ground operation to be launched against them in May. The speed of partisan reaction to the airborne attack was not the result of lack of security, as the Germans believed, but was the product of strict and careful training. The post-battle report of the 'Prinz Eugen' Division pays tribute to the skill and the ability of the guerrilla forces and includes the sentence, 'Their mobility vis-à-vis the German troops is well known . . . knowing the countryside as they do and being familiar with the mountains, unencumbered by a huge Train and enjoying the support of the local population, the Red troops are capable of marching enormous distances.'

No new tactics were encountered by 'Prinz Eugen' units but, as the report acknowledged,' The partisans are on the defensive and do not need new tactics.'

Each side accused the other of torture, summary executions, atrocities and reprisals. The actions on the Drvar battlefield can best be understood if one sees them from Command level and not from that of the combat soldier. At Command level the German military authorities considered that any armed uprising against the Occupying Power (themselves) contravened the Geneva Convention which gave them the right, as they saw it, under the terms of that document, to summarily shoot armed civilians as *francs tireurs*.

The partisans saw themselves as soldiers in an army fighting a war against an implacable and ruthless foe. German post-battle reports accuse the guerrillas of binding round the legs and arms of SS wounded prisoners, lengths of explosive fuse which blew off their limbs. Partisan sources describe the fury of the SS men and of their brutality towards civilians in Drvar.

Partisan warfare and anti-partisan operations are perhaps the dirtiest form of fighting and it is a tragedy that the record of the bravery shown by both sides during Operation 'Rösselsprung', should have been besmirched by brutal and inhuman deeds.

10

UNEXPECTED OFFENSIVE

Special Forces in the Ardennes, December 1944

In December 1944 an offensive was launched by the German Army in which three of the military special forces described in this book took part. That winter offensive came to be known as the Battle of the Bulge and the special units involved were Brandenburg, paratroops and some of Skorzeny's own groups.

In so far as this offensive, decided upon and planned by Hitler, can be said to have had any strategic intent, it was to capture the port of Antwerp and by driving a corridor between them to split the British Army in Belgium and Holland from the American Army in France. What Hitler intended the German forces to do once they had reached Antwerp is unclear, although he spoke of bringing about another Dunkirk. What the Führer with his ability to reject unpalatable facts chose to ignore was that the Allies had unchallenged air superiority and that they were quantitatively stronger than the Germans. Also, with qualitative superiority in supplies, fuel and weapons, they could replace their losses quickly and easily – and the Germans could not. A sober appraisal of Operation 'Watch on the Rhine', which Hitler saw as a thrust from the Ardennes to the North Sea, produces the conclusion that its only result would be the forming of a long and narrow salient against which Allied ground and air forces would strike until the Germans withdrew.

The idea for this counter-attack had come suddenly to Hitler and, by this stage of the war, deeply suspicious of his military commanders, he told them nothing of his plan until the first week in November. His obsession with security prevented the commanders from briefing their staff until the last possible moment and, in fact, regimental commanders knew nothing but the bare outline of the operation until the day before 'Watch on the Rhine' opened.

Hitler had wanted the operation to be launched in the late autumn, but the date proposed had to be postponed several times; the final date chosen was 16 December. Four German Armies were to carry out the operation: from north to south they were: Fifteenth, Sixth SS Panzer, Fifth Panzer and Seventh Armies. To build up the military force Hitler created twenty-five Volksgrenadier divisions. Each of these had a lower infantry establishment than that in standard infantry divisions, but this was compensated by a higher establishment in automatic weapons.

Volksgrenadier divisions, the Nazi Party's attempt at creating an army, did not merely maintain the same fire of a normal division, but exceeded it. In order to strengthen the armour components for the forthcoming battle, the Führer created ten new Panzer Brigades, each equipped with Panthers and Tigers. In a discussion with Skorzeny, Hitler ordered the special forces to be employed in such a way that the enemy front would be ruptured quickly, for the key to victory lay in speed. The armour would crack open the American defence on D-Day. The River Meuse would be crossed on D-Day plus 1, using bridges at Englis, Amay and Huy, which would have been captured intact – and held – by Skorzeny's commandos. The infiltration of commando troops dressed as Americans would ensure that the roads were kept open so that the armour could move quickly, 'bounce' the Meuse and then race on to Antwerp. Teams of men would infiltrate, moving ahead of the advancing Sixth SS Panzer Army, not only to seize bridges but to hold cross-roads and sow confusion among the American forces.

In this major operation Hitler intended that the main burden should fall upon Sixth SS Panzer Army and to give them the greatest 'punch' he allocated them the special forces and the newest armoured fighting vehicles. Sixth SS would draw behind it the other armies and the whole force would carve a corridor across northern Belgium and southern Holland with Antwerp as the objective.

Hitler briefed Skorzeny on the vital role that he and his units were to play. The Sturmbannführer prepared accordingly. The Führer had told him to recruit men who spoke American/English, and to disguise them as US servicemen. In view of Hitler's demand for absolute secrecy, the SS officer had intended to recruit his men as discreetly as possible, and he was alarmed when he read an Order which had been circulated down to Divisional level, in which his name and the address of his headquarters were mentioned. Part of that order reads:

'The Führer has ordered the formation of a special unit of a strength of about two battalions to be employed on reconnaissance and for special tasks on the Western Front. Volunteers from the Army and from the Waffen SS who fulfill the following requirements will be accepted. They must be physically fit, mentally alert and have strong personalities. They must be fully trained in hand to hand combat. A knowledge of English is essential and American dialect terms and military technical terms is required . . . captured American clothing, equipment, weapons and vehicles are to be handed in to equip these volunteers . . . Divisional Quartermasters are responsible for the collection of that material and returns will be rendered by 1st November.'

It was not long before a copy of the order was in the hands of American Intelligence officers whose Appreciation, known as 'Estimate 37', of 10 December, forecast a German offensive, albeit in a different sector of the Front, but one in which special forces would be used.

'The enemy's strategy for the defence of the Reich is based upon the exhaustion of our offensive which he will follow with an all-out counter-attack . . . between the Roer and the Erft . . . A captured Order for selected personnel speaking the American dialect to report to HQ Skorzeny in Friedenthal, near Oranienburg, by 1st November, obviously presages special operations . . . by infiltrated or parachuted specialists . . .

Meanwhile, plans were going ahead for the employment of Skorzeny's special forces which he sought to disguise under the name, 'Panzer Brigade 150'. The brigade was divided into two forces, each with a distinctive role to play. There was an armoured battle group and a commando force of 160 men, subdivided into sets of agents carrying out one of three types of duty. The 'saboteur' detachments, each of five or six men, would destroy those bridges which the US forces might use. The teams would also attack fuel or ammunition dumps from which US units might be supplied. 'Reconnaissance' groups, each consisting of four or five men, were to infiltrate the areas north and south of the Meuse and identify the enemy's armoured and artillery units there. These 'reconnaissance' units were also to confuse the American troops by relaying false information and issuing conflicting orders. They would also change street and direction signs, remove minefield markers and use them to indicate false fields. The third group, the 'Lead' commandos, had the tasks of collaborating with the attacking German divisions, intercepting enemy radio signals and issuing conflicting counter-orders.

The purpose of the Armoured Battle Group was also to confuse the Americans. In appearance it should resemble a US Armoured Group fleeing in disorder from the German assault. Hitler told Skorzeny that this particular part of his Command was to be a hard-hitting armoured fist which was to move fast and create confusion. If his Battle Group had to look like an American one, what Skorzeny wanted was American tanks, halftracks, trucks and Jeeps. The young SS officer was shocked at the discrepancy between what he asked for and what he got. He indented for 150 Jeeps and light cars and received 57. From one demand for 198 trucks only 74 were delivered. Fifteen US tanks were asked for and he received five – all of them German. From a requisition of 26 Armoured Personnel Carriers only eight were forthcoming and six of those were German. Not one of the vehicles he received was in good order and many needed a week's work to bring them up to a 'running' standard. Those which were too badly gone had to be cannibalized for other trucks. Two Shermans were, finally, received. In one the engine was completely smashed and its tank gun was useless. The radio equipment was missing and had not been replaced by D-Day.

Instead of modern US anti-tank guns Skorzeny received obsolescent Polish and Russian pieces. There was insufficient personal equipment to outfit the teams of men who would be dressed as Americans to infiltrate behind the US lines. The requisition for steel helmets could not be met. Even when clothing and equipment was taken from US prisoners it was still insufficient. Skorzeny feared that these shortages might force him to curtail the scope of his operation. Sheet metal was welded to the sides and turrets of German Panzers to change their profiles so that they resembled American tanks. When the conversion job was complete, Skorzeny described it as being capable of deceiving only 'very green troops, at night and when seen from a great distance'.

The composition of Panzer Brigade 150 must have given Skorzeny a headache. It was a hotch-potch of units – some Army, some SS, some Luftwaffe, some infantry, some armour:

2 Battalions of a Luftwaffe para unit known as 'Battle Group 200' This supplied 800 men.

1 Company of Skorzeny's SS 'Jagdverband Mitte' which provided 175 men.

2 Companies of SS Para Battalion 600, which sent 380 infantry.

2 Army Panzer Companies which supplied between them 240 men.

2 Army Panzergrenadier Companies which provided between them 350 men.

2 Companies from the Army equipped with heavy mortars: total strength of 200 men.

2 anti-tank Companies, combined total 200 men.

1 Engineer Company of 100 men.

1 Signals Company of 200 men.

3 Vehicle Repair and Maintenance Platoons, each of 75 men.

The Panzer Brigade was divided into an HQ detachment and three Groups: two Panzer and one Infantry. To move the Brigade from its start-line to the objective, the River Meuse, Hitler allocated three roads from which there was to be no deviation except to avoid a head-on clash. The task of Brigade 150 was to make ground: to clear the way forward for the follow-up Panzer Divisions and to relieve the infiltration teams which would be holding the Meuse bridges.

The shortest distance that the Brigade had to travel was about 55 miles and it was anticipated that the link-up with the commando teams would be made within six hours of the start of the operation. In order for the Brigade to achieve that target Hitler laid down precise rules of conduct. If the Brigade met opposition from a weaker force, Skorzeny was allowed to destroy it before going on towards the river. Radio silence between the three groups was to be enforced.

While his mechanics were making 'runners' out of automobile wrecks and converting standard German tanks to look like Shermans, Skorzeny considered the problems of the men who would form his English-speaking Commando. The volunteers had already begun to arrive at Brigade headquarters. Tests by the SS commander revealed that those who claimed to speak English had varying levels of competency. In Category A, those with an absolutely fluent command of American-English complete with idioms, there were only ten men and most of these were from the Brandenburg units. Those with a good knowledge numbered between 30 and 40 and these were put into Category B. More than one hundred and fifty who could understand English, but had little spoken ability, were Category C, while the greatest number, those who could understand simple phrases if spoken slowly, were placed in Category D. These D men numbered some two hundred.

At 05.30 on the morning of 16 December, the German attack opened and early successes were gained. On the German side of the line the roads leading up to the front were blocked as units struggled through a mass of motor- and horse-drawn vehicles, along country roads unsuited to the mass movement of armies, and in terrible weather. The US front had not fragmented as had been hoped and the German columns could not deploy but had coagulated to form a solid mass. In the middle of this jam on that first day was Skorzeny's Panzer Brigade. His English-speaking teams were behind the American lines, or so he hoped, for he had no communications with them. Unable to force his way through the traffic jam in which he sat, the Sturmbannführer decided to take an active part in the ground fighting around the towns and villages which the Americans were holding. Skorzeny was concerned at the danger of a long flank exposed to a possible US thrust. He took his battle group into action between Baughez and Stavelot and set out to help in the capture of Malmedy. During a tour of his battle group's positions, Skorzeny and his runner were caught in a heavy and accurate US artillery bombardment and the Sturmbannführer was wounded badly enough to be moved out of the line.

What had the special units achieved? Some reversed road signs had confused an American tank battalion moving towards the front. A unit had been bluffed into withdrawing from a village which it held. Telephone wires had been cut and an ammunition dump had been blown up. A few other light-weight blows were the sum total of the results on the ground. There had, however, been a psychological result. The realisation among American soldiers that there were Germans in US uniform active behind the front line produced in some of the non-combatant detachments an outbreak of spy mania. Sentries posed catch questions and the unfortunate who was challenged and did not know, for example, that Harry James was a trumper player or who failed to have a detailed knowledge of the leading baseball teams, was liable to be arrested, beaten up or threatened with execution as a spy.

Of Skorzeny's nine teams, seven were able to infiltrate successfully and one reached the Meuse. The remaining two were quickly intercepted and caught. Men from one of the captured groups, the Einheit Steilau, were court-martialled and shot. Believing that the wearing of an enemy's clothing was not a capital offence unless accompanied by the carrying of weapons, Skorzeny was angered at the American Army's action. He was not to know that a rumour had swept the US forces that the real object of the German special detachments was the assassination of General Eisenhower and that the Americans were determined not to let the Commander-in-Chief fall victim to a terrorist's bullet.

Let us now see how the other special force, the paratroops, were conducting themselves in the offensive. The paratroop battalion that was dropped to carry out Operation 'Stösser', a special mission within the Ardennes offensive, is less well-documented than Skorzeny's units and it did not achieve even the Panzer Brigade's modest results.

General Student, Commander-in-Chief of the German airborne forces, chose Oberst Baron von der Heydte, a veteran of Crete and Commandant of the Fallschirmjäger School at Alten, to lead the parachute special force. When the two officers met on 8 December, Student could give his subordinate only an outline of the forthcoming operation. He could give no details of the part that the paratroops would play, saying only that their role would be vital. Von der Heydte was to form a battle group made up of one hundred men from each battalion of II Para Corps. The men of this composite battalion would come from miscellaneous detachments and not from a single regiment in order to preserve secrecy.

Heydte was permitted to select his own company and platoon commanders to whom he gave such details as he himself had been given. At his unit conference it was decided that the battalion would be organised along the standard lines of four infantry companies, a heavy weapons company armed with twelve machine-guns and four mortars, a signals platoon and a pioneer platoon. Student had already ordered the battalion commanders of Second Para Corps to send in one hundred of their best men. Few commanding officers complied with the terms of the order and, on the principle that special mobs are made up of riffraff, sent their worst men, the hard cases. Von der Heydte returned one hundred and fifty of these misfits to their parent units and had them replaced by better soldiers. Most of them were completely inexperienced and had made no operational jumps. The few that had dropped by parachute into action had fought in the battle for Crete, three and a half years earlier, but these were a very small minority; for the mass of the battalion this was to be their baptism of fire. Yet with these men von der Heydte had to carry out an operation of whose details he was still ignorant, but of the importance of which there was no doubt.

Within a day, for such was the flexibility of German military administration and organisation, the companies had been formed and equipped. The next step was for von der Heydte to establish from his direct superior, Dietrich, General Officer Commanding the Sixth SS Panzer Army, exactly what the role of the para battalion was to be. The result of the discussion with the SS General was the following operational order:

'On the first day of the attack, Sixth SS Panzer Army will capture Liège or the Meuse bridges south of the city. Before dawn on that first day, the von der Heydte battle group will drop into the Baraque Michel mountain area, 11 kilometres north of Malmedy and secure the multiple road junction there for the advanced guard of the SS Panzer Army. The armoured advanced guard will probably be from 12th SS (Hitler Youth) Panzer Division. If for technical reasons this drop is impracticable on the morning of the first day of the attack, then Battle Group von der Heydte will drop, early in the morning of the following day, into the area of the River Ambleve or at Amay and secure the bridges there, to facilitate the advance of Sixth SS Panzer Army's armoured point.'

The task which Dietrich had been given was clear and daunting. The Oberst's inexperienced paratroop force was to drop by night over wooded mountains. The drop was to be made immediately before the barrage which would open the offensive. To von der Heydte's comment that the high ground winds that could be expected in mountainous areas would bring the risk of injury or even death to the paratroops, Dietrich was unsympathetic. He was not, he said, responsible for the poor standard of training in the Luftwaffe's para arm. From practical experience the Oberst knew how temperamental radio-sets were in mountainous terrain and feared that a breakdown in communications could nullify his battalion's gains and prevent it from carrying out another part of its task, that of reporting the US units present in the area. He asked for carrier pigeons as a back-up. The SS General replied that he was not running a menagerie and that if he could lead an Army without pigeons von der Heydte could lead his battle group without them. Neither could he supply the paras with photographs of the landing area nor would he authorise the sending out of recce patrols for fear of a breach of security. Although the birds could not be supplied, other necessary equipment was promised, including dummy paratroops which would be dropped over Spa and Stavelot to confuse the American defenders. The dummies were procured just before the battle opened.

D-Day for von der Heydte's group was 16 December, the dropping time between 04.30 and 05.00. On the evening of the 15th the Oberst's battle group began to move towards airfields at Padeborn and Lippespringe, but shortage of petrol reduced the vehicle numbers in the transport column and only one third of the para battalion got to their departure points on time. The operation would have to be postponed for a day. Dietrich, whose operational maps showed that the SS Panzer Army had not gained its first-day objectives, gave orders that the operation was to take place on the morning of the 17th. Radio intercepts showed that the Americans were bringing in reinforcements from the north, via Baraque Michel down to Elsenborn. The task of the para battalion was to cut the road and halt that flow of troops, and not to drop in the River Ambleve or Amay area.

Shortly before midnight on the 16th, the JUs took off. The one hundred and fifty aircraft which formed the armada were soon meeting head winds which blew across the heights of the Hoher Venn. Many of the inexperienced pilots did not take into account the fact that head winds reduce the speed of aircraft, which in turn reduces the distance flown. Most pilots were working on a time basis to determine when they had reached the target area. The adverse winds gave them a false answer so that when they dropped the troops few of them came down in the actual drop zone. Two hundred troopers landed on or near Bonn in Germany, others fell in Holland. American anti-aircraft fire broke up the formations and drove them off course. Only ten of the whole armada of transport machines reached the target area. One of those was the JU in which von der Heydte was flying. The Oberst was depressed and in great pain. His left forearm had been shattered earlier in a training accident and he had also damaged his right arm. He had had little or no sleep since Student had given him his Command some days earlier, and he felt that the entire 'Watch on the Rhine' operation was running out of true. The Oberst and his string of men jumped into the dark snowy night, against dangerously high ground winds of more than 30 miles per hour. That wind had already blown the mass of von der Heydte's battalion off course and away from the target. The Oberst landed alone in the bitter darkness. The rest of the string were widely dispersed and by 03.50 only six men had joined him. By 04.50 there were twenty-six, but by the evening only one hundred and twenty-five men of the entire battalion had rallied. Among them was an artillery observation officer from the SS and two of his radio-operators. The sets had been damaged in the drop, as the Oberst had feared, and the signallers unsure whether their messages were being received sent out blind the information that American armour was moving southwards down the road. The paras were without heavy weapons because the containers had been lost in the drop, and so could not carry out their given task of cutting the road and stopping the flow of US troops to the battle area.

Although the drop had been unsuccessful, morale among the paras was still high and their Commander sent out reconnaissance groups in the direction of Malmedy, seeking to link up with the SS spearhead units. None were met. In the afternoon of the 17th, von der Heydte pulled his group back north-eastwards into the woods and there made contact with a further hundred and fifty men of his scattered battalion.

The Americans, of course, were fully aware that the paras were in the crossroads area, but they grossly overestimated the numbers of the German special force. The battalion had been widely dispersed and reports had come in from widely-scattered units of the American Army of the presence in their areas of German parachute troops; so many reports, in fact, that it was believed that whole divisions of Fallschirm-jäger had been put in. To meet the implied danger the American deployed troops who should have been employed in other parts of the Bulge and this over-reaction kept infantrymen out of the line at a critical time. Paradoxically the failure of the paras to drop as a concentrated force succeeded in creating confusion among the enemy.

Luftwaffe attempts to air drop supplies to the hungry, frozen para-troops were inept. The containers dropped by one JU were all lost except for one which held only drinking water and packets of damp cigarettes. After three days von der Heydte realised that no link up with the SS spearheads would now come about and that there was no way in which his battalion could influence the course of the battle. His men were without food and they lacked sleep. He decided to reduce his Command by sending back the unfit, and as a first step he sent the wounded paras out towards the German lines. He then formed his remaining men into a battle group and led them into a thrust aimed at penetrating the ring of American forces which he knew now sur-rounded his Command. The attack died in the fire of US tank guns and the paras fell back into the woods. Von der Heydte reasoned that if the US ring was too strong for a large unit to break, perhaps small troops of men might be able to filter through. During the 21st, he broke up his special force and sent detachments of two or three men out into the night. He himself set off with his adjutant and a runner towards Monschau, unaware that the town, which had been an objective to be taken on the first day of the offensive, was still uncaptured. Two long days later the Oberst, in agony from his broken arm and weak from lack of food and sleep, ordered his companions to leave him and stumbled into a house in Monschau where he surrendered to US troops.

For one special force the Ardennes offensive was over. For Skorzeny's Brigade it was continuing, if in a different role. His special force was not now thrusting aggressively towards Antwerp, but was on the defen-sive, fighting tenaciously and very successfully against the Americans.

When 'Watch on the Rhine' was over, it was calculated that it had consumed twenty German divisions which, between them, had lost 24,000 men killed, 63,000 wounded and 16,000 taken prisoner; all of them lost in an operation which made as much sense as driving up a cul-de-sac at full speed.

11

THE END OF THE SPECIAL FORCES

It will be remembered that Skorzeny had formed Jagdverbände in battalion strength and had named these after the regions in which they were to fight. The collapse of Army Group Centre released the Red Army to flood across eastern Germany sweeping away everything in its path. Into that maelstrom of defeat Skorzeny sent some of his battalions to hold fast while all around them was collapsing and giving way.

By the end of August 1944 Germany's allies had begun to desert her. Among those who now abandoned the Nazi cause was Roumania. That country held a strategic position for it was the buttress of the German Army's right wing. It was feared in Berlin that a hostile government in Bucharest might seal in the mountain passes of the Carpathians and thereby trap the divisions of Army Group South fighting desperately against a new Soviet offensive launched by the 2nd Ukrainian Front. Hitler ordered that the vital passes be captured and held. In obedience to his command two platoons of the 'South Eastern' Jagd Battalion were sent and carried out the task. The passage of the German Army through the Carpathian passes was relatively uninterrupted. There then remained the task for the men of those platoons to bring themselves out of a Roumania now allied to Russia and, therefore, hostile to the Germans.

The platoons were divided into four groups which then set out to reach the German lines. To assist them the men of the 'South East' battalion adopted a number of disguises. Some were dressed in the uniform of Hungarian tank crews. Others wearing civilian clothes submerged themselves in the crowds of refugees flooding westwards. One group, dressed as Roumanian soldiers, was led by a Roumanian-speaking Brandenburg soldier, and was greeted with flowers and wine. This good fortune did not last and the SS group was halted by suspicious Russian and Roumanian soldiers. Very quickly their captors identified them. A hastily convened court martial condemned them and they were executed in a quarry.

While part of the 'South East' battalion was being destroyed in Roumania the 'Eastern' battalion had been sent on an almost totally hopeless mission, 'Operation Poacher', to Minsk in White Russia. Reports from an agent behind the Soviet lines spoke of about two thousand men holding an isolated position deep behind the Russian front. This group, commanded by an Oberstleutnant Scherhorn, intended to form a 'wandering pocket' and reach the German lines. It says much for the confidence that the Germans had in themselves, of the fear that they had of being taken prisoner and of the trust which they reposed in the efforts their High Command would make to rescue them, that such 'wandering pockets' were a feature of almost every Russian offensive. A hedgehog moves with an outside surface bristling and armed, and in like fashion pockets of Germans, isolated groups by-passed in Soviet offensives but determined to regain touch with their own army, passed through the great woods of Russia and of western Poland.

The composition and tactics used by 'wandering pockets' depended upon the numbers and arms available. It was usual for strong infantry patrols to continually sweep both flanks of the advance. Armour if available led the forward movement and Panzer Grenadiers formed the rear guard. In the centre were the soft-skinned vehicles, the artillery and the wounded. Air drops supplied ammunition, food and information on Soviet troops in the area. The progress of a pocket was necessarily slow and anxious, for at every clearing or cross-roads there was the likelihood that heavy armoured fighting vehicles of the Red Army might be waiting to intercept and destroy the German group.

It was to make contact with Scherhorn's pocket that the men from the 'Eastern' battalion were sent out. His group differed markedly from other pockets. His men were exhausted and wounded. He had no armour and very few trucks. Being without radio he had been out of touch with the German forces for weeks. In addition the pocket was located some five hundred miles behind the Russian lines. But Scherhorn's men were filled with a fierce determination to return home and to aid them in this endeavour the 'Eastern' battalion formed four groups. Each was made up of two Germans and three Russians. The parties were to be dressed in Red Army uniform, would carry Russian arms and food. They would be taken by air to a point as close as possible to where Scherhorn's pocket was believed to be and the whole group would then parachute down.

At the end of August the first detachment was dropped east of Minsk to be followed days later by the second group which was also taken to the same area. Six days and eight days later respectively the third and fourth sections were dropped between Dzersinsk and Viteys.

Consider the feelings of the German men of the groups. They were being transported to a wild and remote area with whose vast forests they were unfamiliar. They would be dependent, once they had landed, upon the loyalty of the former Red Army men who had dropped with them. Their task was to find, somewhere in the extensive and almost impenetrable woods a group of men who did not want to be found easily. And all this they must undertake while anti-partisan patrols of the Russian forces made periodic sweeps with armour and planes and vast masses of infantry to destroy the pockets which still held out.

Radio signals from the first group of the Eastern Battalion soon after it had landed indicated that it was under fire from a strong group of Soviet units. The hasty messages gave only the barest information and soon communications were broken off, never to be restored. The second detachment found the Scherhorn group and radioed a harrowing account of the suffering of the wounded and the pitiful condition of the remainder of the group. A doctor was parachuted in but he broke both his ankles on landing. A second doctor was sent in. The radio link between Skorzeny's Battalion HQ and the pocket functioned well and with this restoration of communications planes were sent into drop supplies and food to the encircled men. A shuttle service was set up, but the intention to build an airstrip in the forests from which machines of KG200 could evacuate the seriously wounded had to be abandoned when Red Army patrols found the strip and occupied it. Meanwhile the remaining groups of 'Eastern' Battalion had had their own experiences. The fourth section having searched in vain for Scherhorn's pocket returned to the German lines after an epic march. The third group vanished silently and completely into the vastness of the Soviet Union and nothing more was ever heard of it.

With a radio link established and a shuttle service in operation the time had come to formulate plans for the return of the Scherhorn group to the German lines. The front had moved further westward and they were now nearly 500 miles inside Russian territory. A march westwards was out of the question. The countries to the south, Hungary and Roumania, were now hostile. There remained only one possible direction and that was northwards, marching to reach the town of Dünaburg in Lithuania. But to reach that place, nearly 200 miles distant, meant that the group would have to cut across the lines of communication of the Soviet armies fighting at the eastern approaches to Germany. It would be a trek filled with danger but it was the only choice. Once in Lithuania the aircraft of KG200 would land on the frozen lakes and take off again carrying the wounded of Scherhorn's command.

By this stage of the war the demands made upon the Luftwaffe and the shortage of fuel had reduced the number of missions which could be undertaken. The sustenance of one small group of two thousand men isolated deep in the forests of Russia received at first a low and then an even lower priority. Fewer missions were flown to supply food and ammunition to the beleaguered men. Winter had set in and the soldiers in the Scherhorn pocket were not equipped to cope with its bitterness. They had been out of touch since the late summer and had none of the special clothing or footwear which would help them to survive. They were, however, still resolved to continue with the march. Although Skorzeny and his officers appreciated that the march rate of the 'pocket' would be low, none thought that it would be only ten miles per day for just four days of the week and that this would be followed by three days of recuperation.

Scherhorn formed his group into two columns. The first of these was led by the experienced soldiers of the 'Eastern' Battalion and the second by the Oberst himself. On 15 November 1944, the columns set out trusting in the Luftwaffe to keep them supplied as they moved towards the Baltic and their final destination. But KG200 had been forced to reduce even further the number of sorties which it could make and ever fewer supplies were dropped to the two columns now making their painful way and dwindling in effective fighting strength with each passing day. The messages from Scherhorn's group were increasingly ones of despair as the hopelessness of the situation became more apparent to them.

Scherhorn's men never reached Dünaburg. A destination 180 miles removed from the starting point in the huge and silent woods should have been covered, even at the slow speed of ten miles per day, in less than a month. But the odds against the German columns were enormous. There were furious battles against Soviet patrols; hand-to-hand fighting as the Germans tried to force a passage through strongly held cross-roads. The effects of the winter climate slowed down the pace still further and the weakened men could no longer fight against all the factors that were opposing them. Late at night in the first weeks of May 1945, as German units across the length and breadth of Europe prepared to lay down their arms in unconditional surrender, Skorzeny's headquarters received the last faint radio signal from the Scherhorn pocket before its soldiers, too, passed into captivity.

During January 1945, a major Soviet offensive opened. Skorzeny's Jagdverbande battalions were grouped as a division under his command and were flung into the fighting for the Schwedt bridgehead in the role of conventional infantry. This was a terrible misuse of those men, for each of them who became a casualty represented a loss of a highly trained and skilled specialist. But such considerations had little significance in the embattled Germany of January 1945. Every man, specialist or recruit, was needed to hold the collapsing front and there were few opportunities for Skorzeny to mount the raiding operations which were the *raison d'être* of his specialist groups. One mission which did present itself was the infiltration of a team into the Red Army's rear in Poland. This small detachment of twelve Germans and twenty-five Russians, commanded by Obersturmführer Girg, a 25-year-old, had orders to disrupt the Soviet supply routes. The journey which they undertook began in East Prussia and took them 500 miles through enemy-held territory, during which their skills and abilities were tested to the full. They disguised themselves in Roumanian Army uniforms and wore the insignia of a specialist unit. Initially they moved in partisan fashion, using the tricks they had learned during the fighting on the Eastern Front. The early stages of the mission were soon completed, but knowledge of the presence of the German group was soon with the NKVD whose officers mounted a large-scale cordon and search operation. From its positions deep in the Soviet rear areas the little group had to fight its way back to the German lines and lost heavily in this fighting retreat.

This seems to be the last raiding operation undertaken by the units of Skorzeny's organisation. The remnants of his Command were regrouped and put into the line as tank-busting teams. The Soviet offensive of April 1945, crushed those detachments in a welter of barrages and tank assaults. Only a few individual soldiers escaped from the battlefields.

There remains to be mentioned only the SS Paratroop Battalion, the last of Skorzeny's special forces. This had been renumbered '600' and reinforced. Towards the end of March 1945, the battalion, now at full strength of nearly 800 men, was put into the German bridgehead on the east bank of the River Oder at Zehden. The paratroopers held their exposed positions for over three weeks, even though on either flank other units had crumbled and died, or had given way under the terrible pressure of the Soviet thrusts. The SS paras held fast. On 26th March, thirty-six of them, all that was left of the battalion, swam across the Oder as the last outposts on the eastern bank, held by a small rearguard, were overrun. But this was still not the end for 600 Para. Heavily reinforced once again and this time with volunteers from the SS training schools, a new battalion was formed round a cadre of the survivors. The para formation was fleshed out by convalescents and other men who left hospitals to rejoin the colours and to serve with their unit in the battles which marked the end of the Third Reich.

The SS Para Battalion was the only full strength and properly organised unit among the forces which had been flung together for the defence of Neuruppin and the burden of the defence as well as of the attack, fell upon it. On one day in April, No. 3 Company, which had 'stood to' at dawn with a strength of 84 men, had only 30 left alive by sunset. Starting at first light and persisting until the onset of darkness, Soviet Guards tank *divisions* backed by Guards rifle and cavalry *divisions* had flung themselves against the thin line of SS defenders, only a company in strength.

Panzerfaust and Panzerschreck, the German rocket-propelled weapons had all been used up before the third attack came in at 14.00, but across the wooded heath of Neuruppin were scattered the blazing or shattered wrecks of a battalion of Soviet tanks. Until rear echelon men or the Company runners could bring forward fresh supplies of tank-busting weapons the men, exhausted now from days of unequal combat, would have to fight the armada of Red tanks which flooded against them, armed with only hand-grenades and satchel charges.

At 15.15 the noise of tank engines and a short bombardment of Katyusha rockets and field guns heralded another attack. The T34s and JS tanks rumbled across the fields towards the paratroopers who waited, each trooper evaluating the vehicles of the oncoming mass just as a matador weighs up the bull which might kill him. The SS men allowed the tanks of the first wave to close to a point where they themselves could not be seen by the Red crews and then clambered on to the rear decks and went to work.

Some did not climb on to the machines, but ran alongside the tanks so as to place upon them a magnetic, hollow-charge grenade. A tug on a blue-beaded cord set off the nine-second fuse and then the paratrooper dived into the nearest cover to protect himself from the force of the explosion which was often sufficient to blow a tank apart. Many German soldiers had been killed by blast before they had reached cover; killed in the moment of their triumph.

Into open hatches grenades were dropped; Teller mines were wedged between tracks and running wheels to explode with shattering detonations which blew off the track leaving the huge vehicles spinning helplessly on a single caterpillar. Some paras flung satchel charges under the broad tracks and soon more and more Soviet machines lay shattered on the Neuruppin heath.

A further five times, massed Soviet armour came in against No. 3 Company and five times the Red machines were flung back. The last attack shattered the Company and its commander knew that his dying Command could not withstand a sixth major assault. To his relief Battalion Headquarters ordered a withdrawal and the survivors of the Companies assembled on a dark road in a night lit by the fires of burning German farms and Russian tanks. A roll call showed that from the 800 men who had entered the fight there were only 180 survivors. These few then fought their way westward through the Russian encirclement and back into battle. Nothing more is known of them for in the general collapse of the Eastern Front the SS Para battalion No. 600, disappeared as a fighting force. There could have been only a few survivors.

PART TWO

THE NAVY'S SPECIAL FORCES

1

THE K MEN

On 1 January 1943 a task force of German surface ships, including the battleship *Lützow*, the heavy cruiser *Hipper* and a number of destroyers, intercepted a British convoy in the Barents Sea. The German group was driven off by an inferior number of Royal Navy ships and the convoy reached Murmansk without further challenge. The blame for this failure of the German battle group to destroy the Allied convoy lay not with the German seamen nor their officers, but in Hitler's directive that the ships of the Kriegsmarine were not to be risked.

Despite the fact that the commanders of the task force had complied with his orders, Hitler was furious at the Navy's poor showing and in a blinding rage declared capital ships to be an unjustifiable drain on men and equipment. All the capital ships were to be scrapped and their heavy armament was to be mounted in coastal-defence batteries. These were orders that no sailor could accept and certainly not Admiral Doenitz, the new Commander-in-Chief. He ignored them and retained the ships for further operations.

Hitler's outburst showed the narrowness of his strategic vision. That the self-confessed 'greatest military genius of all time' understood as little of aerial strategy as of the special problems of war at sea, is illustrated by the remarks he made in April 1945, to General Koller, the Luftwaffe's Chief of Staff. 'Why', the Führer had demanded, 'should the Luftwaffe need Air Force officers to lead it? A General of any Branch of the services could lead the Luftwaffe just as well.'

The tirade against the Navy made it clear that for as long as the war continued, the Kriegsmarine had no prospect of obtaining authority to build any new type of surface vessel. U-boats, the only naval units still carrying the war to the enemy, were doing so under almost impossible conditions. Nevertheless, and Doenitz made this very clear, they would have to continue to bear the brunt of Allied air and sea attack until there was a change in the Führer's attitude towards the Kriegsmarine. Although Hitler was aware that U-boats were his most important weapon, he still saw the Service with the vision of a man tied to the concept of land warfare.

Despite his attitude the admirals, their officers and men served the Third Reich and its leader with the utmost loyalty. In view of this loyalty, it is surprising that the Navy's special units when they were formed, strived so long and so hard to remain independent of Skorzeny, whose control, in theory, would have been the most sensible harnessing of the national effort.

The Navy had had no need of special units during the first years of the war. Its surface ships had fought well, albeit mainly in coastal waters. A few armed raiders had sunk British ships and a few blockade-runners had broken through the Royal Navy's screen to bring home war materials otherwise unobtainable. There had also been the skilfully directed U-boat campaign whose successes, particularly in the Atlantic Ocean, had been impressive. Early proposals to form special units were rejected as being unnecessary. Then the Navy's war changed. Its surface ships were bottled up in port or had only the freedom of the Baltic Sea in which to operate. British radar, able to locate surfaced U-boats even on the darkest night or in the thickest fog, forced them to spend more time submerged. That British scanning device and the possession of Enigma combined with the growing skills of the officers of the Western Approaches in anti-submarine operations, forced the U-boats onto the defensive. There were no more surface raiders or blockade-runners. It was at this time that Doenitz and the senior officers of the Navy began to consider special forces and their methods in the prosecution of the war at sea. In the naval archives they found much that was informative; details of plans suggested years before, but which had been rejected as impracticable or unnecessary.

Far-seeing men in the navies of the major Powers had long argued that the era of air power and torpedo-carrying aircraft had made the battleship, already shown to be obsolescent in the First World War, now obsolete. Capital ships were also vulnerable to attack by motor-boats or other small, but powerful weapons. Proposals to employ manned torpedoes, motor-boats packed with explosives, and miniature submarines had all been submitted a decade or more before the outbreak of the Second World War. On the German side, all these proposals had been rejected by the Naval Staff of the time.

During the early years of the war there had been attempts by the Kriegsmarine to imitate the raids of the British Commandos. A German amphibious expedition to attack Allied meteorological stations in the Arctic had failed to achieve its purpose, chiefly because the hastily-formed force had lacked suitable vessels and adequately trained men. This failure and that of early raids, reinforced the arguments against the raising of special naval units. Then in 1943, the case for special groups was re-examined in the light of the contemporary naval situation, and this time was accepted. It was decided to train along British lines, units of submariners in small craft to attack enemy ships in harbour, and to form amphibious assault detachments along the lines of the British Commandos.

Both the Italian and British Navies had units equipped with underwater chariots, whose frogmen riders could bring them beneath an enemy ship in order to fix explosives to its hull. The Italians had also used light and fast explosive motor-boats and directed them at enemy surface vessels. OKM now considered it appropriate that motor-boats of similar pattern be brought into service so as to maintain a naval presence on the seas by conducting aggressive action against the vessels of the Anglo-American Powers.

Doenitz entrusted to Konteradmiral Helmuth Heye the task of forming small units (Klein Kampf Verbände) to use ideas, tactics and techniques most suitable for employment against Germany's enemies. By this late stage in the war (1943), there were difficulties in the procuring of supplies and in the production of new weapons, but Admiral Heye, was given unrestricted authority to requisition what was required. Then, too, the naval engineers whom he approached were intrigued by the problems he set and which required all their considerable expertise to resolve. It was as well that they were inventive and skilled, for fast action was soon demanded of them. The 'K' units were needed urgently. The sudden and pressing need allowed for none of the usual routine of designing, testing, refining and developing of new craft before they were taken into service. Speed was vital and while the naval constructors toiled with the problems of designing and building the special naval weapons, those seamen who had volunteered for unspecified but risky duties were being interviewed, selected and trained. The men had been recruited by word of mouth and by invitation. The approaches had been confidential yet news had spread and the response to the discreet call had been wildly enthusiastic. From the many hundreds of volunteers, thirty officers and men were finally chosen and it was around this small cadre that the German Navy's special forces were built.

It was no time for the German Navy to stand on ceremony or to be insular in its approach to the problems of the new type of warfare. The leaders of the special force were prepared to accept advice from any source. The Italians were the principal authority and, specifically the detachments led by Prince Borghese which had attacked British ships in the harbour at Alexandria and at Gibraltar. The only other force which had the required disciplines was the Royal Navy. The K-men and their officers studied captured British handbooks and copies of operations orders picked up at Dieppe. These, together with information gained from the skilful interrogation of prisoners, provided the new German organisation with a great deal of knowledge. Then came a singular piece of good fortune for Admiral Heye and his men. A sunken British 'X' craft was recovered and repaired, and its qualities evaluated.

At the end of 1943 the first group of thirty officers and men of the K units were assembled in a barracks in the Baltic port of Heilingenhafen, where the unit was officially designated Marine Einsatz Abteilung (Naval Assault Detachment). More volunteers arrived until, with a unit strength of four officers, four ensigns and one hundred and fifty other ranks, the first training sessions began.

Life for the crews was almost monastic. There were to be no contacts with civilians and, therefore, no shore leave given. Total exclusion from the world would ensure that the new and secret unit remained secret. The one outing per month to the civilian cinema was made by the K-men under such heavy guard that the local population thought them to be naval criminals of the worst sort.

Commando-type training was given by Army veterans of the war on the Eastern Front, specialising in close-combat fighting and survival. Submarine specialists taught the use of escape apparatus and the K-men underwent a short, but intensive course in naval engineering. There was instruction in foreign languages, particularly English. Various types of navigation were studied long and intensely. In short, there was no aspect of seamanship or military training that was not taught and practised until its use became a second nature. The courses were hard and brutally demanding. Failure in any subject usually meant being returned to unit and with it the sober warning never to speak of the MEA or its activities, under pain of death.

Now the pace stepped-up. At Halling in Pomerania, Army instructors demonstrated the use of hollow-charge grenades, similar to those placed on the turrets of the fortress at Eben Emael, but modified for use on the hull of a ship. The Army instructors drove the sailors hard. Forced marches across sand were the norm; and the recruits were made to fight their way through dense forests in an effort to toughen them. There were night alarms which roused the men from their sleep into the icy conditions of late winter along the Baltic coast. It was no place for weaklings. One of these night alarms tested the courage of the recruits who were ordered to leap over a cliff whose height was unknown to them. More and more men dropped out until only those remained who, in Admiral Heye's words, would, 'with a few members and with less means still be able to cause the enemy great loss'.

Heye considered the difficulties facing him and produced the only possible answer to the problem of shortage of time to raise, train and bring his force into action. He would not concentrate upon the production of a small number of ship types, but would go for short runs of a wide variety of vessels, simple in design, construction and operation. His justification was that any weapon or tactic is only successful until its counter is found. The Allies, he felt sure, would soon find a defence against any weapons he could employ, but if he could ring the changes with a wide variety of vessels, each mission might prove successful.

Reviewing the progress already made, Heye found that among the Brandenburg units there was one which had under command a motor

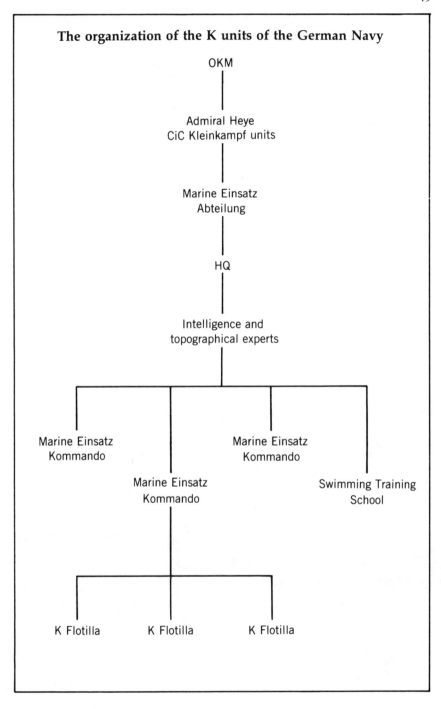

The organization of the K units of the German Navy

OKM

Admiral Heye
CiC Kleinkampf units

Marine Einsatz
Abteilung

HQ

Intelligence and
topographical experts

Marine Einsatz
Kommando

Marine Einsatz
Kommando

Marine Einsatz
Kommando

Swimming Training
School

K Flotilla   K Flotilla   K Flotilla

torpedo-boat flotilla. These could be used to train his men in the explosive motor-boat technique employed so effectively by the Italians. The MTBs were commandeered and were soon *en route* to the Baltic. The 'X' Craft was also undergoing tests and if found suitable could soon be in production. Then, too, there was a new method of launching torpedoes in which only one man was needed; just the sort of weapon and tactic for K-men. It was time to form the Abteilung into separate Kommandos which would operate in the Field independent of MEA HQ. The Kommandos were numbered 60, 65 and 71 respectively, and were commanded by Leutnants Prinzhorn, Richard and Walters. Each Marine Einsatz Kommando was made up of one officer and twenty-two men and on the unit strength were fifteen trucks including a radio truck, three amphibians and trucks to carry equipment. Each MEK was fully motorised and was so fitted out with supplies and equipment that it formed a self-contained unit able to operate for six weeks without replenishment.

2

HUMAN TORPEDOES AND MIDGET SUBMARINES

The first of the several types of special vessel used by the K units, the Neger, floated just below the surface of the water so that the head and shoulders of the 'Captain' were visible. The disadvantages of such a craft are obvious: a large bow wave, and water sweeping over the vessel. The Neger's open cockpit was likely to be flooded in anything but the calmest sea. The first trials proved that unless the sea was as smooth as a millpond the danger of flooding was acute. This problem was overcome by enclosing the open cockpit in a plexiglass dome, but this produced another problem – that of supplying the 'Captain' with fresh air. Any increase in weight, such as the fitting of oxygen tanks, not only upset the trim of the boat but reduced its radius of action. The answer was to supply the 'Captain' with a supply of potassium cartridges of the type used to purify the foul air in submarines. The crewman was responsible for opening the cartridges and thus keeping himself alive.

A very simple set of controls for the two torpedoes was found to be quite effective, but the suspension of the second torpedo beneath the upper one presented problems. In the first trials the 'live' torpedo, which was fired electrically by the 'Captain', fouled the suspension hooks and dragged the carrier torpedo and the 'Captain' through the water at a speed of 30 knots. This was impracticable, and for the sake of stability and to prevent the Neger from nosediving, it was necessary to reduce its speed considerably. The voltage of the electric motor was brought down and down until a speed of about three knots was reached. At this rate the craft was stable and controllable. The fact that the Neger was electrically propelled meant that its radius of action was severely limited. Thus, the base from which it would be launched could be no more than fifteen nautical miles from the target area, for there would have to be sufficient time to find the target and get back home. At a speed of three knots any mission fifteen miles distant would require the crew to be in the water for eleven hours and all the time they would have the problems of oxygen supply, navigation and keeping the vessel trimmed. Such a low speed restricted them to attacks against ships at anchor and in coastal waters where the sea would be smoother. Attacks would have to be made at night and the 'Captains' would have to take tidal ebb and flow into consideration.

Then came the question of how the linked torpedoes were to be put into the water. They would have to be brought in secret to launching points where there might be neither cranes nor lifting devices. The solution was to build a number of what were in effect, 'prams', on to which the vessels were lifted. The whole apparatus was then rolled down the beach and into the water until the Neger floated.

The Neger programme was one of constant improvisation and luck played a great part: there were plenty of torpedoes available, and plexiglass domes produced for bombers. What was very impressive was the speed of the entire operation: from Admiral Doenitz' discussion with Heye and the Neger's designer, to the first mission at Anzio in Italy took just five weeks. The first K units of the German Navy entered the water on the night of 20/21 April 1944, to attack Allied shipping off the Anzio beachhead.

It is my personal conviction that the officers and men who undertook that initial Neger mission were sacrificed in an attempt to determine whether operations by K units were a practical means of fighting a limited sea war. Anzio was chosen because Italy was the only active theatre of war. This first operation might supply answers to the many problems encountered by the K units. Tactics and weapons could be improved upon in time to meet the Allied invasion of Europe which surely would be launched in the summer of 1944, that is to say in only eight weeks' time. But now the first K units manning Neger craft are *en route* to their attack upon shipping at Anzio. Let us accompany them on this their first active-service operation.

The Allied campaign in Italy was, in that early spring of 1944, concentrated upon two areas on or near the Tyrrhenian sea. Monte Cassino barred any advance by the American Fifth Army, and to bypass that dominating mountain the Allies launched an amphibious operation at Anzio and had formed a bridgehead. To supply the troops in the perimeter, Allied convoys sailed from Naples, past the German front lines and docked in the harbours of Anzio or Nettuno. It was in order to destroy the Anglo-American ships that 261 'K' Flotilla and its Neger craft were put into their first action by the German Navy. Orders from the Supreme Commander of the South Western Theatre of Operations laid down that the whole strength of the flotilla, some 40 craft, was to be used. The date for the operation was to be not later than 15 April.

It will be recalled that the Neger's radius of action was only 35 nautical miles, and the craft had to be manhandled into water deep enough to float it. The nearest point to the Anzio beachhead from which deep water could be reached within 90 feet of the shore line was near Practica di Mare, some eighteen miles from the target area. Thus, the Neger 'Captains' would set out knowing that they had insufficient power in their batteries to make the round trip. To preserve the secret of the Negers each 'Captain' would take his craft from the operational area out into deep water where an explosive charge would sink her. He would then, with luck, swim to shore and find himself behind the German lines.

This first operation was dogged by bad luck almost from start to finish. The pram-like structures on which the Neger were carried had been specially fitted with aircraft tyres for ease of movement. The third-class Italian roads along which the first prams travelled tore some tyres to pieces. To prevent further destruction the Germans employed Italian civilians to remove sharp-pointed stones which littered the road surface between the houses in which the torpedoes were stored and the departure beach. A stretch of two miles had to be cleared and the use of civilians was a breach of security, even though the Italians never saw the Neger craft.

The operation had to be postponed until the night of the 20th. The sky that night was cloudless which was an advantage to the 'Captains' who would have to navigate by the stars. To aid the attackers it was arranged that a bonfire would be lit at midnight to mark the German front line, and light Flak guns would fire tracers at 20-minute intervals in the direction of Anzio. According to reports, the target area was filled with vessels of a recently arrived convoy. Clear weather and a suffic-iency of targets gave promise of a good operation.

At 21.00 on 20 April, the 'captains' reported for the operation which was scheduled to begin at 22.00. The difficulties encountered in the launching of the Negers was evidence of how little time there had been to prepare and showed up the lack of foresight on the part of the senior officers. It had been thought that to get the craft into deep water would require the labour of more than five hundred soldiers. These were com-mandeered and detailed for duty. Fifty to a Neger, they sweated and shoved the heavy vessels through the deep clinging sand, struggling to bring the craft through the shallows and into water deep enough to float them. The sea was icy cold and many soldiers taking the easy way out, abandoned the Negers. It took more than an hour to launch only a handful of the manned torpedoes. These, formed into three battle groups, set out for Anzio and the ships reported to be lying at anchor. Left behind stranded on sandbanks were fourteen craft and in the shallow water was one Neger which was not found until the following morning. Its 'captain' was found to be dead. Contrary to orders, the soldiers manhandling the pram had tipped the Neger off the carrier into shallow water and left it. The K-man had died of asphyxiation.

The first of the three flotillas, commanded by Koch, had the farthest distance to travel. They were to carry out their attack in the bay of Nettuno. Serbicki's second group was to attack ships in the port of Anzio and Potthast's third flotilla was to fire its torpedoes in the harbour at Anzio. The course that each flotilla was to follow was due south until 02.00 and then due east, which should bring them to the target area.

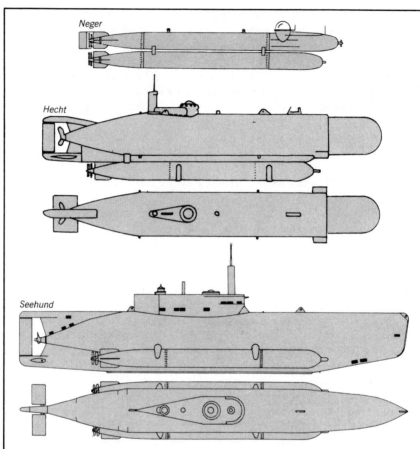

Neger

Hecht

Seehund

German midget submarines and human torpedoes

Neger
A manned torpedo fitted with a dummy warhead and having a hollowed out section of the casing forming a cockpit in which sat the single crewman. The Neger could not submerge completely, but swam just under the surface of the water. Carried below the dummy torpedo was a live torpedo which was launched by the 'Captain'. The Neger had a radius of action of about 35 nautical miles at 2½ knots; its standard cruising speed. Weight was 3 tons. An improvement upon the original design was the fitting of a plastic dome over the open cockpit to improve sea-going qualities. This dome could only be opened from the *outside*. The Neger was designed by Engineer Mohr and was approved in order to use up the vast number of torpedoes which had accumulated in naval stores.

Hecht
A boat built to the design of the U-boat construction Department as U-boat Type XXVII A. The Hecht could dive to a depth of 150 feet, had a maximum speed of 6 knots and a cruising speed of 4 knots. At that speed it had a radius of action of 60 nautical miles. The craft carried a torpedo and a mine, and had a two-man crew. The Hecht was a disappointment and the 50 craft that were constructed were all used for training.

Seehund
Another submarine type which could carry two torpedoes. Cruising speed was 5 knots, at which rate the Seehund had a radius of action of 270 nautical miles. Maximum diving depth was 150 feet. Weight 15 tons. Known as U-boat Type XXVII B, the Seehund was a development of the Hecht.

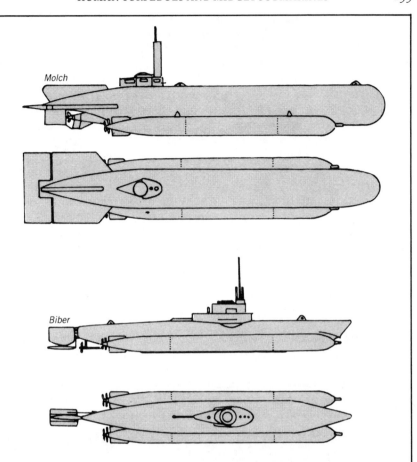

Molch

Biber

Molch
A small submarine boat crewed by one man, it could dive to a depth of 90 feet. At a cruising speed of 5 knots, it had a radius of action of 105 nautical miles. Armament was two torpedoes. Weight 10.5 tons. Although used in Italian waters and in the coastal waters of the Low Countries, the Molch was a badly designed craft.

Biber
Designed by Hans Bartels, the Biber was the lightest type of submarine, weighing only 6 tons. It could be propelled either by batteries or by a petrol engine. Using batteries alone, the radius of action at 5 knots, the usual cruising speed for electric propulsion, was 10 nautical miles. When the petrol engine was used, the speed increased to 7 knots and radius of action was 90 nautical

miles. The Biber was armed with two torpedoes and could dive to a depth of 90 feet. A total of 324 boats of this type was produced and they were used in coastal and inland waters of Holland. A two-man version was never brought into service, nor was the Biber III, which had an increased radius of action.

Linsen
The German Navy's version of the Italian explosive-filled motor boat. The Linse had a maximum speed of 31 knots, but this was only reached when the boat was sent against its target. Cruising speed was 15 knots and at that rate the craft had a range of 80 nautical miles. The weight was 1.2 tons. It has been estimated that 1,201 Linsen were built.

The feelings of the 'captains' can best be imagined. Riding low in the water, their radius of visibility limited and their direction-finding entrusted to the stars and a compass strapped to their arm, they set off. Within seconds each man was alone in the dark night, on a dark sea. Their senses were heightened by the knowledge that this was not a practice run on a German lake, but a naval operation which would allow the German Navy to strike a blow against the enemy. The men in the second and third groups, tense and expectant, waited for the shock waves that would indicate that their comrades of the first wave had unleashed their torpedoes.

The first group of Negers reached the target area well after midnight and Koch's men were astonished and depressed when they found that the bay was empty of ships; the freighters had already unloaded and sailed away. Two small warships were torpedoed and a gun mounted on the mole in Nettuno harbour was attacked and destroyed by a torpedo. For a gain of two small patrol vessels and a gun, the German Navy's secret weapon was compromised, for the Allies found one Neger afloat with its 'captain' dead from carbon dioxide poisoning. He was one of the two crew men who died that night in an endeavour to prove that the Neger was a practicable weapon.

The last words on that first K mission are included in the radio message transmitted on 21 April. It read in part: 20th April. Between 22.30 and 00.15 on 21st, Neger craft were brought to the water. Three non-starters en route to the dispatch point. Of 37 craft brought to the water 23 were started. 14 were stranded on sandbanks. Observers at Cap Cicero reported loud explosions and sheets of flames at 05.45. Followed shortly afterwards by three or four other detonations. Returned by 10.00.'

Three months later came a second opportunity for Neger to be used. This operation was against the great concentration of shipping around those beaches in Normandy upon which the Allied armies had disembarked in June. A small port southwest of Trouville was selected as the site from which the Neger would be launched and the most intensive preparations were made in the harbour so that those launching problems which had complicated the Anzio operation would be avoided. The K Flotilla War Diary of 4 July, recorded the intention to use thirty Neger of Kapitän zur See König's 361st Flotilla in an attack to be mounted on 5 July and which was to be followed some two or three nights later by a second wave of manned torpedoes. At almost the last moment a car accident caused command of König's flotilla to be passed to Koch who had led the Anzio operation.

Employment of the Neger in the waters of North-West Europe was dependant upon so many concordant factors that it is surprising the weapons ever came into active service. The tide off the Normandy coast had a current which flowed faster than the Neger's cruising speed.

ight The balcony and wooden hut in hich Tito worked while he was at rvar. Behind the hut can be seen the left in the rock through which the ugoslav leader escaped.

elow, right Another view of Tito's cave n the hillside outside Drvar. The amouflaged balcony can be seen early. The water course had dried up hortly before the attack in May 1944, nd it was up the dry bed of the stream reached from the balcony by means of rope — that the partisan leader made is escape.

Top Men of the 7th SS Mountain Division 'Prinz Eugen' w
the jeep belonging to Tito that was taken during the raid
the partisan headquarters.
Above Man-portering supplies in the hostile terrain of weste
Bosnia.
Left A 7.5cm Skoda 1918-pattern mountain gun, manned
men of the 7th SS Mountain Division artillery regiment,
action in western Bosnia during the sixth offensive mount
by the Germans against the partisans.

Above One of the three-man teams Skorzeny sent into the Ardennes battle of December 1944 was caught on the 18th; the members were shot as spies after being granted the last request of hearing German nurses, prisoners-of-war in the next cell, sing Christmas carols. This photograph shows an American Army chaplain granting absolution to Manfred Pernass before the execution. (Courtesy US Army Dept)

Below The wreckage of one of the aircraft in which Baron von der Heydte's paratroop detachment was carried into battle during the Ardennes offensive. The aircraft was shot down with the loss of the para 'stick' that it was carrying.

Above The Neger human torpedo was the German Navy's first close-combat weapon. The 'captain' in the specially-fitted top torpedo casing lined up his target using the vertical rod in front of the transparent cupola; once on target, he released the lower, 'live' torpedo, which then ran towards the objective. **Below** Admiral Heye, Commander-in-Chief of the German K forces, seen here decorating a man from the Neger units afte a mission off the coast of Normandy in 1944.

Right The caption to this photograph asserts that it is 'captain' of a Neger after his return from a mission off th Normandy beaches; he claimed that he had sunk a Britis destroyer.

Right Bartels, designer of the Biber submarine and one of the commanding officers of the K organization.
Below The method of launching a Biber — by lowering it into the water.
Bottom A Seehund submarine.

Above Linsen, explosive motor boats, seen here in a Normandy harbour before setting out to attack Allied shipping. Note the railing around the bow of each boat; this contained a small explosive charge that blew the bows off the boat, causing it to sink so that the main charge would detonate underwater with the force of a sea mine.
Below The pilot of a Linse in training prepares to leave the craft at high speed.

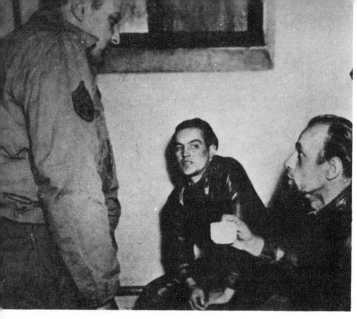

Left Two German frogmen under interrogation. These K men, part of a six-man team, had been flown from Berlin to the Rhine with orders to destroy the Remagen bridge and the new pontoon bridge that had been built alongside it. **Below** A frogman of the K units demonstrates to Admiral Doenitz and other senior officers the protective clothing and compass with which he is equipped.

Thus, all operations depended upon the craft using the tide to carry them to the target area and back again to the base from which they had been launched. Tidal conditions were favourable on only four days in each month and the wind had to be less than Force 4. Any higher reading produced a choppy sea which cancelled the operation. There was no combination of favourable conditions in June so that the first operation was not undertaken until early in July. The target was the massive fleet of Allied ships supplying the invasion armies. The nearest beach was Sword and the closest point from which an assault could be launched against Sword was Villers sur Mer, just outside Trouville. The Neger and their prams were hidden in barns and in a small wood near Trouville.

The Negers were to be launched between 23.00 and 01.00 and this would bring them into the target area between 03.00 and 05.00, to coincide with a period of slack water as the tide turned. During that short period the 'captains' would select their targets, and at about 06.00 the torpedoes would be fired. In the ensuing confusion the Negers would escape, using the tidal stream and their own power to bring them back behind German lines.

The beach at Villers was of the same fine sand as in the Italian operation, but in France there were three distinct advantages. The first was a pair of concrete ramps which led down into the water. Secondly, the high tide covering the ramps made the launching easier and thirdly, close liaison had been established between the commanders of the K unit and the men of a pioneer battalion which had been detailed to help launch the twenty-six craft. Two difficulties were encountered. The Neger could not be brought out of concealment at Trouville until darkness fell and there were only two hours in which to take advantage of the tide flowing down to the invasion beaches.

Allied air superiority prohibited the preparation of the launching ramps by daylight, but at last light teams from the pioneer battalion moved out to clear gaps through the barbed wire and the minefields laid between the Villers road and the beach. Other pioneers covered the concrete ramps with boards and while that work was proceeding trucks had already left Trouville carrying the Neger and their prams. To direct the drivers through the dark night, a chain of men stood with torches along the narrow Normandy roads to the beach. There the prams and the Neger were pushed along the concrete ramps and down into the sea until the depth of water was sufficient to float them. A proper dispatching procedure had been introduced to prevent a recurrence of the tragic accident that had marred the Anzio operation. Once afloat, the 'captains' were guided through the German sea minefields and out into the stream, *en route* to the target area. The raid was on. The night was moonlit and there were stars by which to navigate. Despite the cold the crews were sweating inside their closed hatches and visibility was affected by condensation fogging the plastic domes. The attacks took place, though not at 06.00 as ordered, but much earlier.

The German Navy's High Command announcement of the raid reported it to be highly successful and attributed to the flotilla the sinking of an *Aurora*-class cruiser, two destroyers, a 7000ton steamer and two Tank Landing Craft. In addition, a further two landing-craft, a destroyer, two steamers and a cruiser were reported to have been hit by torpedoes. These claims do not accord with the British official figures. Losses reported by the Admiralty during operations on the night of 5/6 July, do not mention a cruiser or destroyers, but do admit that a frigate and a minesweeper were lost. A post-battle report by Kapitän zur See Böhme, Chief of K Operations in France, expresses his conviction that 80 per cent of the torpedoes fired during the operation had scored a hit. His detailed chronological list, compiled after debriefing the 'captains', opens with the sinking of the cruiser at 03.05, continues for nearly two pages and concludes, '. . . at 05.40, at 05.50 and 06.00 separate detonations were heard, which were not to be confused with the explosion of depth-charges . . .' Seven Neger according to Böhme's report, returned to the place whence they had been launched.

By comparison the second operation, carried out on the night of 7/8 July, was a total disaster. Not one 'captain' returned; they were all killed, wounded or taken prisoner. Yet the operation had started well. The careful planning of the first mission had proved itself and the drive from Trouville to the launching site had run so smoothly that twenty-one Neger had been put into the sea in only fifty-six minutes. The targets selected were ships of the convoys which had sailed into the beachhead areas that day.

The actual results of this raid by 361 Flotilla cannot be positively known. Only through details obtained from sightings by army and navy units could the German Navy High Command claim some successes. One thing is clear. The Allies were expecting the second attack and had taken countermeasures. Files in the Public Record Office include reports from Admiral Ramsey in which he states that he had been aware that human torpedo units were being deployed off the landing beaches on 5 July. It follows, therefore, that on subsequent nights all ships would have kept a very sharp look-out. Such simple measure as explosives charges dropped into the sea kept the human torpedoes at a distance and continuous air sweeps over the sea caught many Neger on the surface during their journey back to Villers. It is a human, but fatal, reaction after a mission for the attacker to relax his vigilance. The Neger 'captains' in their little cockpits could not keep an all-round watch and fell victim to the swooping attacks by squadrons of Mustangs and Thunderbolts. The effect of air superiority can be appreciated from the words of Kapitän zur See Böhme who, in the first months of his time as a prisoner of war, wrote down his impressions on the conduct of the war and particularly the K Flotilla operations in both the North-Western Europe and Italian theatres of operations.

'At the mouth of the Orne river in France, I used my small one-man submarines, as a surprise weapon against Allied steamships. These submarines carried one torpedo, which they released at 300 to 400 metres from the target. In all 120,000 to 150,000 tons of Allied shipping were sunk in these operations. The largest number of these submarines I ever employed in one operation was 60.

These submarines used a plexi-glass hood instead of a periscope, and accordingly could be used only under cover of darkness, from around 11 or 12 o'clock at night until dawn. Otherwise at least twice as many Allied ships would have been sunk.

Frequently, day broke before my one-man submarines had returned and Allied fighters strafed them on the way back to the mouth of the Orne river. Of the submarines I sent out, I recovered only 10 or 15 per cent. Approximately 200 small submarines were lost through Allied strafing attacks. I have seen at one time as many as 50 to 100 fighters circling the bay like hawks hunting for these submarines. They were very persistent. Once they mistook a wreck caught in a strong current for a submarine wake, and attacked and re-attacked it for half an hour.'

One of the last of the weapons which the MEA introduced in the final year of the war was the Biber, a one-man craft. This was not a true submarine although it had the configuration of a small U-boat. Rather it was a vessel with diving capabilities, but which fired its two torpedoes from a surface position. Its inventor, Leutnant Bartels, also led the first mission undertaken by these craft on the night of 29/30 August. Eighteen Biber were launched from Fécamp in France, but only two reached the target area. Bad weather had forced the other 'captains' to abort the mission. Later, a second operation was undertaken with a flotilla built around eighteen brand-new craft – the ones in Fécamp had had to be destroyed before the Germans evacuated the town, or else had been lost in Allied air raids. The new base for the flotilla was now Rotterdam and the targets were the Allied shipping using the River Scheldt. The distance from the Biber base to the open sea was 28 miles. As with the Neger, there was in the Biber the danger of carbon dioxide poisoning. The Biber too, had a limited range. The ships left on an ebb tide to conserve fuel and energy and returned on a flow tide. Departure was always by day in order that the Biber would arrive in the target area after the onset of darkness. From December 1944 to February 1945 Biber Flotilla No. 261 operated from Rotterdam. The number of times that the ships could put to sea was limited by bad weather, but a total of one hundred and ten Biber took part in operations before the flotilla was withdrawn from active service.

The Seehund which, by January 1945, had made its appearance, was a true submarine with a crew of two. The greatest number of successes of any of the naval special units was achieved using this vessel type although its introduction into service was inauspicious. The first mission, on New Year's Eve, 1944, was a disaster and from a total of eighteen ships which put to sea only two returned. After improvements to the design and a retraining programme, a second wave of ten Seehund went out in the second week of January. Not one Allied ship was sunk during that mission, but the safe return of all the Seehund proved that although the vessels were small they were seaworthy. The continuing bad weather reduced the scale of operations, but from the first successful sortie in January 1945, to the end of the war, groups of Seehund craft were in operation and between them sank 90,000 tons of Allied shipping.

3

EXPLOSIVE MOTOR-BOATS AND FROGMEN

There were other attacks carried out by the K Flotilla using both human torpedoes and Linsen, the explosive motor-boats. Linsen were small, radio-controlled, wooden shells, seventeen feet long with a 4½-foot beam and a draught of only sixteen inches. A standard Ford V8 engine producing 90hp was the power unit. The explosive charge, weighing nearly 1,000lb, was carried aft, directly behind the 7 metre band UKW receiver through which sound or tone signals guided the Linse to its target.

The use of manned speedboats to bring an explosive charge against an enemy ship was not new, it having been found effective by the Italians during the First World War. Such craft had also been used by the Brandenburg in operations in Russia, but early in 1944 the craft were commandeered by OKM and handed over to Admiral Heye. The K-men soon found that there was a great deal of difference between piloting the fast craft in the calm conditions of the training lakes and in the stormy waters of the North Sea. A complete redesign had to be undertaken. By mid July 1944, No. 211's flotilla of thirty Linsen was ready for operations.

Tactically, a flotilla was based on a series of Rotten (sub-units) each consisting of a command vessel and two explosive boats. Four Rotten equalled a Gruppe and four Gruppen equalled a Flotilla. Thus each flotilla controlled sixteen command boats and thirty-two explosive hulls. Among the several negative features of the Linse, the principal one was that it could only be used at night so as to maintain the element of surprise. A second disadvantage was that its short range required it to be towed to a launching-point near the target area. This proved to be both difficult and wasteful and many of the boats under tow were damaged so severely that they could not be used in the attack. A crash programme of construction produced boats built to the specifications and requirements of those who would ride them. The new craft had a 95hp engine and larger fuel tanks, which increased speed and range and the new hulls had better seagoing qualities.

The tactics of Linsen operations was for each Group of the Flotilla to make its own way to the operations area. On arrival, targets would be selected individually by the skipper of the command boat. Each Rotte would move to a point some two to three miles from the target and upon a torch signal one of the two explosive boats would move ahead of the command ship, and advance, with engine throttled back, to within a few hundred yards of the target. The crewman would then open the throttle and the boat would leap forward at top speed, too fast for the victim to take evasive action.

As the Linse raced towards its target the pilot would adjust his paratroop-style helmet, flick on the switch of the radio-receiver and thus pass steering control to the command ship, and switch on an electric fuse. The K-man would then fall sideways off the racing craft into the sea. A rubber suit kept out the worst of the cold until one of the three-man crew of the command vessel picked the swimmer out of the water. The captain of the command ship controlled the vessel while the third crew member, with the radio control box between his knees, directed the Linse towards the target.

To enable the controller to follow the course of the small, black-painted, explosive vessel, a pair of lights was fitted: red in the bow, green in the stern. When the red light shone directly above the green the boat was running true. Any deviation from the correct course was corrected immediately by the radio-controller. When the Linse struck its victim the force of the impact broke a spring-loaded rail which ran round the bows. This rail contained an initial explosive charge which detonated on impact with a force sufficient to tear away the bows of the boat. The after part of the vessel containing the explosives sank immediately and exploded a few seconds later, with all the force of a sea mine. The second explosive Linse of the Rotte would already be *en route* to its target and once its pilot had been retrieved the command boat would break off the action and turn away, to disappear into the darkness of the night and the smoke-screen which it laid as it fled.

On the night of 2/3 August, K Flotilla 211 carried out a combined raid using both Neger and Linsen. It is a truism that a weapon is only effective until its counter has been found and the Allied navies had soon found counters to both these weapons. Suspecting this, the German Navy hoped to confuse the enemy by switching from one type of attack to another during the one night. A short period of combined training for the Neger and the Linsen men was sufficient to show where problems existed in co-ordinating the proposed attack and for these to be overcome.

The fifty-eight Neger were the first to leave. They were slower than the Linsen and needed time. In the target area the 'captains' were able to pick out their targets in the bright moonlight and to see the results of their torpedo action. At a debriefing on their return ten men reported that their torpedoes had failed to hit the target or had not detonated. Two other craft were caught and held in anti-torpedo nets draped around certain major units of the Allied fleet. The number of Neger missing from the operation was 41; a percentage casualty rate of 80. The few successes gained by the Neger did not compensate such severe losses of highly-trained men.

The Linsen group had gone in with a strength of thirty-two vessels, twelve of which were command ships, one of which was lost. Successes claimed included a cruiser of the *Fiji* Class and a 10,000ton steamer, two destroyers, an ammunition ship and a 3,000ton freighter. In addition, torpedoed and probably sunk, were one large transport, one medium-sized ship, a destroyer and a corvette. Few of these claims were accepted by the Royal Navy.

The bulk of Flotilla 211 went home to be fleshed out with new men, but the rear party still had strength enough to carry out another Linsen operation during the night of 8/9 August. Four command craft were lost and eight enemy ships were claimed. In this connection it is interesting to note the German statement that no Linse command ship or explosive vessel was ever lost by enemy action. All losses were attributed to bad weather or accidental collision.

During the nights of 16 and 17 August other attacks by human torpedoes took place, but it was clear from the few gains that the flotilla had shot its bolt and was becoming weaker. This time only eleven of fifty-three craft could be launched because of bad weather and on the second night from the forty-two craft which did enter the water, twenty-five were lost. The Germans were being driven out of France and there were no longer any bases from which the manned torpedoes could set out to harrass Allied shipping. The bad weather, rough seas and other conditions which prevented the employment of the Neger may have caused them to be withdrawn, physically, from the scene of operations. *Psychologically*, however, they were often thought to be present for the Germans took to casting into the sea numbers of plastic domes which looked like Neger and which caused anxiety to look-outs on Allied ships who saw the sinister little domes shining in the moonlight.

While the Neger and Linse units had been in action in Normandy, more K units were being equipped and prepared for service. Flotilla 261 received the Biber type of submarine and Flotilla 411 was outfitted with the Molch. At Honfleur a group of seven frogmen commandos from another flotilla blew up coastal guns and ammunition stores to deny these to the Americans. During the following weeks K units were sent to Italy and to southern France and from 10 September to 30 November, fourteen new flotillas were formed and posted to areas in Holland, Denmark, Norway and northern Germany, but the continuing bad weather and Allied air superiority reduced the number of operations that could be undertaken and many that were begun had to be cancelled. Although the operations at sea were reduced they did not cease altogether. In addition, several flotillas made raids against fresh-water targets.

Mention has already been made of the frogmen commandos who went into action at Honfleur. It can be said that, with the introduction of frogmen, the Navy found its perfect, all-purpose, small naval-action weapon. Although frogmen could be used with effect against ships at anchor, it was clear that the war at sea could not be influenced by such attacks. The Allies had now occupied the whole of the coastline in North-West Europe, except for a small area of northern Holland. The MEA was now forced to take its operations inland and frogmen provided the answer to the demands for action against bridges. Their units did not need to wait for calm seas as had the crews of the Neger; nor upon the radio-control of a pilot-boat as did the Linsen. Frogmen carried with them the weapons of destruction and placed them by hand and in such a position as to inflict the maximum possible damage.

The reader will already have noticed that in the naval special units a need had grown up, parallelled in the other Services, to close with the enemy in order to destroy him. The MEK men no longer fired a torpedo at medium range or directed a boat at short range but, by physically towing or pushing, brought an explosive warhead to its target. The call from OKM to raise such a specialist unit had come in January 1944, and by the eve of D-Day in Europe, thirty men had been trained.

Experience was gained through contact with the Italian frogmen of Prince Borghese's Decima MAS and it was in Italy, in the area of Venice, that the German crews trained for action. The first two groups of K frogmen were sent into action only two weeks after the Allied landings in Normandy, to attack the River Orne bridges across which passed the British Army's supplies for an offensive aimed at breaking out of the bridgehead. Both frogmen groups took with them the standard explosive head of a torpedo fitted with a timing device set to activate shortly after sun up. The approach to the Orne took fourteen hours, but the frogmen reached and destroyed their targets. This success was gained for the loss of only one man and the operation set the pattern for all future missions. The number of such raids which could be carried out was limited because there were few men who embodied the requisite physical strength, mental resolve and determination. They had to be strong swimmers and be able to withstand extreme cold. A mission might last for eight hours or more and the frogmen would be in the water for most of that time.

The K man wore a rubber suit elasticated at the wrist and ankle. Flippers on his feet gave him increased swimming power. Breathing equipment on the chest allowed him to work submerged when he reached the target area. Beneath the rubber two-piece suit the frogmen wore woollen underwear and layers of warm clothing over that. These layers of clothing gave him a certain degree of bouyancy and, if the balance of air to weight was correct, enabled him to stand in the water with the upper part of his torso exposed. When fully dressed the frogman on land moved slowly and awkwardly, sweating in his tight layers of clothing. Once in the water he was in his natural element and moved with ease and grace. He had been taught to conserve his energy by making use of tidal currents to drift him towards the target, and to swim on his back using only his flippered feet and his legs to propel or steer. To move the explosive charge required the full and unrestricted use of his arms.

To camouflage hands and face, which might show white against the dark surface of the water while the frogman was swimming on his back, a cosmetic cream was used in conjunction with a camouflage net. These aids made the swimmer invisible at even close range for on a dark night he could be mistaken for a patch of weeds drifting with the tide. Commando frogmen attacked the lock gates at Antwerp and put them out of action for weeks. Another assault was made on the river bridges at Arnhem to prevent the movement of British Second Army's supplies for the forthcoming offensive into the North German Plain. The raid was successful and for a loss of ten of the twelve frogmen the great railway bridge was destroyed and the road bridge severely damaged. The principle had proved itself that success comes to small groups of determined men set against accessible targets, and frogmen were used against the Oder bridges as well as against other targets on both the Eastern and Western fronts.

The sinister hand of the SD played very little part in the operations of the Navy's special forces. Despite attempts by the SS commanders to bring Heye's men under Skorzeny's direct control, the Admiral insisted that all operations connected with the sea or with naval landings must be *his* responsibility. He was permitted to retain his standpoint – in principle – for Skorzeny would not allow himself to be totally excluded. He had managed to insinuate some of his men into the first Neger operations off the Normandy coast and others had collaborated in the raid against the Arnhem bridges. The frogmen put in against the River Oder bridges in the first months of 1945, were nearly all SS men, but the Linsen attack against the Oder bridges was a purely K operation.

It will not have escaped the reader's attention that the principal targets of the Navy's special units were the Western Allies. This is understandable for the German Navy had little opportunity to operate against the Soviet Union. One planned operation against the port of Murmansk in January 1945 had to be aborted. Six Biber were carried on the open decks of conventional U-boats to a point off northern Norway from which the attack was to begin. Checks carried out before launching showed that four of the vessels had been so badly damaged during the voyage as to be unserviceable. The raid could not succeed and did not, therefore, take place.

Other K groups carried out operations of a minor nature on the Eastern Front, using either Linsen or going in as frogmen, but their raids had only limited results and it can be claimed that the MEA was formed and trained to operate against the American and British Navies. They, with their numerical and technical superiority, destroyed the German Navy's special forces.

For all their undoubted bravery the gains made by the K men were few and minimal in effect and their losses were severe. Although not measured in thousands or in tens of thousands, but rather in twenties or thirties at a time, it should be remembered that those who were lost were brave, highly skilled and very professional warriors, and that the loss of each one represented the loss of a potential leader. The moral fibre which enables a man, completely alone, to persist in some daring action against incredible odds of weather, the sea and an overwhelmingly superior enemy, is not too common a characteristic in even very brave men. But it was found in the bravest of the brave whose story has been told in this chapter; it was to be found in abundance among the K-men of the German Navy of the Second World War.

PART THREE

LUFTWAFFE SPECIAL FORCES

1

DEFENDING THE SKIES OF THE REICH

Air operations conducted during the Second World War demonstrated that the commanders of the Anglo-American Air Forces and those who led the Luftwaffe differed fundamentally in their interpretation of the role of the bomber. The German leaders considered it as a tactical weapon to be used in support of ground operations, while those who led the RAF and the USAAF considered the bomber Force as a strategic weapon, the purpose of which was to destroy the enemy's morale and his economy.

In their application of that policy the Anglo-Americans were guided by the principles of such pioneers of strategic bombing as Trenchard of the RAF, the American General William Mitchell and the Italian, Douhet. On the German side only Wever, Chief of the Luftwaffe General Staff, and a very few other officers considered the bomber Force in such a role and were greatly outnumbered by those in the Luftwaffe who thought of the bomber as little more than an extension of the artillery Arm. When Wever was killed in an air crash in 1936, his strategic vision and the long-range aircraft which would have entered service in support of his idea were abandoned, and it was the viewpoint of the tacticians which prevailed and their policy of concentrating on short-range aircraft that was adopted by the German Air Force.

It would be an over-simplification to suggest that it was the conflict of strategy versus tactics which alone determined the Luftwaffe's shape; political and economic considerations also played their parts. Hitler's demand for an air force large enough in numbers to be used to intimidate those who resisted his political blackmail was acknowledged in Goering's statement that, 'The Führer does not ask how big the bombers are, but how many do we have.' Hitler's insistence upon quantity as opposed to potency was justified by the economic equation that the same amount of material used to build two long-range, four-engined bombers could have produced five short-range, twin-engined machines. Therefore, in the years immediately preceding the Second World War; given the Führer's demand for numbers, Germany's shortage of strategic materials and the Army's concept of warfare consisting of short campaigns fought across Continental Europe, a Luftwaffe was created whose standard bombers were fast aircraft designed to carry only a small bomb-load and that over short distances.

The campaigns of the first years of the war had indeed been Blitzkrieg-type operations and the victories gained would have seemed to prove correct those who believed in a tactical bomber Force supporting the Army's ground operations. Confident, arrogant, in its capabilities, the Luftwaffe did not develop greatly its bomber Force. The Royal Air Force did, and by 1942 Bomber Command had grown in numbers, had improved both its skill and its tactics and had been equipped with aircraft capable of carrying a great bomb-load to almost any city in Greater Germany. Goering had been able to dismiss the early raids of Bomber Command as pinpricks, but by the end of 1942, these had become hammer-blows and were a forecast of the wrath to come.

When the American Air Force joined the strategic bombing offensive in January 1943, there began for the German cities and people a Calvary of suffering. The RAF came by night and the USAAF by day. Against this round-the-clock assault the bomber Force of the Luftwaffe could do little in the way of retaliation or retribution. American cities were too far distant for the Luftwaffe to reach and those raids which the Luftwaffe carried out upon targets in the United Kingdom caused them losses which were out of proportion to the destruction caused. Not only in the West but also in the East, the lack of long-range bombers in the German service could be seen to be a terrible defect. The Russians had removed factories, powerplants and steel-producing complexes into areas east of the Urals where, far beyond the range of German aircraft, workshops were able to pour out weapons and equipment for the Soviet forces. The German bomber Force was impotent to act against its enemies with the weapons at its disposal and in an effort to strike back produced a succession of short-term improvisations which were intended either to enlarge the radius of action of standard bombers or to increase the destructive power of the bombs carried.

This criticism of the Luftwaffe High Command should not lead one to think that Germany had no long-range aircraft on establishment. She had some, but they were too few to form a strategic Command and were used principally and in small numbers on extensive reconnaissance duties or on patrol missions over the Atlantic.

The Luftwaffe fighter Force, too, faced difficulties among which was Hitler's insistence that in all circumstances the Air Force must be an offensive weapon. He would not accept that Germany must go on the defensive in the air as she had been forced to do both on land and at sea. To his mind, fighter aircraft had a defensive role and did not, therefore, accord with his demand for attack. But bombers did fit that demand and as a consequence factories continued to make standard, short-range machines, when the emphasis should have been on producing fighters to attack the Allied bomber fleets.

The Luftwaffe had begun the war with first-class fighters which had been improved in performance during the years of combat. It should be mentioned that most of the Luftwaffe commanders had been fighter pilots during the Great War and that this Arm was of particular interest to them. They had enthusiastically supported the development of jet propulsion and their support ensured that the Luftwaffe was the first air force in the world to have such aircraft in operational use. Neither did the Service lack sufficient pilots or aircraft. What was wrong was that fighter aircraft defending the Reich were wrongly employed and often incorrectly deployed. In addition, Allied interdiction of the railway system brought about a chaos which resulted in an uneven flow of components from factories which had been dispersed to avoid destruction by aerial bombardment. For example, transit delays might produce a glut of fuselages coinciding with a chronic shortage of wings or engines and, to compound the effects of this confusion, Allied command of the skies above Germany made it harder, and at times almost impossible, to bring together the individual aircraft parts for final assembly.

Although Luftwaffe training schools produced a steady stream of capable young pilots, these men seldom were able to improve upon their basic training. A growing shortage of aviation fuel reduced to an absolute minimum the essential landing and take-off drills, nor were they able to sharpen their reactions or to burnish their fledgling abilities by simulated air combat. Pilots often had little more than a dozen flights before they were sent up against the Allied squadrons.

The Luftwaffe's two main Arms, bombers and fighters, were confronted with problems to which there seemed no solutions. It was the task of the fighter Arm to destroy the Allied aircraft whose raids were destroying the cities of Germany. The bombers had to increase flight range and the power of the bombs which they carried in order to make good the defects from which the Force suffered. Adolf Hitler still looked to the bomber Arm to carry the war to the enemy. The German Air Force had begun the war well, but once it was faced with enemies possessing greater power, higher technical output and better equipment, there began a deterioration which started in 1943 and which continued until the total defeat of 1945.

In 1943 the Luftwaffe had been fighting for nearly two years on two battle fronts: in the East against the Soviets, and in the Homeland against the Allied bombers. Luftwaffe commanders evaluating battle reports and Intelligence appreciations from the Eastern Front concluded that the Red Air Force could be held in check. The skill in combat of the German pilots balanced the manifold superiority in the aircraft which the Soviets could put into battle. The situation in the East would remain stable for as long as a sufficiency of German fighters and pilots reached the Russian front.

The aerial defence of the Reich however, was a problem to which there seemed to be no answer and it was the efforts made to overcome that inferiority which produced some of the special forces that will be described in this chapter.

When considering the bombing offensive mounted by Germany's Anglo-American enemies, the Luftwaffe's commanders faced two distinctly different problems. The British came by night, precision bombing strategic targets all over Europe. By day, armadas of American bombers dropped their bomb-loads simultaneously and created a single carpet of destruction in which one crater overlapped another. The combating of the two enemy forces required a different approach for each. The British flew in a loose stream, each machine acting independently until the target area was reached. Ahead of the bomber stream flew special Pathfinder aircraft which directed the approaching bombers on to targets marked by flares. The bomber stream used these as aiming-marks, bombing on the slowly descending coloured lights. It was not necessary for bomb-aimers in British aircraft to see the target, except when very high precision was required. Bad visibility did not affect greatly the accuracy of RAF bombing, for each machine was fitted with a radar set which saw the target even through the thickest cloud. The aircraft stream could therefore, hide in the clouds and bomb 'blind'. It was the difficult task of the German night-fighter pilots to locate the British bombers racing through the night and taking advantage of every piece of cloud cover.

The British raids showed up a fundamental flaw in the German defensive system. The night-fighters had no reliable electronic device which would enable them to find and intercept the intruders. Until they were equipped with an efficient machine they could not destroy the RAF aircraft in numbers large enough to make the bombing campaign uneconomic in terms of men and aircraft lost. German night-fighters relied upon visual contact and the sky was a large space in which to find a blacked-out bomber. Even though German ground control of the night fighter Force was very efficient in directing the pilots towards the general area of the bomber stream, even the finest of the Luftwaffe night-fighter pilots spent many nights without making contact with a single RAF bomber.

As the war progressed the British air assault grew in strength as increasing numbers of four-engined bombers, capable of high speeds and of carrying a heavy bomb-load over great distances came into service. So great was the growth of Bomber Command that on 25 July 1943, it was able to launch seven hundred and ninety-one aircraft against Hamburg in a raid which devastated the city. Bomber Command had gained a spectacular victory for a loss rate of only 1.5 per cent of aircraft committed. The lavish use of short strips of metal foil known as 'Window' were in part responsible. These strips fluttering through the air produced distorted images on the poor-quality radar sets with which the German night-fighters were equipped.

To combat the US Air Force, which flew from airfields in the United Kingdom, required a different set of tactics. The American enemy could be seen. Indeed it would have been hard to avoid seeing him for the USAAF flew in huge formations; row upon row, line after line, layer upon layer building up into a single 'box' of shining, silver bombers. The principal bombing aircraft of the American Air Force were the Liberator and the B17, well named the Flying Fortress, for each plane was defended by thirteen, heavy-calibre machine-guns. A 'box' of three hundred bombers bristled with three thousand and nine hundred machine-guns forming interlocking defensive zones; a daunting prospect to the Luftwaffe pilots who went in to attack the compact armadas. The Americans strove to fly in tight formation. The Germans sought to disperse it for, once the 'box' had been split up the individual bombers were very vulnerable.

These, then, were the two problems facing the Luftwaffe which had to be resolved. The commanders conceded that the night bomber would always get through if for no other reason than that the British lead in electronics gave the bombers the advantage over the night-fighter. It was a bitter fact, but one which had to be accepted. The attention of the Luftwaffe thereupon swung to the task of defeating the Americans.

Conferences called to deal with the problem produced the same conclusions: either the American machines had to be blasted out of the sky by a major explosion, or pilots had to deliberately sacrifice themselves by ramming the bombers. Hitler, to whom was put the idea of heroic sacrifice by ramming, rejected it out of hand; suicide was unacceptable, but he was prepared to sanction any tactic in which the pilot had a chance of escaping alive. The Führer's qualification was used as an escape clause by those who were organising the special units, each claiming that the pilots did stand a chance. It was proposed, among other ideas, that specially-constructed, simply-built, light aircraft would be flown into the bomber 'box' and there detonated. Developing from this idea of a flying-bomb, was the proposal to tow a glider to a point above the enemy formation from which the pilot would bring it down in a dive, attacking the bombers with machine-guns before ramming his machine against an enemy aircraft.

Reichsminister Speer, the Head of the German Armaments programme, set out in cold and objective statistics the targets which had to be attained if ramming attacks were to be a success. He calculated that since the Americans had an overwhelming superiority in manpower, a one to one result would represent a defeat for the Germans. The ratio of US aircraft which had to be downed for the loss of a single German plane and its pilot was at least three. For a German fighter/rammer to destroy three bombers gave parity. Anything above three was a profit.

By the time that the conferences had drawn their conclusions, the military and political situation of the Third Reich had become critical.

The running sore of the Eastern Front had so worn down the Army that it was no longer able to mount a summer offensive. Instead it was forced to accept the blows of a Red Army whose winter offensive had rolled and rolled and shown no signs of ending. The German Army was withdrawing from the East and those other nations of Europe which had entered into the war against Russia were now seeking to come to terms with the new super Power in Europe, the Soviet Union.

In the West the invasion could not now be long delayed and a successful assault would give to the Western Allies airfields on the Continent from which their fighters could more easily fly escort to the American bombers. They would no longer have to carry drop-tanks to give them the range. From airfields in France the fighters would be able to escort the bombers all the way to the target and back. When that came to pass, German fighter-pilots, already facing overwhelming odds in their attacks upon the bomber 'boxes', would have to fight their way through swarms of US fighters and then go on to face the massed machine-guns of the Flying Fortresses. It was a fearful prospect.

2

FALCONS AND FLEDGLINGS

In the consciousness of senior Luftwaffe officers the idea was growing that ramming was the obvious tactic to destroy the US bombers. It was clear that attack by fighters against the massed machine-gun fire of an American 'box' was nothing short of suicide and if the chances of survival were small, as indeed they were, why not take the last little step and ram the enemy. To ram and to survive was possible. A Luftwaffe officer, Walther Dahl, had perfected a technique and from his ideas evolved 'Storm' detachments formed from existing Fighter Wings. The tactic which these Detachments were to employ was for them to attack in a wedge formation, engaging the enemy with 'on board' weapons at close quarters and if the American bombers did not fall to machine-gun fire they would be rammed.

It was stressed that the only targets for the Storm units would be the heavy bombers. Under no circumstances would combat be accepted from the US fighters which formed the protective screen; they would be taken out by other Luftwaffe detachments. There were early successes for the new German techniques and during one raid the Americans lost forty-nine aircraft. Made bold by such success, plans were laid for other Storm groups to be formed in the Jagdgeschwader of Luftflotte Reich, the Air Fleet charged with defence of the Fatherland. But new tactics produce a counter and once the initial surprise of the new assault methods had been overcome, the Americans produced theirs. The size of the fighter escort was increased, it was made more flexible and there was a tightening of control at Squadron level. The Storm detachments lost the initiative and as a consequence were shot from the skies by US pilots who found them easy meat.

Concurrently with the development of the Storm technique there had grown up among the Luftwaffe's fighter Aces the idea of a 'big bang'. To produce this required the building-up of a strong reserve of perhaps a thousand aircraft and pilots. That force would be unleashed in a mass attack on an American 'box', aiming to destroy every plane in the US air fleet. Such a massive blow would, it was confidently predicted, frighten the American crews and disturb the US High Command. It was a plan that was accepted by Hitler to whom the idea of a single, annihilating blow appealed. Pilots and aircraft were assembled, but all the careful planning and conservation came to naught when the Allies landed in

Normandy. Operation 'Overlord' caught the German Air Force in the process of re-deploying its squadrons in France and as a result it was unable to give fighter protection to the ground troops. In a desperate endeavour to provide air cover, pilots and aircraft were taken from every Luftwaffe Command and thrown piecemeal into the fight where, outnumbered and inferior in training to their enemies, they were destroyed.

The idea of the 'big bang' did not die. With the redeployment of the squadrons completed, the Luftwaffe began again to collect pilots and machines for the mighty blow. By November 1944 a force of seven hundred aircraft and pilots were ready. All that was needed was, first, the target and, secondly, the order that would unleash this mass against the enemy. The bad weather of that autumn and winter of 1944, reduced the scale of operations mounted by the Allies and as a result of this respite and the careful husbandry of resources, the Luftwaffe commanders came within sight of their target of a thousand fighters for 'big bang'. By 18 November the tactics of the assault had been worked out. Seven Jagdgeschwader would attack the fighter screen and either draw it off or destroy it. In the resulting mêlée eleven other Jagdgeschwader would strike at the bombers and destroy them.

At this juncture came a change of objective. Hitler had decided on a ground attack in the Ardennes to take place in December and as part of that offensive ordered a massive air strike against Allied air bases in Belgium, Holland and eastern France. Most of the carefully hoarded fighters would be thrown into Operation 'Bodenplatte'. The attack went in on the early morning of 1 January 1945, with waves of MEs and FWs roaring in at roof-top height and catching unawares personnel and aircraft on American and British airfields. Allied losses were heavy, but two hundred and fourteen of the 'big bang' force were lost including fifty-nine experienced officers whose knowledge and expertise would have been invaluable during the coming months of trial and tribulation.

Reichsminister Speer, determined to co-ordinate the German economic war machine, demanded that the Luftwaffe obtain a breathing-space for industry. The US bombers must not get through. They must be held until factories were operating again; until the new weapons, already designed, could be produced. If that could be achieved, Germany might force a stalemate.

It was left to Goering to find a method of gaining this breathing-space. It was clear that the Luftwaffe's remaining strength would have to be restructured to meet the unequal battles and the proposal was accepted that a special force be formed. This would be made up of jet aircraft flown by the most experienced fighter-pilots of the Luftwaffe. This squadron of Aces was approved by Hitler and on 24 February 1945,

Jagdverband 44 was formally raised. Command of this élite special force was invested in Galland, the former Officer Commanding Fighters, in the rank of General. It was a measure of the desperation of those days that it was believed that a single squadron might win time against the Allied superiority.

The fifteen men who formed the squadron were equipped with the ME 262, a twin-engined monoplane whose jet engines gave it a top speed of 540mph at 20,000 feet. It was obvious that the machine should be a fighter, but Hitler, with his insistence upon the need of a fast bomber, ordered that the 262s be fitted with bomb-racks; an alteration which reduced the speed of the machine and brought it down to the combat level of Allied piston-engined fighters. The advantages of speed and surprise were lost. The squadron was raised in February; the ground crews and pilots had assembled by the first week of March and within a few weeks of that date, JV 44, was operational, ready to engage the Allied bombers.

The experienced German pilots quickly spotted the flaw in the deployment of the US fighter screen, the aircraft of which flew ahead of the slower bombers to intercept and beat off fighter attacks. The solution was simple. The ME pilots held back and let the American fighters roar on towards the target. Then the Aces went in against the now unprotected bombers. For these battles, fought out at speeds in excess of 500mph, the jets needed armament that would destroy a large bomber. It had to be accurate and able to produce a wide spread of shot. The aircraft were fitted with 5cm rockets, twelve under each wing. With such power the MEs could stand off from their targets at distances up to half a mile. A 262 pilot, who was himself out of range of American machine-gun fire, could launch a salvo of rockets at the aircraft 'boxes' and observe that they had the effect of a shot-gun blast upon a flock of pigeons.

One of the first missions flown by Galland's Aces against US bombers heading for targets in Westphalia, showed the capabilities of a first-class fighter flown by an experienced airman. The 262s attacked in the open Kette formation – a shallow arrowhead of three machines, with the other jets of the Jagdverband echeloned above and behind them. The Americans in their Fortresses watched in dismay as the German fighters swept down, literally 'bounced' their jets and then hurtled them through the sky until they were astern of the bomber formation. The first three MEs levelled out and while they were still a great distance away fired their rockets. The trails of fire streaking towards the B17s unnerved some of the pilots whose aircraft were positioned at the back edge of the 'box' and they tried to take evasive action. They were too late. The projectiles were already among them bursting into the shining steel sides of the Fortresses.

The first Kette of jets did not follow the rockets, but climbed steeply up through the bomber 'box', so fast that the US gunners had no time to aim and fire at them. Yet within those few seconds another Kette had already attacked, had roared away and had been replaced by a third wave. Their rockets launched, the German pilots then attacked the American aircraft with cannon which poured out 96lb of shells in three seconds, giving the fighters a strong back-up weapon. Within minutes nearly thirty of the US aircraft had been destroyed, but not all of them by German fighter action. Some, whose pilots had tried to evade the rockets, had collided with others in the formation and had gone down, locked, falling and turning in the bright spring air. The speed, the fury of the Messerschmitt attack had overwhelmed the Americans who abandoned the mission, each aircraft releasing its bomb-load before swinging back towards the safety of the Home airfield.

Successful tactics were not all on the German side. Allied Intelligence officers were aware of the terrible weakness from which jet fighters suffered. They were potential fireballs because of the great load of highly inflammable liquid which they carried. The 262 also had a structural defect. The front wheel of its tricycle undercarriage was weak and would collapse under strain. The jet needed a very smooth runway for take-off. If the surface were rough there was the possibility that the front wheel would give way and if that happened a single spark from the mass of metal which was the jet screeching on its belly along the runway, would ignite the fuel erupting from punctured tanks. Incineration was the fate of many of the Luftwaffe's jet pilots.

The Allied tactic therefore, was to bomb German airfields regularly and often. The mass raid by a force of nearly one thousand American aircraft upon Riem turned the airfield there into a lunar landscape. Squads of German workers laboured flat out to restore the runways to their smooth state, but as fast as they levelled and smoothed one landing strip, the bombers came back to undo all their work. The Allied intention was to prevent the German machines from using the fields. Some foolhardy and skilful pilots of JV 44, did manage to fly off, bouncing and roaring along the landing strips, but each second of the take-off posed the fearful prospect of being burned alive. To combat these daring German pilots, the Americans evolved a new tactic based on the fact that for the first seconds of flight an aircraft is vulnerable and most easily overcome. The Americans introduced the cab-rank system pioneered by the British in Normandy, whereby US fighters patrolled the skies over Riem airfield and attacked any aircraft trying to take off.

SONDERKOMMANDO ELBE

The squadron of Aces was not the last attempt to combat the US 'boxes'. Bowing to Speer's demand for more time, the Luftwaffe commanders returned to the familiar problem. Among the items on the agenda during a meeting in March was again that of a squadron which would ram the enemy. This would not be another Storm unit, but a more ruthless variant. In Storm detachments to ram an enemy had been the last resource. Now it was to be the only resource. Recruits from every Luftwaffe unit volunteered eagerly for the ram squadrons. The last months in the life of the Third Reich produced the bitter paradox that there were men who did their duty to their Fatherland; willingly accepting death for Germany's sake, while senior Party members were striving to escape from the ruins of their dying country, to cover by deception the evidence of the crimes they had committed and to take up employment in countries where their gallows talents would be made welcome.

The term 'Werewolf' was suddenly common. The politico-military understanding of the expression will be explained in the next chapter. Its use on Luftwaffe tongues referred to the grouping of all the ram units into a single, administrative formation under the code-name 'Werewolf'. Because of possible confusion this title was dropped and the unit was designated Sonderkommando Elbe (Special Force Elbe). It is not for me to question the morality of ram units, but to record the operation which they flew. It is certain, however, that many hundreds of men came forward of whom only a few hundred were accepted and trained. It cannot be believed that they were all Nazi fanatics, dedicated to the concepts of Aryanism and influenced by belief in Nordic deities. There must have been in those groups serious-minded men who saw in their self-sacrificing action a chance to bring down at least one bomber before it dropped its bombs on another German city.

The volunteers for the ramming squadrons were assembled on the airfield at Stendal, to the west of Berlin, and there the pilots were given instructions in ramming techniques. Those of them who had attacked and had survived with the Storm detachments, described their techniques to the others. Films were shown of American aircraft that had been shot down over Germany and restored to flying condition. These captured Boeings were flown by men of KG 200, who demonstrated the capabilities of Flying Fortresses, Liberators and other booty aircraft, and their defects.

There were demonstrations on aircraft models, and lectures given by Party officials to strengthen resolve played a part in the political education of the young men. Talks were given by men from the Eastern Front who told of the brutal experiences of German women and children in areas overrun by the Red Army. Others described the destruction caused to German cities by the Anglo-American bombers and built up in their listeners feelings of revenge and hatred. It was not all work. There were skiing trips, good food, excellent billets and the warmth of knowing that the sacrifice would not be in vain.

The period of training, education and rest did not last long. On 5 April 1945, Luftwaffe High Command issued operational orders to 9th Flieger Korps. Operation Werewolf – OKL was perhaps still unaware that the name had been changed – was to be launched. To the Quarter-master General orders were sent to prepare one hundred and eighty ME 109s for the operation and listed the airfields to which the aircraft were to be ferried. From 9th Flieger Korps the orders went out to its subordinate units, naming the fighter groups that would protect the swarms of MEs as they rushed upon their victims. Two Jagdgruppen, Nos. 7 and 54, both jet units, would escort the rams. The finer details of the operational planning: take-off times and rendezvous, were dependant on the enemy, but the higher speeds of the ME 262s meant that the jets would leave at least thirty minutes after the standard aircraft had taken off. Once the German ground controllers had determined, from radio intercepts and by experience, which targets would be attacked by the US bombers, the final details could be issued: which 'box' of American aircraft was to be taken out; where and at what height the Sonderkommando aircraft would strike home and how much fuel each would need for the one-way flight. Fuel was very very scarce and just the bare amount would be put into the tanks of the 109s.

Early in the morning of 6 April, the aircraft had been flown in, parked and camouflaged. This work had to be carried out quickly to avoid the strafing and bombing by the Allied fighter bombers which, now on a roving commission, attacked any target that showed signs of activity.

Reveille also was early for the ramming volunteers. First parade brought them the news. They would be leaving Stendal that afternoon and heading for the airfields from which the mission would be flown. Now the time had come and most were grateful that the waiting was over. By late evening all the volunteers were at their new stations from which they would fly out to almost certain death. Their reception by the host ground crews and flying personnel alike was cool. Strangers, at this stage of the war, might mean that the old campaigners were going to lose their machines to these young men. Flyers' keen eyes noted that few of the newcomers had any medals or decorations. They were very new, this lot. Neither side talked much; the volunteers because they had been ordered not to speak of their mission, and the old squadron members because they still did not know who these strangers were or what their business was. In the hangars the ground crews worked on the recently delivered machines, under orders that each ME had to be operational on the following morning. It was to be a one hundred per cent effort. Darkness brought to an end the fears that an American bombing raid might destroy the planes on the ground. The RAF would probably put in its main effort against Berlin that night. The ramming pilots and their hosts, the Squadron in residence, could sleep without fear of air raids. The crews settled down in the darkness of the April night. Over Stendal was a fine starry sky. Tomorrow, 7 April, would be a nice day.

It dawned bright and clear. It would be warm and sunny this day when for the first time German fighter pilots would use massed ramming techniques against the American daylight bombers.

The atmosphere in the Luftwaffe messes can well be imagined. Hours before an operation there is a certain lightness of spirit; a relief from the pressures of doubt and uncertainty. The knowledge that it is only hours to the operation; that one has in a psychological sense crossed the Rubicon, makes for a seeming light-heartedness. That the condemned man ate a hearty breakfast is a cliché, but a true one. On the morning of an 'op' the food was better then usual and the portions were larger. The appetite seemed somehow larger too. Between the end of breakfast and briefing, the youthful gaiety went and was replaced by a sense of foreboding. A realisation of the dangers that the day would bring was already sinking in and it influenced everyone on the Station; even those who would not be going out that day.

The 7th was a glorious morning and on such a day with a high, bright and cloudless sky, it was certain that the fleets of the 8th US Air Force would be in the air, *en route* to bomb targets in the rapidly shrinking area of Germany as yet unoccupied by Allied troops. The question nagged at each of the German pilots – when would the Amis come?

In England, adverse weather had already postponed take-off, but at 10.20, in conditions which were poor but forecast to improve, the four-engined bombers of 1st, 2nd and 3rd Air Divisions of the 8th Air Force began to take off from airfields strung out across East Anglia. The first hours were spent in forming up; an arduous process when aircraft from scores of bases had to meet and settle into a pre-ordered formation. The confusion can be imagined when a thousand bombers, some early, some late, are sorting themselves out in a very restricted air space.

The great concentration of Flak in occupied western Europe, once the first hurdle in any mission, were silent now, and the crews could relax and consider the targets for today: the remaining airfields in northern and central Germany. In the opinion of many of them this was not really an essential operation. The air war was over. For weeks there had been little enemy opposition; the bombers cruising over Germany at will, without sight of a German fighter. The Luftwaffe, it was confidently thought, was dead; destroyed by the Allied fighters, now based in France and the Low Countries, that would give complete protection to the bombers on their outward and homeward journeys. Today should be an easy mission.

It was a few minutes after 10.30 when the giant, silver bombers of the three US Air Divisions had assembled over the North Sea. At that time the pilots of the ramming squadrons, at a dozen airfields in Germany, received the pre-op warning, 'Thirty minutes to readiness.' The first obscene and frightening thought, 'Oh God have I less than an hour to live?' is blocked out as the essential checks of oxygen mask and parachute are made. 'Parade for briefing,' and the pilots, hardly looking at one another, enter the underground room where maps cover the bare concrete walls.

The briefing is short. Now the veterans realise that these youngsters have been called on to give everything for Germany. The young men look at their hosts and note with awe the medals. These jet men who will take on the Yankee fighters are all highly-decorated Aces. There is a mutual feeling of respect.

The Tannoy blares again, 'Pilots to machines.' German radar has made contact with the US bomber fleet. In the cockpits of their single-seaters the ram pilots observe the departure of the planes that will protect the airfield during take-off. The defence patrol is airborne now. No sound comes through the earphones, the sky above must be clear. Slowly the minutes pass. A drowsiness overtakes the pilots and they loll on that threshold between sleep and wakefulness. 'Achtung! Achtung!.' They are immediately alert. 'Take off. Rendezvous at 30,000 feet above Magdeburg.' Immediately all senses are in overdrive. Sight is clearer, hearing sharper, sense of smell so acute that the blended stinks of the cockpit are suffocating. It is the normal reaction of the hunter.

The old-fashioned fighters roll out and down to the starting position. It is encouraging to know that at other airfields all over Germany the scene is the same. The words of the briefing officer are recalled: 'Today two hundred of you will be attacking the Amis.' There will be two hundred comrades in the air, shoulder to shoulder, a glorious feeling of solidarity.

At Stendal, where the paras had trained in the early days of easy victories, the take-off is like a ceremonial parade. As the first machines reach the starting position, a Luftwaffe band, an Escort to the Colour and the Standards of the Luftwaffe unit and of the Reich are marched on to the grass of the airfield. Round the perimeter the fitters, the mechanics and off-duty men gather to watch the 'Geier' and the 'Falken' as they go out to battle and to die. The eyes of the pilots are fixed on the flag in the hands of the starting-officer. He raises it. One last look round takes in the beautiful countryside, the airfield itself and the Guard of Honour, rigid now at the Present Arms. The band is playing lustily, the Standards unfurl and then the starting officer's arm drops. Operation 'Werewolf' has begun; the squadron is airborne.

Once in the air, the ram fighters close into a tight formation, twenty yards or so separating the machines. There is again the feeling of community, of a brotherhood. There is noise in the earphones: military music, the music of the old Germany and of the new National Socialist Germany. The marches and the singing are an inspiration. All Germany is behind us in this struggle.

Over Magdeburg the squadrons form, waggling their wings in recognition and greeting. Cutting through the marches comes the Controller's voice; the mass of fighters moves on an interception course towards the American 'boxes' flying serenely and quietly through the thin, cold air. As the MEs and FWs turn they see on their right, high and clear, the vapour trails of the jets which will attack the US escort fighters and leave the 'boxes' unprotected. The Controller's voice announces that the enemy is flying at between 15,000 and 21,000 feet. The first wave of ramming fighters forms up. A voice comes through the earphones; not that of the Controller, but of a woman demanding revenge. A voice that moves the pilots to fury as they listen to the impassioned words shouted in that high, piercing, demanding voice; demanding that those who have been killed by the Allied bombers should be revenged; screaming the slogans of the old days before Hitler came to power twelve years before. Most of the pilots were children in the days of the struggle to power, but the slogans inspire a grimmer determination to win, or die.

It is just past noon when, in the distance, shining like a castle, the pilots see the huge boxes of the USAAF's 452nd and 388th Bomber Groups. It has taken them too long to assemble over the North Sea, and the three Air Divisions are scattered. The German fighters will not be met by the concentrated power of thousands of machine-guns. The ram fighter commander, aware of the relative weakness of his force, uses guile and experience to compensate for the disadvantages of having to fight with old slow aircraft in the hands of inexperienced crews. His formation swings in a wide curve miles out of gunshot range, climbs as a group above and behind the bombers and hides in the vapour trails which spread long and wide in the sky. There are thinner trails on the port side – moving fast. It is the jets, the MEs, and they stream almost like lightning through the American 'box'. Vapour trails below and to the right show that the American fighters have taken the bait. The bombers are undefended.

Suddenly it is time. The old-fashioned, piston-engined ram fighters close on the bombers. So far they are undetected. Such immunity cannot last long. Instinctively each pilot chooses his target. The Controller on the ground knows that his crews are ready. It is a matter of seconds now. A last command comes through the earphones, 'Attack! Attack! Sieg Heil!.' A quick look round. No Yankee fighters in sight; the ME jets have drawn them off. The comrades to the right and left are flying close and steady. There below are the huge bombers. Streams of cannon shell, the tracer almost invisible in the bright noon light, flick past. The leading ram dives suddenly. The Squadron dips and attacks. Battle is joined.

During an air battle concentration is so total that the conscious mind cannot reflect upon the dangers that lie ahead. Instinct takes over and the world is suddenly compressed to a few miles of sky and the aircraft in it. Reports from both sides contain almost identical phrases: 'The sky was a whirling mass of aircraft.' 'There were plumes of smoke in the sky as burning bombers spiralled to earth.' 'An ME tore into the upper gunner position of one Fortress and skidded from that Fort into another. All three machines went down.'

In the skies above northern and central Germany on that sunny April day, nearly two thousand aircraft were engaged. The Americans were astounded that the Luftwaffe could still put up so strong a force against them. True, their Intelligence officers had warned against over-confidence, against slackness. Now they knew why the most recent missions had been so trouble-free. The Luftwaffe had been saving its men and machines for this final effort.

Within minutes of the first echelon of ram fighters diving to attack, there was neither sight nor sound of the intense air battle which had just ended. Far away on the ground dark clouds of oily smoke rose from wrecks which littered the countryside. The rammers had done their work. One hundred and eighty-four had attacked; now they were gone. Most of them had fallen in combat; others had failed to find a target and had moved westwards to attack a second great box of American aircraft from 2nd Division, which was flying south-east of Bremen. The 262s had gone screaming back to their Home bases, arriving only minutes before the bombers whose destruction they had intended dropped their bomb-loads upon the airfields. As the American bombers began to land in England, on the German fields, the first priority after dealing with the dead and wounded was to level the runways so that tomorrow's missions could be flown. Tomorrow there would be another Yankee raid. Tomorrow there would be fresh casualties, but not to the surviving ram pilots. Their secret was out and the survivors were sent southwards to airfields in and around Klagenfurt in southern Austria. In the minds of some German commanders, the Alpine Redoubt existed and it was for future ramming missions in the skies above the Redoubt that the ram pilots were gathered. They waited out the war's end in that beautiful part of Austria.

It is strange to consider that so excellent a propagandist as Josef Goebbels should not have sought to demoralise the American and British aircrews by boasting of the modern, aerial Berserkers who, scorning death, would claw down the 'air bandits' from German skies. It might have had some effect. As it was, US Combat Reports spoke of a large number of air collisions, but attributed these to the inexperience of the German pilots. It did not occur to the compilers of these reports that men would deliberately seek death. The attacks were described as having been carried out with a greater than usual resolve, and the writers commented favourably on the bravery of the Luftwaffe pilots who disregarded the heavy defensive fire. This praise was reserved for the German pilots. Most reports by US officers condemn their own fighter pilots for leaving the bombers unprotected. Then, too, the authors praise the skilfully co-ordinated ME and FW attacks made by groups from above and below the bomber formations.

All these positive things are mentioned, but the realisation that the US formations had been victims of the first mass ramming operation in Europe was just not appreciated. The moral shock which the Luftwaffe had hoped to give to the Americans did not succeed. Nor, too, were the German Air Force's physical objectives realised. One hundred and thirty-three German aircraft were lost of the one hundred and eighty-four that went in. Only seventy-seven pilots from the destroyed aircraft survived. The Luftwaffe had managed to destroy only twenty-three heavy bombers and six fighters.

If one accepts Speer's cold-blooded mathematical equation as valid, then on 7 April 1945, above central Germany, the Luftwaffe suffered a catastrophic defeat. A total of one hundred and eighty-four rammers had to achieve, according to Speer, the destruction of five hundred and fifty-two American aircraft. The 8th Air Force had sent in 1,304 bombers and seven hundred and ninety-two fighters and had lost, in this last effort by the Luftwaffe, only slightly more than on a normal day. The verdict of history must be that the Luftwaffe's Operation 'Werewolf' had been an abject failure.

The real failure of the Luftwaffe was that of the leaders of the Third Reich who did not produce a strategy in a war situation, but planned instead a tactical Air Arm – a form of long-range artillery. The ad hoc measures which they were then forced to adopt, vis-à-vis the Allies, forced them into misusing, in order to gain local and temporary successes, the weapons which were produced and of which the ME 262 was one. It also forced them to fling men into unequal battles, facing death with resolute calm, not knowing that their leaders were incompetent.

The final word on the decline of the German Air Force must be that of the Americans. As if to show contempt for the mission flown by the German pilots on 7 April, the 8th Air Force carried out raids on the days following the ramming operation, usually with more than a thousand machines on each day. They could afford to take the losses and the Luftwaffe could not, that was the content of the message which their high, shining squadrons wrote in the German sky.

4
KG200

The catastrophic losses on the Eastern Front had reduced the Luftwaffe personnel in both numbers and ability. The commanders deemed it essential to conserve those with specialist skills and not squander their talents in routine missions. They decided to imitate the highly-successful RAF and group the specialists together and hold them in reserve for unusual operations. The Luftwaffe already had within its establishment a number of squadrons of particular ability, but the proposed new formation would embrace all the aeronautical skills. The decision was taken and Kampfgeschwader 200 was born. It was intended to be special in every sense of the Luftwaffe's understanding of that term and it did, in its brief life span, contain detachments of rare talent and unquestioned ability.

Even now, very little is known about Kampfgeschwader 200. Certainly the public did not know that the Luftwaffe's order of battle included a formation specifically for clandestine and special missions. Few of the exploits of KG200 were acknowledged publicly and even fewer were documented. The secrecy which surrounded KG200, its men and its operations, is only now being lifted as the few official documents which do exist come into the public domain. These records, if one reads between the lines, are eloquent testimonies to deeds of great skill and daring. Even today, four decades later, surviving members of KG200 are still reluctant to talk about what they did. This is not altogether surprising for, when the war ended, Allied Intelligence sought the personnel of this unit, and may still have an interest in certain, unrecorded, long-range missions flown during the last weeks of the war in Europe.

The order from Luftwaffe High Command to form KG200 was issued on 20 February 1944 and placed it under the direct control of Luftflotte Reich. The proposed establishment was two Groups, each having three operational squadrons. In addition, there would be a fourth squadron common to both Groups, the Training and Replacement unit. The operational squadrons would be sub-divided, as necessary, and each would have its own airfield, called an outstation. The headquarters of an outstation was to be located in thick woods and the airfield/outstation was to appear to be deserted by day. The reason for this was that the USAAF attacked any field thought to be still operational. So outstations only came to life on those nights when operations were undertaken.

The first formations to flesh out the bare bones of the newly-formed KG200 were a Testing and Research Unit and Transport Group (East) No. 11. Around this nucleus the Squadron HQ and the HQ of No. 1 Group was quickly formed. The various aircraft which would be used by the KG were flown in and within a matter of days there were thirty-two different types ready for action, and seventeen fully-trained crews.

By the end of March 1944 the first sections of No. 2 Group were being formed together with the Training and Replacement Squadron. Concentrated courses were begun immediately and by the end of July, five completely new crews had been trained and refresher courses had been given to seventy-five more. Clandestine operations were already being flown. Armed with documents which gave them almost unlimited powers, the officers of KG200, could demand the services of other Geschwader or Staffeln. Where crews were considered by their parent unit to be essential to their own operations and could not be posted permanently to KG200, it was understood that for certain special and secret missions the men would be temporarily detached.

Although KG200 was undoubtedly a Luftwaffe unit, part of the establishment of Luftflotte Reich and administered by the German Air Ministry, so many of its operations were special that *de facto* control rested in the hands of Sturmbannführer Skorzeny. From him the chain of command ran upwards to Schellenberg and thence direct to the most senior echelons of command in the Third Reich. Those at the highest pinnacle of power issued the commands which descended, via Schellenberg and Skorzeny to Oberst Baumbach, Commander of KG200. It was he who organised the mission from Geschwader HQ at Gatow in Berlin, deciding whether the operation which had been ordered was viable and which of the two Groups would undertake it. Baumbach also specified the type of aircraft to be used and directed the supply station at Finow to prepare and to deliver the specified machine. The aircraft and the specialists who would brief the crew then flew to one of the Group's outstations. These had a certain autonomy in the conduct of operations, subject always to Group and Squadron approval. A Group operated over a specific geographical area and each outstation had its own operational area and its own code-name. Outstation Olga covered western Europe, including the British Isles, from Spain to Holland. Outstation Carmen covered the western Mediterranean, the Arab countries of the southern Mediterranean and West Africa.

The wide variety of aircraft operated by the KG included the standard types in German service, Italian and French machines as well as British and American planes which had been shot down over Germany and repaired. The KG pilots must have been extremely versatile, and the problems of obtaining spares must have been well-nigh insuperable.

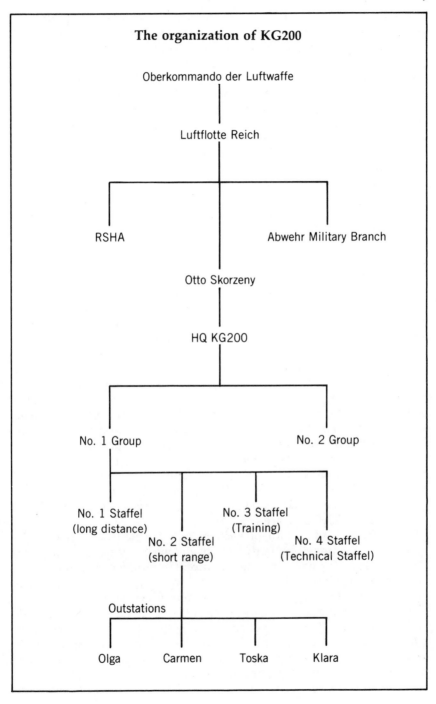

The organization of KG200

By the final years of the war the increasing scarcity of supplies and equipment meant that those with the greatest 'clout' gained the most. Even under peace-time conditions the priority given to a mere colonel commanding a single squadron would have been low. In the abnormal conditions which obtained during the war the CO of KG200 would have had no priority at all. Nor was there any covert way in which Oberst Baumbach might obtain the things he needed for his unit, for both it and its operations were classified as a State secret. But KG200 was responsible directly to Skorzeny and thus, indirectly, to the Party hierarchy. Such an affiliation had its compensations as well as its disadvantages. KG officers worked on Skorzeny who, in turn, influenced Schellenberg to act on behalf of the Luftwaffe's special force. Through that intercession the Squadron was usually assured a sufficient supply of those materials it required to execute the bizarre operations which were ordered by the highest authorities in the Reich. These men considered it vital to the German war effort to place and recover agents from behind the Allied lines, an activity which formed one of the principal duties of KG200 and which required the most precise navigation, pilot skill of the highest order and strong nerves.

It is, principally, in its role as an intruder unit into Allied rear areas that KG200 is most celebrated. One of its outstations flew into Russia the Red Army deserter, Tavrin, who was assigned the task of assassinating Josef Stalin. Other flights from the same outstation dropped a whole wave of Russians who were prepared to work as agents or spies for the Germans. These groups were sent in to report on Soviet troop movements and several years after the war had ended, signal messages from some of these isolated and abandoned men were still being received. Other disaffected Russians were used to carry out partisan activity behind the Red Army's front lines and with such success that even in the 1950s bands of them were still operating. The last group, a Ukrainian nationalist detachment, was only destroyed after a total of twenty-two Red Army and KGB Divisions, including armour and aircraft, had been launched against it. Such were the agents that the RSHA trained and KG200 delivered.

Nor was the infiltration of such men conducted only in the east. Agents were dropped by both Olga in the west and by Carmen in the south. Despite the deteriorating situation the number of such missions increased until they were being ordered on an almost daily basis without consideration being given to the military situation, the availability of aircraft or the state of the crew. Professionalism has the built-in danger that it makes the accomplishing of even difficult tasks seem easy and the undoubted success of KG200 had the result only that the impossible had to be repeated over and over again. The KG200 crews who went out on what seemed to them to be one seemingly senseless mission after another, could only assume that the Supreme Commander saw the 'big picture' and that if Hitler decided the operation was important, then it must be so. The highest echelons of OKW and those of the RSHA both claimed that there was a need to drop agents in the rear of the Allied armies and to sustain them with arms and money. It was held that many of these agents were 'sleepers' that is to say operators who would lie dormant and who would be activated at some future date when Germany's star was again in the ascent. No one in KG200 could imagine that the need for such 'sleepers' would ever come, for even at crew level the chaos facing Germany had by now become very apparent.

If Skorzeny was surprised at the type and frequency of the operations which KG200 was ordered to carry out, he did not betray it, but he was not alone in thinking that his political masters were out of touch with the true situation. It has been established that the men around the Führer had little or no idea of the true war situation or of the hardships which the German people were suffering. Hitler and his closest aides lived in a seclusion from which reality was excluded. He moved phantom armies across maps, ignoring the strategic limitations of time and space, and gave tasks to divisions which had long since been burned out and whose strength existed only on paper. It was this basic ignorance of the real state of things that was responsible for the unreal orders that were given to KG200.

Divorced from reality; the victims of faulty Intelligence often doctored to make it acceptable to Hitler, those around the Führer drew up plans and issued orders that had no correspondence with true facts. To their minds it was no more difficult to fly a blacked-out aircraft across enemy territory in foul weather than to carry out a short, cross-country flight in daylight. The notion that fog might close an airfield was brushed aside as an irrelevance and the adversities of ice and snow were dismissed as being of no consequence. Nor was there any understanding among the men in Supreme Command of the dangers which faced German aircraft even when flying above their own country. Allied fighters were a constant threat by day. By night German fighters might well make a mistake in identification and shoot down a KG plane. Such errors did occur for now the once efficient Luftwaffe tracking and ground-control organisation could not maintain the same excellent standard of former days. All in all, the pilots of KG200 were faced with risks whether they flew by night or by day.

It was a situation which could not improve. As the Allied armies advanced into Germany and broke asunder the central control of the German State, so more and more decisions had to be made at local level by both military and civilian leaders, for no sense was coming from the Führerbunker in Berlin; only strings of orders, many of which had no relevance. Some of these lunatic commands were acted upon, some were simply ignored. There were many commanders in the field who considered that the Götterdämmerung which was falling upon the Third Reich need not descend on the whole of Germany, and for ever. For example, as the war drew to its close, a general order went out for units to destroy the records of their service. Many ignored this command so that their War Diaries, battle orders and files remain today intact or very nearly so. Others, and among this group is included KG200, obeyed the instruction. Not that there was much written material to destroy in the case of the KG. Many of the orders it had received and those which it had transmitted had been by word of mouth. Nevertheless, the KG did have some war records and these were burned so that it will never be possible to write the definitive history of the Luftwaffe's special force, nor will the full extent of their missions ever be known.

It will be appreciated that to undertake a short hop into the densely populated countries of western Europe required not merely a different type of aircraft but also a technique different from that which would be used to drop an operator in the wilder terrain of Russia. Flights into western Europe ran the gauntlet of alert Allied forces whose command of the air was undisputed and whose radar coverage extended from southern France to northern Holland. It was, therefore, out of the question for KG200 crews to fly by daylight and at high level. They had to rely upon a night intrusion at low level in a slow, light aircraft and preferably in bad weather; a climatic condition which the KG pilots used almost as a tactic.

In the task of placing agents behind the Allied lines the role of KG200, initially, was simply that of a carrier. This arrangement changed as the war situation deteriorated and the officers of the Squadron were drawn into very close contact with the agents and their 'dispatchers'. The road which an agent trod was intended to be a short one. Within hours of completing his training for the special job for which he had selected, he would travel via 'safe' houses together with his dispatcher and arrive at the departure field under cover of darkness. There he would meet the KG crew which would fly him on his mission as well as the experts from Finow who would brief him, would ground train him in parachute jumping and give the final polish to his abilities. Then he would leave.

To jump into the inky blackness of a winter's night without any parachute training was frightening enough, but at least those who jumped were aware of what was happening. Consider the feelings of those who were carried as 'human bombs'. There were occasions when a team of agents had to be dropped and in order that they would arrive as a group and not scattered, they were placed inside a cylindrical container. This wooden framework, weighing about 1,650lb when holding three agents, was carried under the wing of an aircraft or, less usually, in the bomb bay. They would have been aware of the danger of interception by night-fighters, of the danger from anti-aircraft fire; danger from so many sources and they helpless, strapped in their triple coffin. There is a record of one mission which had to be aborted as a result of night-fighter interception. The KG200 crew, in an effort to shake off the pursuers, took their machine higher and higher, quite forgetting that the agents in the plywood bomb had no oxygen masks. When, at last the crew remembered their passengers and tried to contact them by the intercom, there was no response. The aircraft returned to the outstation. On arrival one of the agents was found to be dead and all showed the effect of severe frostbite.

For obvious reasons the 'dispatchers', often neglected to inform their charges that their descent would be made in a cylindrical container, and it says much for the moral fibre of the agents that they allowed themselves to be fitted into the 'coffin' horizontally, one on top and two below, strapped in to prevent injury during the flight or the descent, and with only their hands free so that they could break out of the container.

Over the target area the wooden 'bomb' would be released. The rate of descent was controlled by three parachutes and the base of the container was an alloy section which crumpled upon landing and thus absorbed much of the impact. When a three-man team was dropped, and such a descent implied that the target was a special one, a similar 'bomb' filled with supplies, including radio and sabotage equipment, was carried under the aircraft's other wing.

The principal purpose of the human 'bomb' was to drop a team, but the container could also be used to recover agents. A slow-flying aircraft would release a cable with a hook attachment which would be fitted to the end of the 'bomb' by ground crew. Working on the 'snatch' principle the 'bomb' containing the agent would be winched into the aircraft.

The RSHA plan to flood the Allied areas of Europe with agents depended on departures being carried through quickly and without any hitches. The dispatch of operators ran smoothly enough except when other missions and urgent priorities were insisted upon by the Reichs leadership. Then schedules which had been worked out for the dispatch of the V-men were frustrated and there were frequently no aircraft available to drop the waiting agents. Inevitably, there would be a build-up of operators who should have been kept isolated but who were now meeting one another in 'safe' houses or even on the airfields. It was a complete breakdown in security. Each dispatcher naturally stressed the urgency of his own V-man's operation. The strain which this waiting placed upon the agents and their dispatchers affected not only them, but also the officers of KG200 who were drawn, unwillingly but inescapably, into the problem of establishing departure priorities.

In an effort to reduce the number of V-men waiting for dispatch, it was decided that the practice would cease of carrying only one agent per aircraft; wherever possible two or even more would travel together. This 'bus service' meant that most operators could not be air landed, but had to be dropped by parachute. The agents, untrained in the techniques of parachute descent, each carried in his arms a large container of equipment. The shock of the canopy opening usually tore the bundle from the operator's arms. In order that it would not be lost, the bag was roped to the agent; an additional weight which increased the rate of his descent, but which left the untrained man likely to fall heavily upon the equipment and either damage its contents or his own person.

Even the approach to the drop zone was not without incident. If the KG200 navigator had directed the pilot with pinpoint accuracy and the drop zone was only seconds away, the agent would be alerted and prepared quickly; for there could only be a single run in. The engines would be cut or throttled back; the aircraft door would be opened; the agent would stand braced in the doorway and would fall through the dark night. Usually he would be met by a small group of Nazi sympathisers who would help to bury his parachute and who might even supply transport to take him to the operational area.

In addition to the conflict of priorities between the Reichs Government and the RSHA, one other factor affected the operations which KG200 was able to undertake. The state of the weather decided, often only hours before departure time, whether a mission was to be flown. As a result of Allied military operations the Germans had lost the long-range weather forecasting service upon which they had relied. Climatic conditions in Europe can change considerably during the autumn and winter, the seasons during which KG200 was operational in 1944 and 1945, and the choice of target was changed, sometimes twice during a single day. The effect upon the morale of the agents can well be imagined to say nothing of how such changes reduced the efficiency of the KG Squadron.

Although a great number of the KG's operations were undertaken for Intelligence purposes, there were others which were combative: pathfinding for other squadrons, target identification and illumination. In addition there were ramming missions and bombing raids of a particular nature. The increased sophistication of weapons and technology used by the Allies was not always matched by the scientists of the Third Reich, for a great deal of German original thought was wasted in the pet schemes of Hitler and the men around him. Thus, by the middle years of the war, the Luftwaffe had no high-explosive bomb as powerful as those used by the RAF, nor any bomber that could lift as heavy a bomb-load as could the standard British heavy bombers. The only way the Germans could bring a massive amount of high explosive on to a target was to fly it in an aerial pick-a-back combination. The Luftwaffe went back to the British pre-war development of a 'mother and daughter' air-craft and modified the idea to their own particular needs.

At this time there were numbers of obsolete bombers some of which could serve as the mother plane and which would be loaded with high explosives. The daughter machine which would bring the mother to the target would be a standard fighter whose limited range could be increased by drawing fuel from the bomber's tanks. The combination was called 'Mistel'. It was, of course, as unattractive to look at as it was difficult to manoeuvre on the ground. Taking off was always a problem. The pilot in the fighter aircraft was seated some thirty or more feet above the ground and had no downward vision at all. Take off could be affected by cross-winds and the pilot had to be constantly aware that below him was suspended an explosive-packed aircraft. Once airborne, most flights were uneventful, since both machines were controlled by the pilot in the fighter. As the combination was not manoeuvrable it could not defend itself and had to be escorted to the target. The pilot would make his run in, direct the bomber at the objective and jettison it. The missile would dive and, hopefully, collide with the target. The daughter machine, freed now of the weight of the bomber mother, would revert to being an independent fighter.

The impression which has perhaps been given in this short account of KG200, is that the missions it undertook were lunatic projects with little hope of success; forlorn hopes carried out by flying fools upon the instruction of short-sighted dilettante despots who were unable to grasp strategic concepts. Admittedly, only very few of the operations flown by the Squadron could have had a profound and strategic effect upon the conduct of the war, but there were some and the story of one of them is a fine example of what might have been. Had the operation for which KG200 planned and trained been mounted, it might have been as great a strategic coup as any achieved by the RAF's legendary ✦ 617 Squadron. The operation was code-named 'Eisenhammer', and was intended to paralyse Soviet industrial capacity through the destruction of the electricity-generating network in the whole of western Russia.

The plan was conceived by Professor Steinmann who, in 1943, had advanced the thesis that Russia's weakness lay in her generating plant. The professor's theory was that the construction of power-plant covers a period of years; the manufacture of turbines alone requires at least twenty-four months. If the Soviet turbines were destroyed, all elec-tricity supplies in western Russia would be reduced, production would halt and the Russians' ability to supply their armies with weapons and supplies would be affected. From Abwehr sources it was learned that there were no store-houses filled with replacement turbines. Thus, each turbine destroyed would have to be replaced by a newly-manufactured one and in the case of those which were just damaged, the only plant capable of carrying out repairs was itself in ruins. Steinmann had also discovered that the entire electricity supply of western Russsia depended upon only three stations of which those at Moscow and that at Gorki were the principal ones. The destruction of these would paralyse Russia for months.

When it was originally proposed, the task was beyond the capability of the Luftwaffe; no standard squadron on the 1943 establishment was capable of undertaking such an operation. Not until the formation of Kampfgeschwader 200 did the likelihood arise of this ambitious, strategic plan being accomplished. Even so there were delays of all sorts. An attempt to mount the raid in February 1945 failed because of the imminence of the Soviet winter offensive. By this time the question of whether the Russian electricity network could be damaged or even destroyed was academic. The Red Army was equipped to capacity and any effects of the raid upon the generating plant would not have been felt for months. Once again it was too late and a plan which in 1943, might have had far-reaching effects was, in March 1945, nothing more than a reflection upon what might have been.

The order to carry out Operation 'Eisenhammer' had, however come from the Supreme Commander, and training was begun. To understand the initial difficulties to be overcome, it must be realised that by March 1945, the most easterly point the German Army held was in Lithuania, and for aircraft to carry out a raid on the generating supplies in and around Moscow would entail an outward flight of about 1,300 miles, and would necessitate frequent changes of direction to deceive the Soviet air-controllers as to the destination of the mission. The home-ward flight, however, could be direct and, therefore, shorter. The out-ward journey would take about ten flying hours and the return, about five. To fly these tremendous distances necessitated the fitting of auxiliary fuel tanks shaped like giant torpedoes under the wings or belly of the aircraft. Even then, only a strong tail-wind on both the outward and homeward runs would allow the crews to touch down in friendly territory.

The crews of KG200 knew the capabilities of their aircraft. They needed no computer to work out the simple equation of how much fuel could be carried and how many miles of flight could be nursed from it. The answer remained constant. Even with auxiliary tanks the fuel load would be insufficient to last them for the two journeys *unless*, and their survival depended on this, there were a very strong tail-wind there and back. Even with that support it was still a terrible risk; without it, they must come down in Russian-held territory.

To assist the crews a mass of Intelligence material was assembled. With the end of the war only a few months distant, it seems, in hindsight, absolutely unbelievable that so much time and effort should have gone into making models of the power-stations in both summer and winter conditions. Vertical and oblique photographs of the plants were obtained. The most detailed flight maps were drawn and every navigational aid which could be incorporated was brought into service. Courses were run on survival techniques in case they had to land in Soviet territory. Crews were shown which herbs, nuts, berries and barks could be eaten. They were taught to trap animals on land and to fish with hooks supplied to them. Special emergency rations were issued, as were collapsible rifles for hunting for fresh meat to supplement their rations. Basic Russian was taught, particularly the most useful phrases; a dictionary was supplied. Large amounts of money – most of it forged – was given to the crews and every type of obtainable escape material was issued. While these courses were being run, special bombs were designed and produced. Their destructive power, so it was claimed, would penetrate twenty inches of steel. The newly-developed – and untried – explosive would be earsplitting and each Mistel bomber was to be loaded with one of the new-pattern bombs.

The tactical plan was that KG200 would send out two flying groups. The first would be pathfinders who would mark out the route from Lithuania across White Russia and who would identify the twelve targets which sat in a half-circle to the east of Moscow. The second group would be the Mistel and their escort of fighters.

Day after day the crews were on standby, but the vital tail-winds never coincided. Then, while KG200 waited, tragedy struck. American bombers laid a carpet of bombs across the airfield and destroyed most of the Mistel which had been prepared for the operation. It was the last straw. Nothing associated with Operation 'Eisenhammer' had gone well. One result of the American raid was to demonstrate that the super bombs did not meet the claim made for them. One of them was actually fitted inside a Mistel when the Fortresses dropped their bombs. It did not detonate as might have been expected, but instead burned gently and for a long time. The operation had to be postponed and then, with the airfields in Lithuania overrun by the Red Army, the decision was taken to cancel it. One of the few strategically-conceived German air operations against an economic or an industrial target was still-born. The undamaged Mistel combinations were posted back to KG200 to be used in another operation; not strategic in conception, but tactical.

The Red Army's offensive in 1944, had faltered once or twice in its triumphant westward march, but each time it had recovered the initiative and had driven forward until, by the end of January 1945, Russian advance guards had reached the Oder. German demolition teams were to have destroyed the great number of bridges which spanned this major waterway, but the work had not been completed and one hundred and thirty fell into the hands of the Soviets. The Red Army poured across the bridges and set up perimeters on the Oder's western bank, out of which their assault would come to capture Berlin. At this late hour it was suddenly deemed imperative by the German Führer that the bridges be destroyed; if not all of them, then certainly the most important ones. Although the Russians had captured so many bridges, they were still insufficient to accommodate so vast an army as the Soviets were building up for the final offensive. In addition to the permanent constructions, the Red Army engineers erected wooden pontoons, and soon there were nearly five hundred bridges across this last major river barrier to the east of Berlin.

Hitler, acutely aware of the threat which these bridges posed, ordered their destruction and KG200 was directed to carry out the Führer's orders. The squadron's first attempts to smash them by dropping a large number of sea mines into the Oder was a failure. It had been anticipated that the mines would float downstream, hit and detonate against the bridges, but the German planners had not taken into account the fact that the depth of water in the river would be insufficient to float the heavy mines. They sank. Next an attempt was made by sailors of the 'K' units and this too failed because the mines which they used lacked sufficient power. To drop aerial mines would not give the desired effect or the necessary accuracy. The choice was either to use a guided-bomb or the Mistel combination.

At a time in the war when chaos was the norm in Germany; when living conditions were terrible and fighting efficiency ebbing rapidly away; when every effort should have been made to concentrate the Fatherland's dying efforts upon some vital objective, nothing in the mind of the Führer had a greater priority than the destruction of the Oder bridges. He set his whole mind to the task and soon a stream of the most precise and detailed orders had been issued. These controlled the times and the rendezvous of the several units which were to take part in the mission. It might be thought that such arrangements could have been left to the men who would have to fly the operation – but no. Sheaves of written orders were issued and resources drawn upon that would have been more relevant to some vast strategic objective rather than the destruction of a single, tactical target.

The bridge whose destruction Hitler finally decided was vital to the German defence plans, was that at Steinau, and the combat report of the mission – one of the few original documents of KG200 extant – records in great detail the preparation and the operation itself. Six Mistel were to take part. On their flight to the objective as well as during the return journey, they would be escorted by other aircraft from the KG, which would act as pathfinders and mark the route. From the depleted squadrons of Luftflotte Reich, twenty-four ME 109s were drawn off to protect the bombing group against the masses of Russian aircraft which flew above the Oder bridges. The raid was ordered to start on 31 March 1945, between 07.23 and 07.35. The Mistel and the Pathfinder aircraft would take off and rendezvous with the MEs above the Oder at 09.05. The explosives-filled bombers would be released in two waves: the first at 09.05 and the second at 09.12. The attack height was to be 7,500 feet. During the flight to the target, three of the six Mistel were forced to abort, so the raid took place at only 50 per cent of strength, which was sufficient for only one attacking wave. The JUs struck home; all three machines hit the target and all three FW launch-aircraft returned safely to base. The whole operation was conducted for the loss of only two Messerschmitts; but for all that enormous effort, the bridge was out of action for just a matter of days.

Between the end of October 1944 and the spring of 1945, Allied armies moved towards and into Germany. As the fronts held by the German Army began to break and the enemy advance thrust deeper into the Fatherland, the airfields from which KG's outstations had operated were overrun. The last months of outstation Olga are typical of all and are described here to show the confusion which obtained in Germany in the closing stages of the war. From its home base at Frankfurt am Main, outstation Olga was forced to move, an operation which involved not only the pilots and their crews, not only the ground staff and the specialised equipment, but also the agents and their dispatchers, for the RSHA was still sending out operators into enemy territory. The machines, men and equipment which made up Olga were shuttled about until finally they found a base outside Stuttgart from which the outstanding operations on the outstation's schedule were undertaken. Little help came from KG HQ, only a string of orders emanating from RSHA and the Reichs hierarchy, demanding the execution of impossible assignments. The KG HQ at Gatow was unable to control Olga once the outstation left Frankfurt, and had been unable to obtain the spares for which the outstation had asked.

As the Americans drove into southern Germany, it became abundantly clear that Olga would have to abandon the Stuttgart base and move to another, more secure and suitable, airfield. This was no easy task for many of the aircraft required an unusually long runway and the number of fields with this facility were limited. The nearest to Stuttgart was at Munich. Olga moved into Bavaria and searched the Munich area for a new base. The movement of aircraft and equipment could not be undertaken by day because of Allied command of the air and night movement was both slow and difficult. On many occasions journeys to airfields proved only that they were already occupied by squadrons in residence. Alternative sites were sought and eventually Olga came to the Dornier aircraft works on whose field the outstation set up again in the hope of resuming operational flying.

The frequent moves had demonstrated one thing, that when it came to keeping aircraft flying it was very much the case of each Luftwaffe squadron acting in its own best interests. Useless now were the special authorisations issued under the hand of the most senior man in the Reich. The carefully sealed and secret red-paper letter, demanding in the name of Adolf Hitler that the fullest co-operation be given to KG200, proved to be just a piece of pretty-coloured paper, having no authority at all when it came to the question of survival as an operational unit.

Back in Berlin, Baumbach was posted away from KG200 and was replaced by a Major von Hernier. The latter's term of office was very brief. On 25 April, the new Commander released from the service the men of KG headquarters group. Not all went back to civilian life. Some set off to join Olga, but there was a general feeling that the war was over and signs of a general dissolution. Some units continued to fight on. A part of No. 2 Staffel in Magdeburg handed over its aircraft to KG66 and the Staffel men, now surplus to establishment, were put into the battle line as infantry. No. 3 Staffel was placed under the direct control of Luftflotte Reich, obviously intended for very special operations, while the remaining Staffeln of KG200 were scattered around the Reich in places as far apart as Flensburg near Schleswig Holstein, and Linz in Austria.

The story of the wanderings of the remnants of the former KG200 through those regions of Germany which had not yet been captured by the Allies, is one of confusion and despair. In the final week of the war, arrangements were made for all men still on the strength of Olga to escape into the American or British lines and thus avoid imprisonment in the concentration camps of the Soviet Union. Each man was supplied with civilian clothes and issued with proper discharge papers, food for his journey and a sum of money equal to a week's pay and supplementary benefits. Those with cars or motor cycles, filled them with petrol siphoned from the tanks of the last remaining aircraft; others left on bicycle or on foot. Secretly and quietly, the groups left the dark airfield and set out for civilian life. The service of outstation Olga had ended, but in the far north of Germany one sub-unit of KG200 was still on duty, waiting to fly high personages out of the country and into the safety of those lands whose governments were still friendly to Germany. Thus died Kampfgeschwader 200. Its men submerged themselves in the chaos of a dying Germany, keeping to themselves as they still do, the memories of the flights they undertook in an attempt to win victory for the Reich through the employment of a special Luftwaffe force.

PART FOUR

'POLITICAL' SPECIAL FORCES

1

PENSIONERS AND CHILDREN

The military disasters which overtook Germany during the late summer of 1944 must have convinced even the most fanatical members of the Nazi Party that, short of a miracle, nothing could stave off defeat and that the best that might be hoped for was a stalemate. Hitler may have declared a German victory to be certain and a great many of his closest comrades may have paid lip-service to his words, but those who could interpret the signs made their own preparations to meet the wrath to come. Those leaders of Nazi Germany who had the most to lose if she were defeated, strove to delay nemesis. There was, however, little that could be done. The wonder weapons, which Hitler had promised would destroy London, had failed and it was admitted, but not publicly, that no new wonder weapons could now save Germany. There remained only the people.

The leaders of the Nazi Party convinced themselves that the German men and women burned with revolutionary fervour and that the political mobilisation of the masses could be harnessed to bring victory out of defeat. The logic of their argument was that the armed forces, the so-called weapon-bearers of the State, were losing the war because their attitudes were old-fashioned. Inspired by National Socialist philosophy, revolutionary ideas and fervour would bring the whole nation under arms and it would become a Peoples' War. The struggle of the masses would confound the plans of Germany's enemies. A military stalemate would be achieved which would weary the Allies and lead to conflict between them. The belief that sooner or later, military hostilities would break out between the Russians and the Western Allies was the conviction that buoyed the German leaders.

The German people had had no experience of total war. This is not to say that there was not in Germany worry, fear and chronic shortages. All these there were and in abundance. Millions of German soldiers had been killed or wounded and Allied aircraft were bombing the cities of Germany almost at will. But it was still not total war. Even though the people had enthusiastically endorsed Reichsminister Goebbels' offer of war to the death only a year earlier, nothing had really changed during that time to bring the German masses to that level of sacrifice experienced by the women of Britain, of Russia and of the occupied lands of Europe. Then, late in 1944 came the conviction that Gemany's salvation lay in harnessing the masses. At that time of anguish and crisis the solution to Germany's problems lay, so it was thought, not in conventional forces but in firing the masses with a 'do or die' spirit. One product of this conviction was Werewolf, an organisation which, had it been organised in time, been more firmly controlled with clear-cut, unequivocal policy directives, might well have played an important part in producing that stalemate which was Germany's only hope. Even badly organised as it was, the Werewolf threat to carry on partisan warfare in the rear of the Allied armies advancing into Germany, was sufficient to influence Anglo-American operations in the last weeks of the war.

Research shows that there were three different bodies to which the name Werewolf was given. The first and most important was a partisan army which was to operate behind the Allied lines. Knowledge of this special force was blurted out by Goebbels in a radio speech which gave details of Werewolf missions. His speech demanded that not just the trained operators alone should be Werewolf, but that the German people should rise up in a national resistance that would 'drown the enemy in a sea of blood'. This proposed rising en masse was the second type of Werewolf and there were cases reported of German civilians actually taking up arms and fighting as part of that force. The third Werewolf was a Luftwaffe squadron whose pilots volunteered to carry out kamikaze attacks upon Allied bomber fleets. We concentrate here upon the first and second types of Werewolf organisation.

The Werewolf organisation, as originally planned, was to be the German partisan organisation. It was inspired and planned by the Nazi Party, but the administration would be that of the OKW, which would give the movement legality and which would nominate the targets to be attacked and arrange the missions that were to be undertaken.

The theory of Werewolf was that, as the Allies advanced into Germany, the secret agents of the German partisan movement would allow themselves to be overrun. They would go to ground and would later emerge to engage in their clandestine operations. These would take the form of attacking enemy units, destroying the enemy's supplies and destroying his communications networks. In addition to fighting a partisan war, the second duty of Werewolf was to ensure that the German people remained loyal to Hitler, even though their cities and towns had been occupied by the Allies. To guarantee this loyalty, any Germans who collaborated with the enemy by accepting office in the Allied administration would be assassinated. By fly-posting placards, by the distribution of leaflets and through the painting of slogans on walls, the German civilians in the occupied areas were to be reminded where their duty lay and that it was an obligation to support and encourage Werewolf and to shield its agents from discovery.

The concept of Werewolf as an élite band of partisans was first given formal endorsement in the late spring of 1944, and the task of recruiting, organising and training was passed to SS Gruppenführer Prutzmann. In order to preserve the secrecy of the organisation, the first recruits were obtained not by public announcement but by verbal invitation or by personal recommendation. Once a nucleus of reliable men and women had been assembled and instructed, a wider circle of people could be admitted into the secret. The results of this wider trawl pleased the Nazi hierarchy for there followed a flood of keen men and women willing to enlist in this secret force. There was never any need for conscription; Werewolf began and ended as an all-volunteer organisation.

The bitter war in Russia and in occupied Europe had given the German Army a vast amount of experience in anti-partisan operations and it was acknowledged that the SS Jagdverbände were the most efficient in combating the hidden enemy. Because their units had the highest success rates, the best men of the Jagdverbände were seconded to the secret schools to teach partisan skills to the Werewolf recruits. The first and best of these schools was at Hulcenrath, a castle in the Rhineland. Other training centres were established at Lubbucke, Waidhofen in Austria, Neustrelitz and Quenzee, the old Brandenburg school. Hulcenrath was the best school because it was able to give a full and thorough training. It had been set up very soon after the Allies invaded Normandy. By autumn there was less and less time to train recruits in the other schools and by the time that the armies of the eastern and western Allies stood on German soil proper, instruction time had been cut so much that the Werewolf agents were given little more than basic training.

A special force such as Werewolf – a partisan army – must be flexible in organisation and in structure. It is a ground rule that such a group must not be large in number, so that in the event of one of the group being taken prisoner and forced to talk, he can betray only a few of his comrades. The officers of the Jagdverbände decided that Germany's terrain and population density could not support within any one area a tactical group larger in strength than a platoon. That formation, numbering about sixty men, would only be grouped for major missions such as an armed raid. Minor operations, such as a road watch, the cutting of telephone wires or assassination, would need no more than four or five agents at any one time. Groups would normally operate in minimum strength, but would be brought together to platoon strength only for special missions.

It will be appreciated that partisan operations are carried out behind enemy lines where agents hide their military identity by wearing civilian clothes. This deception makes them terrorists, so that they cannot be considered as members of a regular army and therefore entitled to the protection of the Geneva Convention. Summary execution was the usual sentence for captured and convicted partisans, but the full implication of the risk that they ran seems not to have been completely understood by the Werewolf nor does it not seem to have been stressed in the training lectures given by the SS.

Efficiency of partisan groups also depends upon regular supplies of food, weapons and forged identity documents. To ensure that Werewolf had all these things, Prutzmann ordered the setting up of hideouts all over Germany and Austria. In these secret and well-hidden depots were the essentials which partisan groups needed to keep them in the field. A team of SD officers was made responsible for the initial stocking of the store depots and with the task of maintaining the level of supplies in the hideouts.

A second group of SD officers was charged with procuring false papers and for producing convincing cover stories for the agents. It was anticipated that the establishment would be on a one to one basis; one SD officer training one Werewolf agent, but this ambition was never realised. Werewolf training was hard and the instructors unforgiving. One mistake, the recruits were told, and you were dead. It was not your death at the hands of the enemy which was of concern, but the fact that your training had been wasted by a single stupid error. Mistakes were unpardonable; they were evidence of a sloppy, non-Nordic outlook. Tiredness and sickness were no excuse for inaction. The ability to cross the thresholds of pain or deprivation were aimed for, and even the youngest recruits were expected to be animated by the task that they had shouldered. Although the Werewolf were all volunteers and could, theoretically, withdraw from the force, in practice this did not work. Indeed, it could not. Quite a few of the very young agents asked at the last minute to be released from the tasks which had been assigned to them. Their SS instructors laid out for them, starkly and simply, the alternatives. Either they could go out and *risk* detection and possible execution; or they could refuse to go on operations and *would* certainly be shot by the SD for refusing to obey a legal order. Most of the Werewolf went.

Trained in weapons skills, explosives and communications, the agents returned after training, to their home areas, there to await the orders that would take them underground and into German partisan operations. They had not long to wait. As early as September 1944, the Western Allies had advanced to the German frontier and had captured the town of Aachen after bitter fighting. In the East, the Red Army was driving towards the pre-1939 frontiers of Germany. In those threatened sectors of the fighting line the Werewolf prepared for battle, and as its fury rolled over them they disappeared from their villages and met in secret locations to await the orders that would take them into action.

Partisan forces do not operate bureaucratic procedures and cannot afford the luxury of maintaining extensive written records. As most Werewolf operations were launched against local targets, they had to be locally initiated and controlled. In a State which was dying, as Germany was in 1945, war diaries, the most usual method of recording a unit's history, were not kept. In those final weeks whole volumes of precious and irreplaceable archives were destroyed by fire as part of a deliberate, nihilstic, scorched-earth policy. Thus there is a whole fascinating area of military history of which no written records exist and which it is no longer possible to reconstruct; as far as Werewolf is concerned, not even personal accounts survive. Even today, people seldom admit to membership of the German partisan organisation. They still fear retribution – forty years on.

In the absence of German official military documents and war diaries, it is not possible to produce a factual picture of what it was like to have been on active service as a Werewolf in those last final months of Germany's death agonies. It is possible, however, to paint a general picture built up from interrogation summaries, statements of evidence and interviews with Austrian civilians who lived through those difficult months. A synthesis of such interviews has produced the following record of what it must have been like to be a Werewolf on the Eastern Front.

'Training took place at Waidhofen on the Ybbs in what was then the Gau Ostmark but which is now the Province of Lower Austria. I had been in the Hitler Youth since before the Occupation of Austria in 1938 and my father had been a member of the then illegal Nazi Party from the early 30s. As we were dedicated Nazis we were among the first to learn of the new partisan movement. A friend of my father's in the Gau administration told my father about it and my parent told me. I volunteered immediately as I knew that was what was expected of me. It seemed to me it would be a more exciting life as a partisan fighter than serving as a gun number in an obscure anti-aircraft battery and I felt very proud to have been allowed to enlist into this special and unknown Force.

'I entered the Waidhofen camp in February 1945, and was told that everything I possessed had to be sent home. No family photographs, no personal possessions were allowed. Firstly, they were a traceable link in the event of capture and secondly, there was to be no reminder of past days, no memories to weaken our resolves. We were told that we were Hitler's – that we owed total allegiance to him. He was to fill all our waking thoughts. Totally and utterly. We were his creatures for him to use as he saw fit. This was the theme of all the political lessons which formed so great a part of the curriculum. We were convinced Nazis before we entered the camp, and the indoctrination we received turned us into fanatics. That is perhaps the wrong way to describe us. We were highly skilled in partisan warfare and could kill efficiently, remorse-lessly and without emotion. Fanatics are emotional killers and are seldom efficient.

'Our fieldcraft lessons were hard; indeed brutal. We would be force-marched for miles and in total winter darkness would have to construct a 'hide' that had, in daylight, to be undetectable to our inspecting officers. If they found our foxholes, discovery meant a beating. We had to run a gauntlet of our SS instructors and they knew how to inflict great pain. My course lasted five weeks. I thought myself tough when I joined the camp. The SS instructors proved to me that this was not so, but by the end of the course I could march all night and then dig a foxhole so narrow it fitted me as tight as a glove. And it was almost invisible. I would kill anybody if I had to. There was not a German or a Russian weapon that I could not use and I was trained in demolition, explosives, radio techniques and survival. Because we were dedicated to Hitler we could not write home or telephone or communicate in any way with our families. It was made quite clear to us that we were expendable and that death would be our punishment for failure. Death and torture from the Reds. We were told that we would never receive medals, or citations or honours, but would have to carry out our dangerous tasks without reward or recognition.

'Towards the end of March groups were sent into action. At the start of our training the papers had reported with confidence German offen-sives which would sweep the Communists out of Hungary. When I went into action in the first week of April the Soviets were already in Austria. I was part of a four-man group – a road watch detail – and the area in which we carried out our tasks was north-east of Vienna, in what is now Czechoslovakia. It was our task to report on Russian troop movements along the road, specifying types of guns, tanks and other arms. Two men kept watch; one kept tally on the vehicles passing along the road and the other protected the watcher. The other two members of the group sent signals, cooked or rested. It was difficult to live off the land even in an area as rich as Bohemia, and we did not dare approach the civilians who would have betrayed us to the Reds. Cooking fires had to be small and were constructed in the fashion described in our handbook. What I missed most were hot baths. We had been told not to wash with scented soap; a stupid warning as German soap at that time was a grey, sandy tablet completely unscented. We had to smell of earth; even BO could be smelt by intelligent and thorough searchers and there was no doubt that the Reds would search for us. None of our group smoked so that the betraying smell of tobacco could not give us away. We must have stunk, but we were not conscious that *we* smelt, just that our comrades did.

'Once, and only once, was our group involved in a killing. A small patrol of motorised infantry approached close to where we were hiding.

There was a cutting, like a very deep river bed through which the Soviet vehicles would have to pass. Before they reached the cutting we had placed a mine and up went the first vehicle of the group. A mine was placed behind the last truck and as the driver tried to reverse it, that went up, too. Then we shot up the vehicles and the men inside them. When the action was finished I was selected to go with the group leader to a hidden dump to obtain supplies. I was surprised at the content and the amount of stuff that was hidden there. Food, clothing, blankets, weapons – enough for years, was all there in that skilfully located 'hide'. It was so well hidden that a yard away and it was unrecognisable.

'One night, probably about 14 April, we were ordered to move farther northwards, and once again we were to report on vehicle movement. Forty years on I know now that the Soviets were swinging up through Bohemia towards Berlin. I did not know it then. All I saw was that armour and trucks, masses of them, were driving day and night past our positions. At night the vehicle columns drove with blazing headlights. There was no sound or sight of any German troops or aircraft. At least, not on our sector. We were watching one day when something happened. What caused it is to me still a mystery. We were dug in on the forward slope of a hill overlooking a road running northwards from Bruck an der Leitha. My three comrades were in foxholes carrying out our road watch procedure. I was sending signals from a position about four hundred yards behind them, up the slope. Suddenly a group of Red tanks swerved off the road and came on in line abreast straight for the foxholes. If my comrades had stayed in position the Soviets might just have passed over them and never known that they were there. As it was one of the three panicked, I suppose. He climbed out of his hole and in full view of the enemy ran uphill towards our Field HQ where I was still sending out the radio messages. The Reds shot him as he ran and then drove very carefully over the ground until they reached the foxholes where the other two Werewolf men were. They crushed both my comrades to death by spinning the tanks on their tracks over the holes.

'Then they came uphill towards me. I had left the radio on, but had stopped sending messages and waited as the enemy armour cautiously approached me. Inside that narrow foxhole I waited to die. It sounds calm and collected now, but I was terrified and I had nothing with which I could fight back, only my MP. The rumble of the vehicles vibrated through the earth and shook me as I crouched inside the hole. One of the T 34s was literally within feet of me. The Red tank men fired their guns and their machine-guns. What they were firing at I do not know, perhaps it was an attempt to flush us out. I was the only survivor and stayed put, stuck inside the hole. When the tanks stopped there were footsteps milling about. I could sense then by the vibrations in the earth. The tank men had probably got out and were searching for the 'hide'. Then it was all quiet again. The tanks drove away, but I still sat quite still and took no chances. It was likely that the Reds had left a small detachment behind to watch and wait for any of us to come out. I sat in the foxhole for hours and hours. Then from my watch dial I could see that it was night time. A cautious peep. Then a longer look round. There was nobody there. All the Reds had left. I did not go back to look for my comrades' bodies. We had been told that sentimentality was a negative emotion.

'The Soviets were heading north so I struck south and eventually joined another Werewolf group. I recognised one of the members of the detachment standing outside a railway station and went through the ritual of recognition. This was to role a small coin over and over between my fingers. When the comrade approached me there was an elaborate exchange of signs and countersigns before we trusted each other. We had been taught caution and for all I knew he might have been a Red agent. So far as he was concerned, so might I have been.

'His group was preparing to paint slogans in a nearby village. These served to frighten those who were collaborating with the Reds. Slogans reminded them that the Werewolf was watching and that Hitler's orders were still to be obeyed, even under foreign domination. This new group did a lot of slogan writing. We wandered about, sometimes minelaying, sometimes slogan painting for what seemed like weeks on end. The whole area was clear now of Russian troops and the group leader decided that we were too far in the rear of the Reds. We should, he said, be immediately behind the battle line, so we marched westwards. Progress was slow. In a village to the east of Linz we were suddenly confronted by a group of drunken Russians. They urged us to drink with them. Hitler was dead, they told us. The war was over. It was a humiliating experience to be told by a drunken enemy that you are a member of a defeated nation. I think I cried – not then – but later on. The villagers who suspected what we were wanted us out of the way. All they wanted was to return to pre-war days. They were not politically-minded. They were sheep really. They did not care who occupied them.

'There was no point in Werewolf activities any longer, so we broke up and set off home. When I arrived at our house I found that my father was in prison for his National Socialist beliefs and that our house had been commandeered for an American officer who treated my mother like a servant. After a few days I left home. The Americans were carrying out one of their infrequent searches for Werewolf members. It was not safe to be at home. It was safer in a large town so I went to Linz and by raiding the secret Werewolf supply dumps, not only ate well but got into the black market. It was a miserable and ignoble end to what had begun as a glorious national adventure.'

2

WEREWOLF IN THE WEST

That there were many serious attacks by Werewolf all over Germany cannot be denied, but it must also be stated that despite the enthusiasm and ability of the five thousand members who passed through the training camps, the partisan force achieved very little. Here and there the diligent researcher will find clues leading to happenings which occurred in the last days of the Reich and which, it can be deduced, were due to the actions of the Nazi partisans. Conversely, there were ambushes, deaths and woundings which, in the hysteria of the time, were blamed upon Werewolf but which can be seen, judged by today's objective view, to have been tragic, unfortunate accidents totally without sinister involvement.

The activities of Werewolf in the areas of the British Army in Germany, were limited to isolated incidents, but one of these killed Major John Poston, a brilliant, young officer of Hussars, who had been with Field Marshal Montgomery in the desert, in Sicily and in North-West Europe. As one of the Field Marshal's liaison officers, it was Poston's practice to drive about collecting for the British commander those small items of military Intelligence upon which the leader planned his battles.

In the last weeks of the war, Poston, driving along a quiet country road back to Montgomery's headquarters from a liaison mission, was attacked by a group of Hitler Youth Werewolves. Their bursts of bullets struck his Jeep which then skidded off the road. Although wounded in the first volleys, the British officer returned fire with his pistol until he was hit again by a long burst of machine-pistol bullets and was killed. Poston died in battle, much as one thinks he would have wished to go, in a typical Hussar fashion, fighting against odds. So far as is known he was the most senior British officer to die in a known Werewolf attack. There were other clashes between the young partisans and men of British armoured divisions, but the veteran soldiers of the 7th and 11th Armoured had not, in the words of Sergeant Ellis of the Royal Tank Regiment, 'come all this way to be knocked out in the last weeks of the war or to be buggered about by those kids. As a soldier I must say their tactics were hopeless, particularly when fighting in towns and villages, where they tried street fighting using methods that only work in open country. They would, for example, throw a grenade and run into a house. We would open fire on the house with our main armament and a couple of shots would bring it tumbling down. Lucky for us they did not have bazookas or anything like that, just machine-pistols and Teller mines. Of course, you can't lay Teller mines in cobbled streets. You have to dig up the cobbles first. They were too impatient. They just laid the mines on top of the stones, probably hoping that we wouldn't see them. Whenever we fired our main armament they did not scatter but bunched together – out of fear, I suppose. It was pathetic really.'

There may have been deeper reasons for the limited Werewolf activity in the British Zone. The Protestant north of Germany had always been less keen on Nazi ideas than the Catholic south. The North Germans had always been more practical than the emotional Bavarians, and they saw little sense in attacking Allied armour with machine-pistols. The war, they thought, was as good as lost. Let us accept the bitter truth. And so they did not encourage partisan activity in favour of a lost cause. Another significant factor was that one of the largest provinces of North Germany through which the British Army was thrusting was Hanover which had strong links with the British Royal Family. The Hanoverians also had fond memories of the years long gone when their men had served with the British Army as the King's German Legion. There was, therefore, a reluctance on the part of these old friends to take part in clandestine operations against the British.

The other Western ally, the United States, met more opposition from the Werewolf bands and were at first uncertain of how to handle the problems of being fired at by children. Realisation soon came that bullets from a machine-gun fired by a 10-year-old are as lethal as those from a gun manned by a 20-year-old. Slowly, reluctantly, the American attitude changed and then occurred an event which caused it to harden overnight. On 24 March 1945, the Lord Mayor of Aachen was assassinated by Werewolf agents. He was not the only US-appointed official to die at the hands of the terrorists, but he was the most important and the broadcast announcing his death on 1 April, gave Reichsminister Goebbels the opportunity to gloat that the arm of the Nazi Party was long and that its agents, the Werewolf, were vigilant, ruthless killers.

Werewolf was a secret no longer. Goebbels had officially announced that a German partisan movement existed and he then went on to proclaim a general uprising of the whole Geman people against the invading Allied troops. This he also called Werewolf. Deutschlandsender radio-station broadcast a call to arms claiming itself to be the organisation of National Socialist Freedom Fighters. The call to action was taken up by another radio-station and very soon a whole programme of propaganda for Werewolf was being transmitted. Once again, as in the days before the Nazis seized power, the old, emotional slogans were brought out and reused. Slogans which had helped to defeat the Reds, were heard once again on German radio and each station broadcast the same proclamation – the charter of the Werewolf organisation, which was:

'The terror raids have destroyed our cities in the West. Our starving women and children along the Rhine have taught us how to hate. The blood and the tears of our brutally beaten men, our despoiled wives and murdered children in those areas occupied by the Reds cry out for revenge. Those who are in Werewolf declare in this proclamation their firm, resolute decision; sealed with their oath, never to bow to the enemy, even though we suffer the most terrible conditions and have only limited resources. But to meet the foe with resistance; to defy him, despising bourgeois comfort and shall face possible death with pride and we shall revenge any misdeed which he commits against our race by killing him. Every means is justified if it helps to damage the enemy.

'The Werewolf has its own courts of justice which decide the life or death of our enemy as well as of those traitors among our people. Our movement rises out of our people's desire for freedom and is bound up with the honour of the German nation whose guardians we consider ourselves to be. If the enemy feels that we are easy game and that the German people can be driven like slaves; as he has driven the Roumanian, Bulgarian or Finnish people to deportation, to hard labour in the tundras of Russia or the coalmines of Britain or France, then let him know that in those areas of Germany from which the German Army has been forced back, there will arise an adversary with which he had not reckoned, but who will be more dangerous to him, who will fight without regard to so-called, old-fashioned, concepts and bourgeois methods of war, which our enemies adopt only when these are of advantage to them, but which they cynically reject if these bring no such advantage. Hate is our prayer. Revenge is our battle cry.'

The proclamation by Goebbels changed the concept of Werewolf from a secret, special force operating behind the enemy lines, into a series of haphazard and unco-ordinated attacks by any German armed with a weapon, upon any member of the Allied armies. In those days and under the conditions then prevailing, soldiers did not allow themselves to be the targets for indiscriminate civilian assaults without having some recourse to weapons. If the Germans fired upon the military, the military would fire back; and the military had the greater firepower. Goebbels' intention to 'drown the enemy in a sea of blood' seemed very likely to drown the German people in a sea of blood. The broadcast by the Reichsminister also gave a name to the armed assaults which had taken place against Allied servicemen and which, so it had seemed, had been the unofficial action of a few hotheads. Now, Werewolf was in the open, but the Allies drew the wrong conclusion from the broadcast. The Americans and the French believed that a national uprising by the German people was either taking place or was about to and resolved to take the strongest measures against this national partisan movement.

Fear of Werewolf was then blended in with another kite which Goebbels had been flying; the idea of the Alpine Redoubt. The Americans were convinced that in the mountainous areas of southern Germany and of Austria, the Nazis would make a last-ditch stand. Senior officers of the US Army firmly believed that thousands of well-trained, German soldiers, aircraft production plants, tank factories – a whole armaments industry indeed – was there in the Alps ready to defend the Führer in his Alpine fortress. Following on from this belief came the conviction that, as the Allied armies drove towards the mountain fastness, the German High Command would fling across the Allied lines of communication, thousands of Werewolf agents to interdict and to destroy. Any Allied advance upon the Alpine Redoubt, so it was believed, would be met at every possible place by the German masses in arms, backed by an aggressive partisan organisation.

British Intelligence Officers tried to persuade the Americans that both the Alpine Redoubt and the *levée en masse* called Werewolf were elaborate bluffs and sought to keep the main thrust of the Western Allies aimed at Berlin. American fears that partisan activity might involve them in years of war in the hostile mountains coloured their judgement. The US Supreme Commander, Eisenhower, accepted the assessments of his lieutenants, regrouped his armies and drove south – away from Berlin and into the mountains. He was more concerned with phantoms conjured up by his nervous subordinates than with the political fate of Europe.

That the Americans were apprehensive about a long-drawn-out war is understandable. They had a war in the Pacific to finish and had no wish to be tied-down in Europe battling for one German mountain peak after another. In view of the pressing need to conclude quickly the war in the European Theatre of Operations, the American armies drove swiftly and impatiently into southern Germany.

Opposition, where it was encountered, was beaten down ruthlessly. The assassination of Aachen's Lord Mayor and the Goebbels broadcast had illustrated the dangers that the US forces believed they faced and they used maximum fire power against minor targets. Then on 8 April, they suffered another terrible blow. The Commander of 3rd Armoured Division, General Maurice Rose, was murdered by the Werewolf in Padeborn. The gloating by German broadcasters over the murder of the 'Jew General', inflamed the Americans and steeled their already firm resolve. Any fire aimed at them by civilians was considered to be Werewolf activity and was suppressed with savage ferocity. Boys as young as 12 years of age were tried and sentenced to life imprisonment by US Courts Martial. Two members of the Hitler Youth, one aged 16 and the other aged 17, were sentenced to death at the end of March 1945 and were executed on 5 June. The report in the US Forces' newspaper *Stars and Stripes*, claimed that they had been snipers in Aachen. The

American fury was not confined to proven members of the Werewolf. At Budeburg near Wesel on 8 April, and in Spitze only six days later, men of 116th Panzer Division were shot without trial by soldiers of the American Army.

The discovery of Werewolf leaflets in their zone of occupation sharpened US resolve. The partisan pamphlets detailed how acts of sabotage were to be committed, and summarised the reason for such operations in the following words. 'The enemy will then have to take troops from the front line to protect his supply routes. The enemy in the battle line will be weakened. Anything of the enemy's that we can destroy forces him to replace it. Anything which damages the enemy helps our troops.' The Americans found, in their advances, that Were-wolf cells existed even among soldiers who were convalescing. Badly wounded officers and even nursing sisters were discovered to be inciting the lightly wounded to commit acts of sabotage and to maintain resistance to the US authorities. The Americans were convinced that they could see evidence of partisan activity everywhere and in their drive southwards towards the Alpine Redoubt, destroyed all opposition, great or small, actual or imagined. The Americans were impatient to end the war in Europe.

3
WEREWOLF IN THE EAST

It was to be expected that Werewolf would operate on a larger scale on the Eastern Front than in the West and, towards the end of 1944, groups of volunteers, chiefly Austrian nationals, were formed into two commando groups code-named Sigrune and Nibelungen. The principal duties of these two bodies were to relay information on the Red Army's movements and strengths from hiding places immediately behind the Russian front lines. A network of detachments was set up in eastern Austria which would receive the agents' signals and relay them to Passau, the Werewolf headquarters in Austria. In the last week of March, the Russian Army crossed the frontier of Austria and there was a sudden increase in Werewolf numbers. Austrian soldiers serving in the German Army were released from their parent units and offered the chance of serving with the partisan organisation. It was expected that soldiers whose home provinces were being overrun by the Soviets would be even more fanatical in their fight against the Slav invaders than the Hitler Youth who formed the bulk of the Werewolf groups. Those army men, mostly from the Signals Corps, were quickly trained in the radio procedures that would keep them in touch with the local partisan headquarters in Graz and in the Vienna woods, before being sent out to infiltrate Soviet lines and reach their operational area in the Leitha mountains to the south-east of the Austrian capital.

When empires die it is usual for their written records to be consumed by the fury of the war that has destroyed the State. Thus it was in the Third Reich. Lacking documentary evidence it is, therefore, not possible to say how successful were the Werewolf agents in Austria. It is quite obvious, however, that any details of military Intelligence which they might have gathered would have been redundant, for they could never have been acted upon by the High Command in those last weeks of dissolution and chaos. With their years of experience, the veteran soldiers must have realised that the Reich was dying and that their radio messages could have neither relevance to, not effect upon, the deteriorating military situation. What could be more logical, they must have asked themselves, than that their little Werewolf groups, miles behind the Russian front, should break up, that they should bury the evidence of their partisan connections and that they should return home. They realised that to survive in the post-war world was a lot more important than to battle around the corpse of Greater Germany. Certainly the Nibelungen and Sigrune groups, both of which had been put into besieged Vienna, very promptly vanished. Were they war-weary and anxious to get back to familiar surroundings, or had they been caught by the vigilant NKVD, whose agents, both Russian and native Austrian, were on watch for any sign of Werewolf activity?

The Werewolf was in action on all the sectors of the Eastern Front, and the build-up in numbers through the release of local men, such as has been described above in Austria, will certainly have been repeated in the other Gaue and Provinces of Germany proper. Little is known for sure. There were partisans active in East Prussia and in the area of Breslau during the time that those places were surrounded and under attack by the Red Army. It is also known that in some parts of the Eastern Front the Russians were forced to withdraw large numbers of men – some reports speak of whole divisions – in anti-partisan opera-tions against the Werewolf. There was one group which fought throughout the battle for Berlin and whose survivors fought their way out of the dying city to resume their activity in the West.

At the height of Werewolf activity, Allied soldiers vanished from their slit-trenches, telephone lines were cut, vehicles were damaged and stores burned. But by this stage of the war not only were the Werewolf under pressure from the Allied armies, but their own commanders wanted to see an end to their activity. Not that anyone, even in the highest echelons of Command had any real idea of how powerful Werewolf was or where it was in action. One thing was very clear to the leaders of the German State who, following the death of Adolf Hitler, were seeking to arrange a cease-fire. It was crystal clear to those senior officers that any sort of partisan activity in Occupied Germany would mean harsher surrender terms and they made every effort to halt Werewolf operations. The letter which is reproduced here, from General Kinzel, to Jodl, and dated 5 May 1945, reported that the Luftwaffe's Home Command was planning to go underground and to undertake Werewolf activities. Keitel, the Head of OKW, replied immediately and in his letter gave orders that, . . .'the situation facing the troops in the West has changed and any such action (i.e. Werewolf), will seriously affect the national interest. I hereby order that all actions against the Anglo-Americans are to cease. . .'

This was not the end of the matter. A signal was received in the head-quarters of Admiral Doenitz, originating from Field Marshal Montgomery, who demanded action against the announcers in the Wilhelmshaven radio-station who were denouncing the surrender and were calling for continued resistance against the Allies. The tone of Montgomery's message was clear and OKW, realising this, took immediate action. Jodl radioed back to the Field Marshal that although there had not, to his knowledge, been any broadcasts of that nature from Wilhelmshaven station, instructions had been given to monitor all German radio and to take the strongest measures against any offenders.

With the end of the war, Werewolf died. That there were isolated incidents and attacks cannot be denied, but the movement which had, at one time, contained nearly five thousand agents had been generally impotent and had grown weaker with every passing day and with each fresh arrest. The French, the Americans and the British carried out checks and raids upon suspects. The French were said to be the most determined in their pursuit of Werewolf agents, and employed officers of their Secret Service, the Deuxième Bureau, to hunt them down. The British were said to be the most thorough and the best organised. They were, therefore, the most successful. The Americans were the most inconsistent. In one army's area the officers of Military Intelligence would spend their time tracking down, trying and sentencing to life imprisonment children who had been convicted of Werewolf activities, while another US Army would employ known Nazis as the only ones who could keep the civil administration going. In the East there was no hesitation. Werewolf agents if caught were either executed or sentenced to life imprisonment in the camps and mines of Siberia. The Russians were taking no chances with the lives of their soldiers.

The Russians, more than any other nation, were aware of the effect upon an army of occupation of a strong and centrally directed partisan organisation. Their own partisans had forced the Germans in Russia to divert strong units from the battle line to fight the guerrillas in the rear areas. The Russians were determined that there would be no German partisan movement in their zone of occupation. Their anti-terrorist organisation, the NKVD, was active and was prepared to wait. It is a matter of record that several years after the end of the war, when Austria was about to be freed from the foreign armies which had been on her territory since 1945, Russian NKVD agents were conducting intensive sweeps through the Soviet Zone of occupation, seeking to determine whether there were any Werewolf agents still at large.

One explanation for the fact that Werewolf died so quickly is that it lacked the essential requirement of successful guerrilla warfare: a base from which it could be supplied with arms and nourished by recruits. With Germany occupied by the four Powers there was no base from which nourishment and support could come. Lacking these, the movement died. There is also the fact that the considerations of personal life eventually overrode political indoctrination. The need to survive in a destroyed Fatherland was more important than the pouring of sugar into petrol tanks or the slashing of vehicle tyres. The need to look forward and to rebuild Germany was a more attractive prospect than the urge to look back and obey the nihilistic commands of the late Reichsminister Goebbels.

Above Flying Fortresses of the US Army Air Force, part of the top section of a bomber 'box', release their bombs through cloud. (Courtesy USAAF)

Below A radio-controlled glider bomb of the type released from German aircraft and used for attacks against Allied shipping. Its success in that role caused it to be proposed for use against the US bomber 'boxes'. (Imperial War Museum)

Above The piloted version of the V-1 'flying bomb'. It was intended that German pilots would fly this machine into American bomber fleets. (Imperial War Museum)

Below The Heinkel He 177A-5 (seen here in RAF colours) wa another of KG200's long-range machines. (Imperial Wa Museum)

Right Josef Thurnhuber, leutnant in the Luftwaffe's KG200, receiving the Knight's Cross of the Iron Cross for his services with 'Carmen'.
Below The Arado Ar 232 was a troop carrier and transport aircraft used extensively by KG200. It had a tricycle undercarriage and carried eleven sets of double wheels, allowing the aircraft to land and take off in uneven and broken terrain.
Bottom The Gotha Go 242 transport glider was used frequently in airborne operations.

Above This photograph shows the Mistel combination. This version is made up of a Ju 88 as the 'bomb' with an Fw 190 as the carrier. Both aircraft have been repainted in RAF colours. (Imperial War Museum)

Below The Ju 352A, the type of machine that KG200 used to carry agents on long hauls. (Imperial War Museum)

Above Among the close-combat weapons used by the German forces and the special groups was the single-shot anti-tank rocket projector, the Panzerfaust.

Below The Panzerschreck was a two-man anti-tank weapon based on the American bazooka.

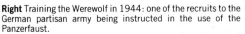

Right Training the Werewolf in 1944: one of the recruits to the German partisan army being instructed in the use of the Panzerfaust.
Below A German youth accused and found guilty of Werewolf activities. This photograph shows him in his cell while officers of the US Army read out to him the sentence of the Court Martial – that he is to suffer imprisonment for life.
Bottom The execution of a Werewolf by American forces in Germany during June 1945. Otto Teuteberg, a former SS soldier, was arrested in Duisburg and accused of firing at US Army units; he was executed in Braunschweig.

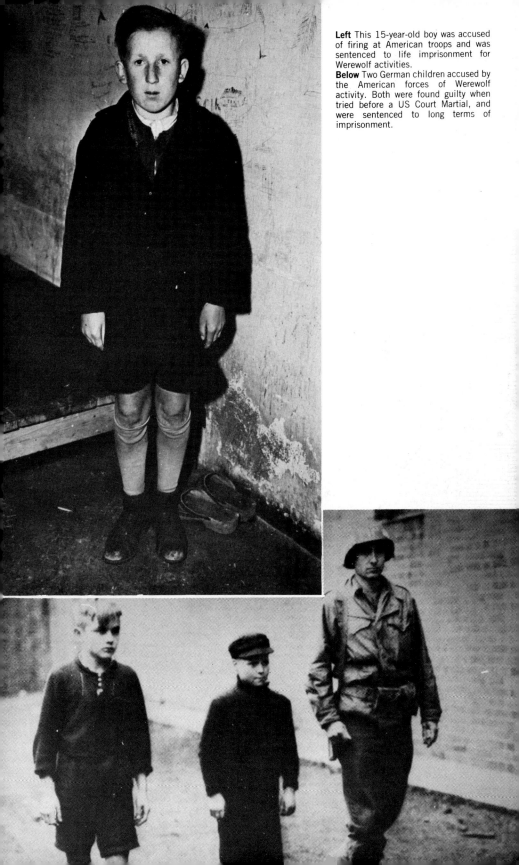

Left This 15-year-old boy was accused of firing at American troops and was sentenced to life imprisonment for Werewolf activities.

Below Two German children accused by the American forces of Werewolf activity. Both were found guilty when tried before a US Court Martial, and were sentenced to long terms of imprisonment.

This photograph of Witzig, hero of Eben Emael, shows him as commander of a para regiment during the fighting in western Germany in the winter of 1944/5.

4
THE FREIKORPS

Werewolf and the Volkssturm were not the only organisations raised by the Nazi Party for the defence of the Fatherland. All over the Reich, groups inspired by the need of the hour, were forming up to strike a blow for Adolf Hitler. Most of these Party-inspired formations were given the name 'Freikorps'. In addition to them, a fresh wave of army divisions was raised, many of them being given the name of some illustrious German soldier, as if the name alone could compensate the shortage of weapons, the lack of men or of training which were factors common to them all. The masses of the Third Reich, in those last weeks of its life, were responding to the call which Hitler, confined now in his bunker in Berlin, had made to Admiral Doenitz. The Führer had insisted that the outcome of the battle for Berlin would determine the fate of the German people and that, compared to that battle, operations on all other fronts were secondary. Responding to Hitler's call, the civilian legions of the Third Reich formed, were armed and marched towards the sound of the guns that were proclaiming the battle for the capital of the Reich.

The chaotic situation in Germany is best summed-up by the accusations which Goebbels made in a discussion with some friends. 'The Generals are in revolt,' he declared, 'Officers are deserting. Ministers are fleeing out of Berlin and officials can no longer control their staffs. Traffic is in chaos; production is stagnant; food is more difficult to obtain and the Führer's closest advisers are alcoholics. Only the people stay loyal. They suffer and sacrifice and do their duty.' Goebbels knew that the German people still stood behind the Führer and would fight for him. Through newspapers and as a result of broadcasts there had been a quickening of the German spirit. Axmann of the Hitler Youth had written: 'Words do not help. Deeds do. The Hitler Youth must be the centre of our national resistance. Our Youth declares passionately that it shall never surrender.'

Among the German masses were many who responded willingly, but whose efforts were undirected. There was such a complete lack of central direction that a miscellany of semi-military and para-military units was raised, equipped and put into the field, often without reference to Berlin and usually at the whim of the local provincial leader. The most interesting of all these para-military groups were the Freikorps, patterned on those others that had sprung up in Germany whenever the need arose. The most recent need had been at the end of the First World War when the nations bordering Germany had sought to exploit her weakness by seizing territory. Freikorps militias had guarded the threatened frontiers where, reinforced by volunteer detachments from all parts of Germany, they had fought hard and had saved the country by their sacrifice. Now, in 1945, with defeat again facing the Reich, the Nazi Party tried to make out that the Freikorps it was raising were directly descended from those that had held the frontiers in 1918–1919. The Freikorps Adolf Hitler was born.

What sort of men could be found in the sixth year of the war to fill the ranks of this élite and special force which carried the Führer's name? Almost certainly they would be neither young, fit nor militarily competent. The war had lasted too long to allow fit young men to lie about in the Homeland. Seen coldly and logically, this special force was a nonsense from its inception to the end of its short and undramatic life. It was seriously proposed that the Freikorps should enter beleagured Berlin and combat the Soviet tank armadas in the city. A corpulent, middle-aged clerk, with a double hernia and six days' basic training was presumably going to halt a wave of T 34s or survive a barrage of Katyusha rockets where the lean, hardened survivors of the Eastern Front had failed. It was a far cry from the blonde supermen of Hitler's SS Bodyguard Regiment, where in pre-war days a recruit was considered ineligible to serve the Führer if he had a single filled tooth of if a tooth were missing. In the 1945 Freikorps it would be a fortunate man indeed who had a single natural tooth in his head.

On 30 March 1945, Goebbels wrote to his comrades at Provincial Governor (Gauleiter) level. In his letter he was pleased to tell them that the Führer had consented to the raising of a Free Corps bearing his name. The new Adolf Hitler unit was to be organised and run by Dr Ley, the leader of the German Labour Front. Any great powers of organisation which Dr Ley had possessed were, to be charitable, past their best. He had a great number of problems – the chief of which was drink. A second, and only slightly less serious, problem was the shortage of almost every type of equipment to outfit the new force, and instructors to train its members. The opening paragraphs of Dr Goebbels' letter were written in a confident, optimistic style which, considering the situation, showed an unreality bordering on madness. It was to be expected, the Doctor claimed, that every true German would fight to the last against the enemies of his Race and Blood. He went on to detail how the new force was to be raised. Each Gau was to raise a contingent of 100 men. There were not many Gaue that could still be considered as being part of Greater Germany at this stage of the war, and their numbers could be certain to diminish with every passing week as the Allied armies moved forward.

The candidates for the 'Adolf Hitler' Freikorps, declared Goebbels, must have had a good schooling in politics and the Party's programme as well as basic military training. Recruitment to the Corps was an honour and no candidate's application was to be rejected on the grounds of his importance to local government affairs. The sacred task of bearing the Führer's name in the titanic struggles to come overrode all other considerations. This new task had the highest priority. In keeping with this high degree of priority, the special task which the volunteers were to carry out on the battlefield was to smash the Allied armour.

The Goebbels directive then went into astonishing and bureaucratic detail. Each volunteer would be issued with three days' rations when he left his home Gau. He would wear his own civilian clothing or, if in uniform, would remove badges of rank and Party armbands. Goebbels did not stress that by such procedure the volunteers would cease to be members of an identifiable military body and would exclude themselves from the protection of the Geneva Convention. If captured the danger of summary execution could face them all. One wonders how many of the Freikorps 'Adolf Hitler', realised the dangers they would face.

All volunteers were to set out as Gaue groups and rally at Heuberg by 2 April. To reach that place they would not travel by train but by bicycle which would be issued and mounted on which they would go into action. The mental image that these instructions conjure up is a sad one: hundreds of middle-aged cyclists pedalling sedately through the German countryside, dressed in clothing 'capable of withstanding hard wear', to quote the instructions, and each with his packed lunch. At the rendezvous leaders would be nominated and without undue fuss the Freikorps would go into action against Germany's enemies.

Little documentary evidence exists of the raising of the Freikorps 'Adolf Hitler', the Freikorps 'Sauerland' or the others, but some details remain dealing with the contingent raised in the Province of Swabia – Gau Schwaben. The Gauleiter, Wahl, wrote to his subordinates a precise of the relevant sections of the Goebbels letter, and in his own covering letter laid down the numbers of men to be supplied from each sub-area (Kreis) of the Gau. He further stipulated that only healthy recruits would be considered. In a situation report a few weeks later, Wahl told his Kreis comrades of the success of the recruiting drive and how from his own personal staff eleven men had gone out. Other comrades from the Gaue Administration departments had brought the recruit contingent up to its nominated strength.

After 18 April, the date of Wahl's last circular letter to his subordinates in the Gaue administration, the Swabian contingent of the Freikorps 'Adolf Hitler' disappears from the official correspondence. It can only be assumed that they did set off for Berlin, but whether they went into action or were captured *en route* can only be conjecture. As civilians, not in uniform and yet using firearms, it may well be that these volunteers were taken prisoner and summarily shot.

CONCLUSION

On 8 May 1945, the war in Europe ended, but only for the Western Powers. Stalin had wanted his allies to accept 9 May as Victory Day, but they had rejected his demand. Thus, while hostilities by the Germans against the Anglo-Americans had ceased on 8 May, there was still fighting going on against the Russians, which would continue for a further day. That twenty-four hour pause did allow, however, a great number of embattled soldiers to disengage from the fighting and cross over into the newness of peace in the West; there to begin the hard but safe life as prisoners of war.

On the Eastern Front, chief among those who sought to avoid captivity by the Red Army and its concomitant of slave labour in a Russian mine, were the men of some of the special units which have been described in this book. Some did not need to bother. As we have already seen, the flyers and the ground crews of KG 200's outstation Olga had already been discharged from the Service and had been sent home. Down in the Alpine Redoubt, the mountainous regions of southern Germany and Austria, a miscellany of military fragments from special forces had congregated, among which were the surviving ram pilots. Then too there were men from Skorzeny's Jäger battalions who had fought their way out of Berlin and there were also Werewolf boys who had been waiting to be used against targets in the German provinces occupied by the Allies. Now it was all over.

In other regions of Germany into which the Allies had not yet penetrated, men of special forces outside of the Alpine Redoubt were attempting to make the transition from specialist soldier to inoffensive civilian by simply heading in the direction of home. One such man was Erich Busch, at that time a company commander in a paratroop battalion, who managed to evade captivity as he trekked from an Austrian battlefield to his home town in northern Germany. Some Brandenburg men were successful in eluding the numerous Allied military patrols; some were not. The British regimental war diaries in those first weeks, include reports of Brandenburgers who had been captured in their unit areas. There were others in that general upheaval who looked for consideration from the victorious Allies. Senior politicians and Ministers of the Third Reich who surrendered, naïve in the belief that their superior status in the German Government would accord them privileges in defeat, and were shocked to find themselves arrested and charged as war criminals. Others, including Hitler, Goebbels and Himmler, committed suicide and died undignified deaths in grubby rooms, having reserved for themselves the privilege of escape by bullet or poison they had denied to their subordinates. Hitler had railed against suicide as cowardice and had persecuted the families of officers who had taken their own lives. There was, even in death, one law for the Party bosses and one for the little men. Then there were the professional survivors – and there were a great many of them – who left Germany for Spain or for those countries outside Europe to which escape routes had already been pioneered; where there was money enough to live like a gentleman and where the laws of extradition did not seem to operate.

The war was over for the men of the special units. Henceforth, the hard-learned skills and the expertise, would be channelled into surviving the terrible years of defeat which lay ahead. As these men struggled through the bitterness of defeat, did they reflect on how the course of warfare had changed during the years of their service? They, and indeed all those who had lived through the war, had seen a revolution in military deployment; a revolution underlined by the acceptance after September 1945 that tactical atomic weapons might have a place on future battlefields.

Throughout history, Generals have proclaimed, in justification of their need for mass armies, that God was on the side of the big battalions. In the early days of warfare, masses of soldiers had formed human walls, a tactic imposed upon the military because of the inaccuracy of their firearms. With the machine-gun and barbed wire came the era of the empty battlefield and trench lines which could not be outflanked. Masses of men, the Generals claimed, were still needed. Then, during the course of the Second World War, which had begun conventionally enough, small groups of highly-trained and ruthless men, whose operations supplemented, complemented and, sometimes even initiated military campaigns, had been formed. These ventures did not provide only tactical victories. Frequently, and in the context of this book one thinks immediately of Eben Emael and of Gennep, the objectives and the successes had been strategic. The special forces of the world's principal armies followed the same lines of development so that the British commandos, the US Raiders and Rangers, the Kamikaze of Japan and the Brandenburg detachments of Germany can all be said to have been cast in the same mould. They fought in small groups and produced results which were out of all proportion to their numbers.

At the end of the war, the world's commanders realised that there had been a military revolution. The destructive power of atomic weapons forced them to accept that the concept of small-unit actions, both in attack and in defence had become now an important means of fighting certain battles. Although combat forces are today trained as if to fight as part of the old-fashioned cohesive force, they are more likely in war to be dispersed over a wide battlefield and deployed in small units, being concentrated in time and space, as required. In such a battle scenario, the conduct of operations will be in the hands of quite junior officers, or even of non-commissioned officers, from standard army units, who will have under their command men whose skill, aggression and professionalism will match that of the specialist soldiers of forty years ago.

There will, of course, still be a need outside of standard units for the specialist groups, for these in an attacking situation will form the point of the spearhead, racing forward, probably adopting disguise as did the Brandenburgers and, like them, aiming to capture important tactical targets. Other special groups will aim for strategic objectives. They will, perhaps drop by parachute on, or be landed by helicopter close to, enemy headquarters, to destroy nerve-centres and to paralyse the defence. There will be a return to the Blitzkrieg concept, but at a much faster pace, and special forces will lead the assault with the mass of the Army, organised tactically into small, hard-hitting units, following closely behind the spearhead. The sophistication of radio techniques will allow this apparently fragmented assault to be controlled and directed as part of a master-plan. Special forces in a defensive posture will carry out selective types of partisan warfare: assassination, urban guerrilla operations against an enemy's communications and supply system, and the destruction of the enemy in his own homeland by sabotage.

When today's soldiers are carrying out NATO winter exercises in the north of Norway, I wonder whether they realise that the survival techniques which they are using were laid down in manuals written by the German Army's special forces which had fought in Russia? Do Allied troops on summer manoeuvres in the deep and silent woods of central Germany know, as they sit in their well-camouflaged foxholes and practise their partisan raids, that the tactics they are using as well as the construction of their holes in the ground were formulated in a handbook which was issued to Werewolf units?

A consideration of the German special forces raises the question as to whether they could have been as effective as Allied special forces, had they been introduced earlier, been supported more strongly and equipped more lavishly?

The answer must surely be that such an efficiency as the Allies had was unlikely given the structure of the Third Reich. We have seen that Germany was a mass of jealous leaders led by a man who would not delegate authority. Political Germany did not have a central intelligence agency until late in the war, but instead had a multiplicity of agencies, each of which worked for its own Minister and each of which operated independently of, or even in opposition to, the others. On the military level, the ten divisions of the Luftwaffe paratroops and the thirty-five divisions of the Waffen SS were outside direct Army control, for their commanders could appeal to Goering or to Himmler, over the heads of the local military men.

In addition to the petty jealousies which diminished the national effort, command at the highest level was too concentrated. Even before the war began, Hitler had assumed control of the OKW and had made it clear that he intended to be no mere figurehead. Then, late in 1941, he dismissed the Commander-in-Chief of the Army and took over the post himself. To further complicate matters he detached OKH from the direct control of OKW and gave to OKH one single task – to fight the war on the Eastern Front. To OKW was given the responsibility of conducting operations in all other theatres of operations. Thus, command of both OKW and OKH was centred in the single person of a civilian politician. To him, through him and from him, went all the plans and battle orders for both Commands. Collaboration stopped there. Below Hitler was an almost total lack of liaison between the two High Commands. It is not hard to imagine the military chaos which such a maladministration produced.

In a situation where the whole burden of the military and political decisions rested upon Hitler, it was obviously impossible for him to give a calm and controlled appraisal of the potential of special forces in the long term. He sought instant victories, immediate solutions although, as we have seen from the Oder bridge mission and the December offensive in the Ardennes, he could involve himself deeply in the tactics of the operations and could produce timetables of unbelievable detail and operations orders of incredible complexity. What Hitler lacked was the all-encompassing, far-sighted vision of a Roger Keyes or a Louis Mountbatten.

Lacking their Führer's direct support and positive encouragement as well as his understanding of their potential, the German special forces could not develop further than they did. The successes which were achieved were brought about by leaders at middle command level who did have the understanding, but who lacked the authority to gain for their units the necessary weapons. Only Skorzeny and, to a lesser extent, Baumbach, were able to do a little to help their organisations.

What did Germany's special forces achieve? The answer must be that in the early days of the war those military detachments under Abwehr control as well as those of the Airborne forces, gained outstanding victories. In those early days they were initiating techniques, tactics and weapons. By 1944, however, the ground forces were not introducing new techniques, but were still using the methods of 1939, 1940 and

1941. At sea, the naval forces had long been impotent and were capable of carrying out only pinprick actions against the Western Allies, while the missions flown by the Luftwaffe's special Geschwader and Staffeln, were almost totally defensive in character.

Could the special forces of the Third Reich have achieved more? I think not. But it is our good fortune that they were given no chance to prove what they might have been able to bring about, had they been raised sooner, been given the support and supplied with the equipment they needed. The special forces of the Third Reich were too little and too late – thank God!

APPENDIX 1
GLOSSARY

ABWEHR: Is an acronym for the departmental group of the Armed Forces High Command (Oberkommando der Wehrmacht – OKW), Intelligence and Counter-Intelligence agencies. Abwehr was led by Admiral Canaris until he was dismissed when control of the Department passed to the Sicherheitsdienst of the SS (SD).

BIBER: The German Navy's version of the British X craft, i.e. a one-man submarine vessel capable of carrying standard torpedoes. Other miniature submarines of the Biber pattern were the Hecht, Molch and Seehund.

EINSATZKOMMANDO: Literally – action group – but more particularly the organisation of armed detachments of the SS, which carried out round-up raids and punitive actions; all to prevent or to destroy opposition in the rear areas of the German Army of Occupation. Chiefly, but not exclusively, the term is used to describe the units responsible for the mass executions of the Polish, gypsy and Jewish populations of Eastern Europe.

GAU/GAULEITER: In the Third Reich the nation was divided into a number of Gau, each of which was controlled by a Gauleiter whose appointment was a political one, approximating to a Lieutenant of a County. A Gau was subdivided into a number of Kreise, the nearest equivalent to which is the English rural district council.

KLEINKAMPFVERBANDE: Small action units of the German Navy, usually known as KKV or K units. The organisation of the K units was the Marine Einsatz Abteilung (MEA) the naval action detachment which was subdivided into Marine Einsatz Kommandos (MEK) or naval action commandos.

LINSEN: The explosive filled motor-boats which were employed by K units against the Allies, and specifically against the Allied invasion fleet in North-west Europe. Linsen were directed at full speed by a crewman against a target. When the Linsen was close to the target the pilot handed the vessel over to the radio control of a commander in a second boat and then jumped overboard.

LUFTFLOTTE REICH: The Luftwaffe was organised into a series of Luft-flotten (Air Fleets). In the deteriorating situation of late 1944–early 1945, the air defence of the Reich was concentrated, and from the remaining Luftflotten the Luftflotte Reich was created.

NAZI (PARTY): An abbreviation for the German National Socialist Workers' Party (National Sozialistische Deutsche Arbeiter Partei), of which Hitler was not the original founder, but was Member Number 7. The Party, under his leadership, obtained power in 1933 and held it until the defeat of Germany in 1945.

NEGER: The German Navy's first 'K' weapon was the Neger. It consisted of two torpedoes arranged vertically. The upper one was modified to carry a 'captain' who piloted the combination to the target area. When a target had been selected the second, standard, torpedo was released electrically and ran to explode against the objective. The Marder was an improved version of the Neger, the difference being that the Marder had submersible capability which the Neger did not.

OKH: The abbreviation of Oberkommando des Heeres (Army High Command). The OKH developed out of the Wehramt (Defence Office) which was the title given to the Army High Command. Under the Weimar government the title was changed to Allgemeines Heeresamt (General Army Office). That title was changed on 21 May 1935, to Oberkommando des Heeres.

OKL: The abbreviation of Oberkommando der Luftwaffe (Air Force High Command).

OKM: The abbreviation of Oberkommando der Marine (Navy High Command).

OKW: The abbreviation for Oberkommando der Wehrmacht, the High Command of the German Armed Forces. The reorganisation of the German military, naval and air arms took place during February 1938, when the Armed Forces Office (Wehrmachtsamt) was reformed into the OKW, under the command of Adolf Hitler. The OKW was divided into OKH, OKL and OKM.

SICHERHEITSDIENST – SD: There was a need in the SS to ensure that its members remained politically loyal and thus a police force was raised within the SS establishment. It was named as the SD. The SD then expanded to control the civil police forces of Germany. Under the dynamic leadership of Heydrich, the SD, which was in competition with the Abwehr, absorbed that Ministry and became responsible for German Intelligence and Counter-Intelligence operations.

SS: The initials of the Nazi Party's élite force, the Schutz Staffel. Formed originally as the guard around Adolf Hitler, to whom the members of the SS swore loyalty unto death, the formation expanded to become an élite para-military force. The Standarten or regiments of the SS Verfügungstruppen eventually became the Waffen SS, a force which expanded to a strength of nearly forty divisions made up of all arms.

VOLKSSTURM: A national army raised from the male civilian population who had not served in the armed forces. Thus the Volkssturm was made up of men either too old for military service or too young for call up.

Those civilians of military age who were eligible for conscription into the Volkssturm were men engaged in essential war work. The theory of the Volkssturm was that the force would be raised within each Gau by the Gauleiter who would decide when it was to be conscripted and when it was to be put into action. Since the Volkssturm battalions were locally raised and intended to fight in their own areas, it may be claimed that they were literally defending their homes and hearths.

WEREWOLF: A description given to several organisations of the Third Reich. 1. An underground, partisan army, carefully recruited and excellently trained to carry out guerrilla warfare against the Allied forces which were overrunning Germany. 2. During 1945, this idea of an élite and secret force was overturned by the speech made by Dr Goebbels in which he urged civilians in the occupied areas of Germany to rise and to drown the enemy in a sea of blood, by recourse to arms. The name Werewolf was also given to an Air Force all-out operation against the Allies.

APPENDIX 2

BRANDENBURG OPERATIONS, 1939–1945

The detachments, units and formations which carried in their title the description 'Brandenburg' descended from a single group of approximately Company strength which was raised by Abwehr before the outbreak of the Second World War. Not until late in 1942, were 'Brandenburg' units considered to form part of the German Army's Order of Battle. Since the purpose of Brandenburg detachments was to mount small unit operations, often using fifteen or twenty men, it is not possible to detail all the missions undertaken. Listed below is a select list of the more important dates, operations and formations in the history of Brandenburg.

AUGUST 1939: Groups of Abwehr men sent out to prevent the sabotage of Polish factories in western Silesia and the destruction of the Vistula bridges.

15 SEPTEMBER 1939: Considered as the day on which Brandenburg was formed. Formal raising of Baulehr Kompanie zbV 800 on 25 October 1939, followed by the raising of a second Company, Deutsche Kompanie zbV.

APRIL 1940: The Campaign in Scandinavia. A glider-borne landing captures bridges over the Grosser Belt in Denmark. Operations in Norway.

MAY–JUNE 1940: The campaign in Western Europe.

JULY 1940: Preparations for the invasion of Great Britain.

AUGUST 1940: Preparations for an attack upon Gibraltar.

AUGUST 1940: Detachments guard Roumanian oil fields against British sabotage attempts.

OCTOBER 1940: Brandenburg battalion reaches regimental status.

APRIL 1941: The Balkan campaign in Yugoslavia and Greece. A Brandenburg detachment captures the Iron Gate on the Danube to allow river traffic to flow.

JUNE 1941: The first Russian campaign. Attacks by many Brandenburg units in the opening phases.

SPRING 1942: Attack upon the Russian rail supply route to Murmansk.

APRIL 1942: Brandenburg groups which have been in Africa since the spring of 1941, undertake Operation 'Salam'. A second operation is undertaken to establish the location of the British supply route – West Africa–Egypt.

235

SUMMER 1942: The second Russian campaign. Brandenburg detachments set out to recruit among the native peoples of the Caucasus.

OCTOBER 1942: Withdrawal from the Caucasus. During the summer and autumn Brandenburg units were on anti-partisan operations in Yugoslavia.

1 NOVEMBER 1942: Brandenburg reaches divisional status and becomes part of the establishment of the German Army and eventually located as OKW strategic reserve.

AUTUMN/WINTER 1942: Brandenburg motor boat patrols against Soviet Naval Commandos in the Sea of Azov.

NOVEMBER 1942: Detachments flown to Tunisia.

FEBRUARY 1943: Rommel's offensive in southern Tunisia.

FEBRUARY 1944: Paratroop battalion raised.

SPRING 1944: Foreign Legions formed of men recruited in the Soviet Union, chiefly from the Ukraine and the Caucasus.

NOVEMBER 1944: The motor boat groups deployed in the Aegean and the Mediterranean. Other Brandenburg units in ground and airborne drops on Leros.

SPRING 1944: Brandenburg becomes part of Grossdeutschland Corps. Operations now conducted by units which do not form part of the Division.

SUMMER 1944: Anti-partisan operations in Serbia.

AUGUST 1944: The para battalion flown to Bucharest and taken prisoner.

DECEMBER 1944: Skorzeny in the Battle of the Bulge.

1945: Jagdverbände in operations on the Eastern Front until the end of the war.

Order of Battle: The Brandenburg Regiment, October 1940

1st Battalion
Depot: Brandenburg/Havel
Operational area: East and West Europe
Companies Nos. 1 to 4

2nd Battalion
Depot: Baden bei Wien.
Operational area: South-east Europe
Nos. 5 to 8 Companies

3rd Battalion
Depot: Düren – near Aachen
Operational area: Western Europe
Companies Nos. 9 to 12

By mid January 1941 Companies Nos. 13 to 17 had been raised and taken on strength.

The strength of a Para Engineer Battalion fluctuated during the course of the War and the numbers given here are those for Africa 1942. A battalion numbered 716 all ranks, and had a weapon establishment of 36 light machine-guns, 8 medium machine-guns, 12 anti-tank rifles and 12 flame-throwers. The Light Engineering Column was equipped with 6 large and 12 small rubber assault boats. Other stores carried included mines, charges, demolition equipment and other explosives selected to meet the tactical requirement.

SELECT BIBLIOGRAPHY

Published sources

Aaronson, S.	*Heydrich und die Frühgeschichte von Gestapo und SS.*
Baumbach, W.	*Zu Spät.*
Bund deutscher Fallschirmjäger.	*Der deutsche Fallschirmjäger.* (Journal of the Bund).
Cooper, M.	*Die Luftwaffe.*
Euler, M.	*Die Entscheidungsschlacht am Rhein und Ruhr, 1945.*
Dierich, W.	*Die Verbände der Luftwaffe, 1935–1945.*
Freeman, R.	*The Mighty Eighth.*
Galland, A.	*Die Ersten und die Letzten.*
Gunzenhauser, H.	*Die Geschichte des geheimen Nachrichtendienstes.*
HMSO	*The Official History of the Second World War.* (The War in France and Flanders; The Middle East; the North-West European campaign.)
HQ US Army.	Civil Affairs Handbooks: German Military Government over Europe; Propaganda in Occupied Europe; SS and Police in Occupied Europe.
Keilig, W.	*Das deutsche Heer, 1939–1945.*
Klee, K.	*Das Unternehmen 'Seelöwe'.*
Kleitmann, K.	*Die Waffen SS:Eine Dokumentation.*
Kühn, V.	*Torpedoboote und Zerstörer im Einsatz.*
Kumm	*Vorwärts Prinz Eugen.*
Kurowski, F.	*Der Luftkrieg über Deutschland.*
Kurowski, F.	*Die Schlacht um Deutschland.*
Lucas, J.	*Panzer Army Africa.*
Lehmann, R.	*Die Leibstandarte.* Vol. III.
Michels and Sliepenback.	*Niederrheinisches Land im Krieg.*
Meyer, H.	*Kriegsgeschichte der 12ten SS Panzer Division 'Hitler Jugend'.*
NSDAP.	*Winke für Jagdeinheiten.*
Price, A.	*Luftschlacht über Deutschland.*
Rose, A.	*Radikaler Luftkampf.*

Salewski, H.   *Die deutsche Seekriegsleitung.* Vols. 1 and 2.
Scheibert, H.   *Panzergrenadier Division 'Grossdeutschland'*
                         und ihre Schwester Verbände.
Schellenberg, W.   *The Schellenberg Memoirs.*
Spaeter, H.   *Die Brandenburger.*
US Army.   *'Impact'.*
USAAF.   *The US Strategic Bombing Survey.* Various
                         volumes.
Warlimont, W.   *Im Hauptquartier der deutschen Wehrmacht.*

Unpublished sources
BAOR.   *An appreciation of the Werewolf movement,*
                         29 August 1945.
Dönitz.   Messages from Dönitz during the period
                         15 April–12 May 1945.
Kriegsmarine.   File 'Invasion'. Post-operations report by the
                         Flag Officer Naval Group West, June 1944.
                         (Trans.).
Neumann.   Kriegstagebuch. Korpsartzt II
                         Fallschirmjäger Korps. July 1944 to May 1945.
OKW.   Die Wacht am Rhein. The German Army's
                         attack in the Ardennes in December 1944.
                         Guidelines of political principles;
                         Directives and Orders. 1 Nov 1944 to 1 Jan
                         1945.
OKW.   Jahresverfügung 1945 über Abwehr von
                         Landesverrat, Spionage, Sabotage und
                         Versetzung in der Wehrmacht.
NSDAP.   Werbung für das Freikorps 'Adolf Hitler'.
                         18 April 1945.
OB West.   Angriff Heeresgruppe B. 16 December 1944.
OAK 7.   Bericht über des Kommandos des
                         Sonderstabes Oemichen. 17 May 1944.
RSHA.   Einsatz des SD im Falle CSR. 1938.
SP/SD.   Tätigkeits und Lage Bericht, Nr. 10. Der
                         Einsatz der SP und SD in der USSR. 1942.
SD der RFSS   File 'ENGLAND' 2 July to 5 September 1940.
SD/SS.   File 'ENGLAND' 27 August to 24 September
                         1940.
SS.   Der Sonderkommando 'Gruppe Kunsberg'
                         July 1942–January 1943.
Student.   Interview of the Colonel General with Rektor
                         Haas on 20 September 1959.
Weichhold.   German Naval defence against the Allied
                         landing in Normandy.
Various war diaries, interrogation summaries and interviews.

INDEX